The New Politics of Gender Equality

The New Politics of Gender Equality

Judith Squires

palgrave
macmillan

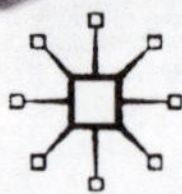

First published 2007 by
PALGRAVE MACMILLAN
Houndmills, Basingstoke, Hampshire RG21 6XS and
175 Fifth Avenue, New York, N.Y. 10010
Companies and representatives throughout the world.

PALGRAVE MACMILLAN is the global academic imprint of the Palgrave Macmillan division of St. Martin's Press, LLC and of Palgrave Macmillan Ltd. Macmillan® is a registered trademark in the United States, United Kingdom and other countries. Palgrave is a registered trademark in the European Union and other countries.

ISBN-13: 978–0–230–00769–7 hardback
ISBN-10: 0–230–00769–4 hardback
ISBN-13: 978–0–230–00770–3 paperback
ISBN-10: 0–230–00770–8 paperback

This book is printed on paper suitable for recycling and made from fully managed and sustained forest sources. Logging, pulping and manufacturing processes are expected to conform to the environmental regulations of the country of origin.

A catalogue record for this book is available from the British Library.

A catalog record for this book is available from the Library of Congress.

10 9 8 7 6 5 4 3 2 1
16 15 14 13 12 11 10 09 08 07

Printed and bound in China

Contents

Acknowledgements

I am particularly grateful to Johanna Kantola and Mona Lena Krook, who together helped me to define this project. More generally, I would like to thank the participants of the ECPR Women and Politics Standing Group for providing the research network that made this book possible. As convenor of this group 2001–5 I benefited from reading the papers presented by its members at various workshops (Mannheim, Edinburgh, Granada) and general conferences (Kent, Marburg, Budapest) and exchanging ideas with the ever expanding number of scholars working on women and politics in Europe. This group provided an inspiring and supportive social and intellectual community throughout the last five years, during which time I explored the ways in which a political theorist might engage with the empirical developments in gender equality being interrogated by political scientists. Women's policy agencies, quotas and mainstreaming have each been subject to extensive scrutiny by ECPR participants and I am indebted to them all for sharing their insights with me.

I am also indebted to the participants of three other research networks, who have informed my thinking on women's policy agencies, quotas and mainstreaming. The Research Network on Gender and the State (RNGS), led by Amy Mazur, Dorothy Stetson, Joyce Outshoorn and Joni Lovenduski, generated much of the scholarship on women's policy agencies that I draw on in this book. The comparative quotas project led by Drude Dahlerup and supported by IDEA (International Democratic Electoral Assistance) brought together scholars from around the world to discuss quotas. I am indebted to the participants of this group for their wealth of knowledge on quotas, which also inform this book. Finally, the ESRC series of workshops on gender mainstreaming led by Sylvia Walby provided an invaluable forum for discussing developments with a diverse range of mainstreaming experts.

Members of the Gender and Governance Research Group in the Department of Politics, University of Bristol (Terrell Carver, Sarah Childs, Penny Griffin, Ana Jordan, Christina Rowley, Laura Shepherd, Carole Spary, Jutta Weldes and Mark Wickham-Jones) also provided a rich, challenging and supportive intellectual environment, in which I have been able to explore this research agenda. I would also like to thank the University of Bristol for funding a semester of research leave and the Arts and Humanities Research Council for Research Leave funding, which together made the writing of this book possible; and Steven Kennedy at Palgrave Macmillan for his enthusiasm and insight.

Last, but perhaps most importantly, thanks to Abigail, Jonathan and Richard for putting up with me going off to so many conferences, being stressed when the deadline looked too tight, and preoccupied when they wanted to play.

JUDITH SQUIRES

Introduction: Institutionalizing Gender Equality

Gender equality has gained a central place on the global political agenda over the last thirty years. It is now widely assumed to be a positive ideal and its pursuit is depicted as a core requirement of social justice. Moreover, gender equality is increasingly framed as central to the realization of both modernization and economic efficiency and its achievement presented as a key to good governance. Both rights-based and utility-based arguments have converged to place gender equality high on the agenda of liberal states and organizations.

The pursuit of gender equality is now widely endorsed as a central policy goal by governments and international organizations around the world (Inglehart and Norris 2003). As a result women have gained greater access to education and labour markets and wage gaps between men and women have narrowed. Governments around the globe have also introduced institutional mechanisms to promote the advancement of women, including measures to increase women's political participation rates and to incorporate women's interests into policy-making. Parity of political participation in particular has emerged as central to both feminist gender equality campaigns and governmental gender equality directives.

This book explores the concern with parity of political participation and the resulting emergence of institutional mechanisms to promote the political equality of women, focusing on gender quotas, women's policy agencies and gender mainstreaming as three key strategies that have come to define the increasingly widespread commitment to gender equality within the political sphere.

These three strategies focus on presence, voice and process respectively: quotas aim to secure increased numbers of women in national assemblies, policy agencies seek to improve the articulation of women's specific concerns, and mainstreaming aspires to ensure that more systematic consideration is given to gender equality issues across the policy-making agenda. The strategies clearly differ, yet while there are conceptual and practical tensions between them, they have generally been advocated as mutually reinforcing ways of securing greater political equality between women and men. Together they represent a distinctive approach to gender equality, and one that has emerged over the last three decades to become a global phenomenon.

While significant and sustained inequalities persist between men and women across the globe, the pursuit of gender equality is increasingly perceived to be a mainstream rather than a marginalized counter-cultural activity; it has been adopted as a central facet of liberal democratic discourse and espoused by leading international organizations and national governments across the globe. At the same time feminist activists have turned their attention to the state, focusing on strategies for greater inclusion within state institutions. The era when the women's movement was defined by its commitment to autonomous separatist action and informal pre-figurative politics has gone, replaced by an increasingly professionalized, state-oriented network of gender equality advocates, who enjoy much greater access to the institutions of power than most early second-wave feminists would ever have predicted.

This new politics of gender equality could be viewed as an unequivocal success story, with feminist concerns transforming mainstream institutional norms and practices. Yet feminist norms and practices have themselves been transformed in the process. The desire to render the pursuit of gender equality compatible with wider policy objectives and existing institutional practices has encouraged feminist actors to adopt utility-based arguments in order to justify greater gender equality, and technocratic processes in order to promote it. This has, almost inevitably, had the effect of marginalizing rights-based gender equality arguments and sidelining more democratic participatory approaches to its pursuit. As this tendency intensifies, the earlier focus on 'voice' is gradually disappearing and a twin-track approach to gender equality emerging, in which 'presence' and 'process' come to function as indicators of parity participation. This book explores the emergence of this twin-track strategy in which governments seek to secure both increased numbers of women in decision-making bodies and greater attention to gender equality in the policy-making process.

Gender quotas have emerged as the central strategy for securing increased numbers of women in national parliaments, generating extensive debate on the pros and cons of a 'politics of presence' (Phillips 1995). More recently gender mainstreaming has emerged as the central strategy for ensuring the inclusion of a gender equality perspective in policy-making, generating debate on the pros and cons of what we might call a 'politics of process'. Where the former gender equality strategy focuses on female parliamentarians and works with numerical indicators, the latter focuses on gender experts and takes the effective implementation of process, such as gender impact assessments, as an indicator of success. Both adopt formal empirical indicators, which render gender equality measurable, but tend to foreclose debate regarding its conceptualization. While there are clear gains to be had from this twin-track strategy, there is also a danger: the earlier feminist emphasis on participatory democracy seems to have lost ground in this new politics of gender equality.

Gender Equality: A Success Story?

Are these developments to be viewed as an unqualified success for gender equality advocates? It is possible that structural change and socio-economic developments, rather than feminist activism, have ushered in this new gender regime, which is simply different from, rather than more equal to, previous regimes. Indeed, this new gender regime is clearly compatible with high levels of inequality in relation to categories other than gender. While gender inequality has apparently decreased, class-based and North–South inequalities have ominously increased; income gaps within societies in many parts of the world have grown, as has the gap between the developed and less-developed regions (Murphy 2003:4).

Of the various egalitarian movements that have campaigned for social change over the last thirty years, the women's movement is frequently viewed as one of the most successful. Yet egalitarian social movements have long been argued to play an important role in facilitating the consolidation of the institutions of governance that allow the economy to be productive (Polanyi 1975). It is therefore entirely possible that the demands of the women's movement have been conceded more readily than those of other social movements simply because they are more consonant with those of the prevailing economic order. To the extent that women have demanded inclusion within existing institutions – educational, economic and political – they have generally found, in the last thirty years, these institutions to be, at least rhetorically, responsive.

Whether this greater inclusion in turn facilitates the transformation of these institutions, as many feminists have hoped, is as yet less evident.

Alert to the dangers of assimilation, the women's movement largely insisted on its autonomy during the 1970s and focused on cultural change rather than on influencing states. Nineteenth-century feminists in western liberal democracies had campaigned for the right to vote and to stand in elections, concentrating on formal equality before the law. However, once secured, these formal rights failed to generate the increased equality of outcome that many had anticipated, leading to a rise in alternative forms of activism during the 1960s and 1970s, with many women organizing outside of state structures in such things as women's peace movements and ecology movements (Millett 1970; Mies and Shiva 1993; Morgan 1970). During the peak of the second-wave movements there were a large number of protest strategies adopted, including spontaneous action, well-organized campaigns of sit-ins, marches and demonstrations, such as the 'Reclaim the Night' actions in England and West Germany in 1977, in Italy in 1978. All these forms of political protest were 'movement events', working outside the formal mechanisms of procedural politics. The women's movement aspired to be open to all, non-hierarchical and informal. Issues of participatory democracy became central, with great attention paid to organizational practice (Pateman 1970).

However, for many the experiences of the radical participatory democracy of the women's movement became paradoxical (Phillips 1991). The emphasis on participation was too demanding for those who were juggling many other demands on their time, and the lack of representative structures raised serious questions of accountability. The absence of formal structures often worked to create an insularity which left many women feeling excluded and silenced. By the 1980s many feminists became again more centrally concerned with the importance of mainstream politics, working to increase the numbers of women present within parties and legislatures, and to pursue policies in the interests of women.

The 1980s and 1990s saw women's issues introduced onto the agendas of diverse social and political groups and institutions, and as feminist activists entered into trade unions, political parties and state bureaucracies the women's movement increasingly engaged with these institutions and feminist attention expanded to incorporate these areas (Banaszak *et al.* 2003:21). Gradually feminist activism adopted a more state-oriented stance (Walby 2002), and the form of political engagement adopted by gender equality advocates shifted from separatist autonomous groups to greater engagement with the state (Chappell 2000, 2002, 2002a; Elman 2003; Kantola 2006).

There are various explanations as to why feminist engagements with the state should have increased in recent years, the most significant of which focus on economic development, political opportunity structures and ideational change. Economic development arguments highlight the extent to which industrialization, urbanization and the growth of an educated middle-class correlate with increased feminist activism. Greater education and labour-force participation have generally been accompanied by higher levels of political participation (Matland 1998), with a minimum level of development being needed to create the conditions in which political opportunity structures and ideational change can begin to have an effect. Within developed countries the shift from Fordist to neoliberal production processes influenced women's political participation rates.

Where the Fordist gender order, which entailed mass production and a stable working class with a nuclear family supported by a male bread-winner and women's unpaid domestic labour institutionalized the family wage (McDowell 1991), the abandonment of Keynesian policies led to reductions in the social welfare services that sustained the male bread-winner model. Many women were propelled into the labour market from economic necessity, signalling a shift in the 'gender regime' from one based on women's domestic confinement to one in which women are present in the public sphere (McDowell 1991; Walby 1997). However, while this process of restructuring has given middle-class women greater access to the labour market and public office, it has also entailed the degradation of the labour market position of many men, and increased the 'double-burden' on working-class women. Nonetheless, the overall growth in female employment intensified women's demands on the state given that the policy priorities of women in paid employment focus on the provision of public services, and led to an increase in women's public participation in the institutions of governance (Lovenduski 2005).

Political opportunities increased with women's growing employment, as women gained not only in terms of economic resources, but also in terms of access to public institutions such as trade unions, which make demands on government, and national parliaments. However, increased economic resources have not always resulted in greater political equality for women, signalling that political institutions and political culture also contribute to the low levels of women's participation in politics (Inglehart and Norris 2003:130). With the recognition that institutional factors mattered, feminist activists devoted increasing attention to electoral systems and party politics (Lovenduski 2005), leading to increases in the number of women elected to national assemblies (Ballington and Karam 2005; Squires and Wickham-Jones 2001). To the extent that the women in national assemblies hold distinct women-friendly policy priorities and manifest a commitment to representing women's interests (Childs 2004a; Mateo Diaz 2005), their increased presence encourages further feminist engagement with the state, which is progressively viewed as open to feminist demands.

In addition to this turn to the state, the informal local organizational structures of 1970s feminism were gradually augmented by activism beyond the borders of nation-states, making strategic use of global communication technologies, and the United Nations women's world conferences to network on an international level (Mendoza 2002:296). Feminists pursuing gender equality goals have made extensive use of transnational links, using the support of international organizations and other (often more powerful) states to put pressure on their own government, in what is known as the 'boomerang effect' (Keck and Sikkink 1998). International treaty commitments have been widely deployed by transnational and local activists to pressurize national governments to conform to international norms by improving national institutional support for the advancement of women. Feminists have also used transnational networks to learn from local struggles elsewhere in the world and to benefit from the organizational support offered by transnational feminist activists. Egalitarian activists have used non-governmental forums to share ideas and expertise, thereby developing a transnational leadership cadre which promotes international learning among gender equality activists. These developments facilitate the creation of new spaces and institutions in which egalitarian aspirations can be affirmed, and so offers new political opportunities that feminists have been quick to exploit.

As a result of these developments state feminism and transnational feminism have emerged as important complements to the social movement feminism that characterized the 1970s. The women's movement has pursued its goals by using intergovernmental institutions and transnational conferences to put pressure on national governments to introduce legislative changes and institutional reforms. While the diversification in the sites and modes of engagement led inevitably to the fragmentation of the movement, causing many commentators to suggest that feminism is in abeyance, the gains secured at the state and transnational levels suggest that this development might better be understood as a change in the repertoire and form of feminist activism, rather than a decline (Walby 2002:534).

Finally, alongside increased economic development and improved political opportunities, comes ideational change whereby traditional attitudes to women's political leadership have become increasingly egalitarian, particularly in post-industrial societies (Inglehart and Norris

2003:29–48), while radical, oppositional anti-state forms of feminism have gradually been eclipsed by gender equality advocates who are committed to framing their demands within, rather than against, the dominant policy paradigms. As traditional attitudes become more egalitarian and as the nature of feminist discourse shifts, away from one of oppression and liberation towards one of human rights and economic efficiency, feminism becomes reframed as an 'inclusionary rather than an anti-system discourse' (Walby 2002:546).

Ideational change has affected not only the extent of support for egalitarianism, but also the way in which gender equality is conceptualized. Within post-industrial countries gender equality strategies tended to shift their focus during the 1980s from questions of redistribution to issues of recognition and representation (Fraser 1995). The first phase of second wave feminism expanded the boundaries of political contestation, beyond socio-economic redistribution, to focus on housework, sexuality and reproduction, whilst continuing to presuppose the key features of the welfare state, and thereby attempting to 'engender' the social imaginary by widening the politics of redistribution (Fraser 2007; Okin 1989; Pateman 1988). Yet with the rise of neo-liberalism came a growing scepticism about the basic idea of egalitarian redistribution (Armstrong 2003; Phillips 1999) and the emergence of identity politics, which frequently appear to valorize cultural difference rather than promote economic equality (Barry 2001). While feminists found that they were unable to make significant headway against injustices of political economy (Fraser 2007), concerns about mis-recognition and under-representation found a more receptive audience. This led to a 'parting of the ways between political and economic concerns' (Phillips 1999:1), which eroded attention to class inequalities while increasing the profile of campaigns for women's political equality. Indeed, many political approaches appeared to jettison concern with economic issues altogether (Phillips 1999: 14–15). This prioritization of political over economic equality further allowed gender equality struggles to be cast as inclusionary rather than anti-system, tending to underplay the extent to which severe economic inequality diminishes access to conventional politics.

One can interpret this new politics of gender equality in two ways, one sceptical the other more hopeful. The first reading stresses that the normalization and institutionalization of a governing neo-liberal economic paradigm has contributed to political disenchantment and disengagement, privileging a largely technical set of devices for managing an open economy that de-democratizes policy-making (Hay 2004:502). Given this, state gender equality mechanisms and policies, which have been actively promoted since the 1980s by the international organizations that oversee neo-liberal governance, might best be understood as part of the de-democratization and co-optation of a women's movement that had previously privileged informal social movement politics outside the state. The coincidence of the normalization of neo-liberalism and the emergence of feminist engagements with the state suggest that these recent feminist strategies may be more complicit in the pursuit of neo-liberal agendas than its feminist advocates have liked to acknowledge. The narrow focus of, and technocratic tendencies within, these strategies is emphasized in this reading, working against the depiction of their emergence as a straightforward success for the global feminist movement.

The second reading, by contrast, suggests that this preoccupation with the loss of democratic politics and changing conception of equality obfuscates the contestation at the heart of the neo-liberal project, in which marginalized groups actively engage in the process of negotiating the emerging concepts and practices that define neo-liberal governance (Larner 2005). From this perspective, the emergence of state gender equality strategies as a central feature of neo-liberal governance suggests that feminist ideas and actors have successfully negotiated a proactive agenda-setting role, capitalizing on the new possibilities for democratic engagement opened up by technocratic governance and state restructuring (Oustshoorn and Kantola 2007) and deploying arguments of economic efficiency to successfully put gender equality considerations onto the policy agenda (Himmelweit 2002). Here feminists active in transnational networks are argued to have used the spaces opened up by a global regime of free trade to engage in politics in new ways (Eschle 2001; Hobson *et al.* 2007). The claim that the normalization of neo-liberalism led to political disenchantment and disengagement is therefore modified in light of the feminist experience of transnational activism and global achievement during this period. This reading therefore offers a more positive account of the new political opportunities offered up by neo-liberal governance.

Making effective use of these changed economic conditions, new political opportunities and altered equality norms, feminists have made increasingly challenging demands of state institutions, insisting that more women be present in state institutions, that the policy agenda be extended to take women's interests into account more systematically than had previously been the case, and that a gender equality perspective be introduced into the policy-making process (Breitenbach, *et al.* 2002). This three-stage dynamic of engagement echoes various other feminist projects, which have generally followed a common pattern of 'adding women in', 'extending the boundaries', and 'reconceptualising the core concepts' (Squires 1999, see also Pateman 1989:2).

Following this dynamic, feminist engagements with the state have taken three key forms: gender quotas, which aim to increase women's participation rates in national assemblies, thereby adding women in and focusing attention on *presence*; women's policy agencies, which create new institutional machineries within the state in order to extend the state's remit to incorporate additional feminist concerns, thereby extending the boundaries of the state and focusing on *voice*; and gender mainstreaming, which subjects the policy-making process to scrutiny from a gendered perspective in order to develop new policy perspectives that avoid structural gender bias, thereby reconceptualizing the core concepts and focusing on *process*. This book explores these three moments of the feminist engagements with the state, evaluating the merits – and pitfalls – of each.

The two most recurrent pitfalls of gender equality strategies are those of *assimilation* and *essentialism*. Throughout the last thirty years feminists have attempted to negotiate the tension between the pursuit of equal treatment and the recognition of difference, oscillating between demands for inclusion into existing institutions according to existing norms, and an assertion of the limitation of these institutions and norms, which have frequently been formulated such that they structurally disadvantage women. Where pursuit of equal treatment generates a strategy of inclusion, the assertion of difference embraces a strategy of reversal (Squires 1999). The concern about a strategy of inclusion is that it may all too easily lead to assimilation, with women being integrated into existing (male-defined) institutions, which remain unaltered by their presence. The concern about a strategy of reversal is that it may all too frequently entail essentialism, with specific identities and interests being attributed to women, thereby perpetuating common sense notions of natural sex difference. Where the former legitimizes assimilatory processes and policies, the latter reproduces essentialist assumptions and stereotypes that were themselves a product of gender unequal institutions and norms. The twin dangers of assimilation and essentialism have haunted the feminist pursuit of political equality, leading many gender equality advocates to argue for a third strategy: one of displacement, which aims to transform the norms and institutions themselves such that they allow for a more equal engagement. Any evaluation of quotas, policy agencies and mainstreaming should therefore be concerned to assess the extent to which they manage to be transformatory while avoiding the pitfalls of assimilation and essentialism.

Emergence, Implementation and Impact

The three political equality measures considered here have been widely adopted throughout the world in a surprisingly short period of time. Gender quotas, first introduced in Western Europe in the 1970s within political party candidate selection processes, have now been introduced in over eighty countries globally, with legislation requiring gender quotas becoming widespread in Latin America and Africa during the last decade. So rapid has been the recent uptake of quota policies in relation to women's candidate selection that commentators suggest that 'quota fever' has affected the world (Dahlerup 1998). Women's policy agencies, introduced following the United Nations World Conference on Women in Mexico City in 1975, have now been established in over 165 countries in a similarly rapid global diffusion of a second gendered democratic policy innovation. Meanwhile, gender mainstreaming, which emerged following the 1995 United Nations conference in Beijing, has been swiftly taken up by supranational institutions, international development agencies, and national governments, and is now also considered to be 'an international phenomenon' (Walby 2005). In light of the widespread adoption of these measures, gender equality within the political arena appears to have become a priority for international organizations and national governments, with these three particular political equality measures becoming part of the process by which states symbolize their commitment both to social justice and to economic modernization.

The three strategies have generally been adopted where a cohesive women's movement has mobilized in their favour; international organizations have put pressure on national political elites to act; political elites have perceived strategic advantages in supporting the measures; and transnational feminist actors have offered expertise in terms of effective adoption and implementation. They have been implemented most enthusiastically in Organisation for Economic Co-operation and Development (OECD) countries by parties of the left which have been experiencing declining support in a period of neo-liberalization and have been keen to appeal to the female electorate in order to enhance their electoral fortunes; and in non-OECD countries by political elites concerned to demonstrate their commitment to women's rights to international funding bodies as a symbol of their embrace of modernization and democratization. Within OECD countries in which domestic rather than international norms remain central, the uptake of the measures has varied, both in frequency and form, with existing citizenship models shaping national responses to demands for greater gender equality in the political sphere (Krook *et al.*

2006). In non OECD countries where international norms have a greater impact, the three measures have most often been introduced from 'above' rather than 'below', either challenging rather than extending existing citizenship norms and practices or operating at a rhetorical level only.

Evaluations of the impact of these measures, usually undertaken by feminist political scientists and gender equality advocates, generally seek to determine whether the mechanisms increase women's participation in and access to political decision-making, and/or transform the policy agenda such that it better represents women. This gives two basic indicators of success, with 'descriptive representation' being used to give a quantitative measure of gender-balance in decision-making, and 'substantive representation' being used to give a qualitative measure of gendered perspectives being included in policy-making. Each of the three strategies offers a different form of political inclusion. Women's policy agencies are judged in terms of both descriptive and substantive representation, aiming to bring 'femocrats' into the state bureaucracy in order to work for women's advancement (Eisenstein 1996; Yeatman 1990). Gender quotas are judged primarily by their ability to secure women's descriptive representation by increasing the number of women in legislatures, though they are also additionally judged by their ability to improve women's substantive representation by female parliamentarians acting for women. Gender mainstreaming is judged primarily in terms of its ability to facilitate women's substantive representation by introducing a gender perspective into the policy-making process.

Evaluations of the success of the three measures in relation to the criteria of descriptive and substantive representation indicate that their rate of adoption has generally been more impressive than has been their impact on women's representation – either descriptive or substantive. Quotas have had a dramatic effect on women's descriptive representation in certain instances, but not uniformly so. The implementation of quotas has been erratic; the impact frequently underwhelming. They have been shown to be most effective in increasing women's descriptive representation where there is a proportional representation electoral system and political parties are supportive, owing either to political will or to effective regulations. The impact of quotas on women's substantive representation has proven hard to measure, with studies focusing on differential attitudes, voting behaviour and issue specialization. Most studies have found that where quotas lead to increased descriptive representation, female parliamentarians have introduced different values, issue priorities and political behaviour. However, the use of differential behaviour as an indicator of success underplays the possibility that issue convergence between genders around new policy priorities may be a more effective indicator of impact.

Women's policy agencies have been shown to improve women's access to decision-making arenas and help realize women's movements' demands in policy-making, but have failed to do so as frequently as they have succeeded. Success has been most likely where the women's movement is cohesive in relation to its demands, where the policy issue in question is a high priority for women's organizations, and where there is a good 'fit' between the approach of the mainstream policy actors of the given policy area and the women's movement's actors. The features of the women's policy agency itself, including scope, type, proximity, administrative capacity, leadership and policy mandate, does not appear to correlate with effectiveness in substantive or descriptive representation, though an unclear mandate appears to be a central obstacle to success.

The impact of gender mainstreaming on women's substantive representation has proven to be extremely difficult to determine, with the effective production of sex disaggregated statistics and implementation of gender impact assessments generally being used as indicators that a gender perspective is being introduced into the policy-making process. An expansion of the range of actors involved in the policy-making process via institutionalized consultation practices has also been used as an indicator of increased substantive representation. Among the assessments of the three political equality mechanisms, evaluations of mainstreaming have generated the least conclusive evidence regarding effective implementation, with many studies finding that its impact is limited to rhetorical change only.

Presence, Voice and Process

While much of the scholarly literature on the emergence, implementation and impact of three political equality strategies treats them as distinct mechanisms, frequently omitting consideration of the other two, gender equality practitioners have generally perceived them to be complementary. Quotas and mainstreaming in particular are increasingly treated as partner measures for the empowerment of women through politics. There is clearly a logic to this in that quotas and mainstreaming engage separate groups of actors and pursue different types of goals: mainstreaming requires that policy-makers take gendered effects into account when drafting legislation but does not require that policy-makers be women, while quotas promote women to the ranks of policy-makers, but do not compel them to consider gender when proposing public policy. Where quotas address the problem of descriptive representation, mainstreaming addresses that of substantive representation. Together, in principle, they promise to secure greater gender equality within political processes.

However, the differences between the two mechanisms may suggest contestation rather than complementarity. The conceptual framing of mainstreaming and quotas is quite different, with distinct notions of equality, representation, gender and politics underpinning each. In relation to equality, gender quotas are defended as a form of positive action, while gender mainstreaming is frequently depicted as embodying an approach to equality and 'goes beyond' both equal treatment and positive action. Mainstreaming therefore has the potential to be used as a means of repudiating and abandoning positive action measures, including women's policy agencies and gender quotas. In relation to representation, advocates of quota policies frequently endorse the link between descriptive and substantive representation, arguing that women-friendly policy originates with female legislators, while gender mainstreaming unravels the link in order to prioritize the pursuit of gender equality rather than the representation of women. In relation to gender, the focus on 'gender', rather than 'women', in mainstreaming acknowledges the relevance of men's lives to gender-equality policies, thus empowering male bureaucrats and legislators in mainstreaming debates, so removing the 'epistemic privilege' apparently granted to female policy-makers in quota policies. Finally, in relation to politics, quotas focus on the vertical distribution of power within party and parliamentary structures, while mainstreaming focuses on the horizontal flow of initiatives across departmental boundaries within state bureaucracies.

While there are conceptual differences between the mechanisms, in practice a combination of the mechanisms might be argued to allow for a more complex understanding of equality policies, in which equal treatment, positive action and mainstreaming each have a role; a more flexible and sophisticated conception of gender, which retains a focus on women as a group; a more subtle understanding of representation, in which descriptive and substantive representative claims can be disentangled; and a wider definition of politics that includes both parliamentary and policy arenas. Consideration as to how the three mechanisms might work together may be fruitful, especially as a coherent strategy embracing all three mechanisms might serve to address some of the concerns raised about each of the mechanisms when viewed in isolation.

For instance, arguments for gender quotas focus attention on gaining access to the institution of parliament, which may delimit wider concerns about gender equality. They also generally appeal to the notion that female representatives will be well placed to represent the interests of women thereby tending to depict women as having unified interests and so obfuscating the differences among women. These quota problems are particularly acute precisely because many advocates anticipate that quotas will lead both to the improved substantive representation of women and to the greater democratization of existing political practices. However, it may be that these expectations are misplaced, and might be more appropriately redirected to women's policy agencies and gender mainstreaming respectively. Were quotas to be viewed 'simply' as a legitimate means of ensuring that a fair number of female candidates get integrated into the existing political structures, and as only one of three mechanisms for engaging in the political sphere, the concerns about essentialism and assimilation might well diminish. Rather than attempting to defend the claim that women's presence alone will lead to improved substantive representation and the greater democratization of existing political practices, gender equality advocates could then make more measured claims about the likely impact of quotas, while paying more attention to the need to complement this mechanism with the other available political equality mechanisms, namely women's policy agencies and gender mainstreaming.

Women's policy agencies, by contrast, are frequently argued to give the women's movement greater access to state bureaucracies. Yet the idea of a singular, coherent movement looks increasingly strained. Women's policy agencies may actively constitute a less than representative depiction of women's interests in order to claim a legitimate representative function, while appealing to professionalized feminist NGOs which adopt an increasingly technocratic mode of operation, as a surrogate for citizen-based democratic participation. In this way women's policy agencies may also manifest the problems of both essentialism and assimilation, reifying the voice of the women's movement while adopting technocratic modes of governance. These problems are particularly acute when women's policy agencies claim to speak on behalf of a movement, making a representative claim that is rarely grounded in mechanisms of authorization or accountability. Where women's policy agencies are regarded more directly as 'feminist advocacy' bodies, promoting specific interests via professionalized policy networks, these problems diminish in that they are no longer viewed primarily as representative bodies and need not therefore be judged in these terms.

Meanwhile, the limitation of gender mainstreaming appears to be that, in practice, it becomes a technocratic process reduced to a series of procedures, such as impact assessments, that eschew both political participation and normative contestation in their reliance of professionalized expertise and evidence-based indicators. Moreover, mainstreaming frequently embraces not only neo-liberal techniques of governance but also marketized economic goals that construe gender equality in an integrationist rather than transformatory manner, relying on utility-based rather than right-based frames of analysis that are ultimately concerned with efficiency rather than equity. Nonetheless, mainstreaming processes do offer new opportunities for bureaucratic interventions that privilege evidence-based policy-making and so empower those 'gender experts' able to articulate their perspectives in these terms, enabling them to speak to all policy issues rather than only to those traditionally considered to be gendered.

The positive potential of mainstreaming may therefore resonate with claims that neo-liberal forms of governance have given way to a new form of governance based on trust and collaboration (Newman 2001, 2006; Rhodes 1994, 1996, 2000). This form of governance relies on professionalized 'social entrepreneurs' who network with community activists and promote change through a process of brokerage (Larner and Craig 2005:405). Together, the strategic brokers within women's policy agencies and social entrepreneurs within women's NGOs have created powerful new forms of governance designed to improve the social integration of women. This has clearly empowered many women politically, but it has also 'governmentalized' their professional functions and political ambitions. In this way, this process-based politics may complement the presence and voice of the other two strategies, but when decoupled from them swiftly becomes a technocratic rather than democratic strategy.

Although many advocates of gender mainstreaming have stressed its participatory function, allowing women's perspectives to be taken into account in the policy-making process, mainstreaming practices actually rely on technocratic data collection and impact assessments carried out by professionalized gender experts. The growing tendency to promote a twin-track equality strategy based on presence and process therefore raises concerns, in that voice is marginalized. Together these gender equality strategies held out the theoretical promise of transformation, yet in practice they frequently appear to be surprisingly complicit with current modalities of governance. The very processes of destabilization and displacement favoured by feminists advocating a transformatory approach to gender equality (Squires 1999), appear vulnerable to new forms of articulation with neo-liberal governance (Newman 2006). Collective struggles for recognition and citizenship rights come to be viewed as part of an 'old' form of politics that is no longer compatible with current practices of governmentality. Meanwhile, a reassertion of voice, in the form of a defence of women's policy agencies, raises renewed concerns about essentialism, which look increasingly vulnerable in the context of the growing concern with diversity and multiple equality strands.

Governance and Diversity

The two most striking challenges now facing gender equality strategies are the reconfiguration of state practices to embrace technocratic modes of governance, and the widespread embrace of 'diversity' as a governmental priority (Benhabib 2002; Liebert 2003). From the late 1990s onwards the 'separate strands' approach to equality – in which sex, race, disability, age, sexuality and religious equality were pursued independently – has gradually been replaced by a more integrated concern with 'diversity'. This places gender equality within a wider equalities framework and demands that gender equality advocates consider other inequality stands and the intersections between them.

These two developments resonate in different ways with the twin concerns that have haunted the three political equality measures under consideration, namely: whether the mechanisms designed to facilitate women's increased political equality lead to the assimilation of women into existing political systems, rather than the transformation of those systems; and whether the mechanisms rely on essentializing notions of women and the women's movement, which fail to recognize a more complex social diversity. While the emergence of a technocratic mode of governance appears to accentuate and entrench concerns about assimilation, the emergence of 'diversity' as a central policy problem appears, by contrast, to confront and unsettle concerns about essentialism. Whether the emergence of a multiple equalities agenda will help feminists to avoid assimilation and essentialism, or will simply accentuate the tendency to retreat into one or the other, is yet to be seen.

The challenge posed by the embrace of technocratic modes of governance requires feminists to engage more directly with theories and practices of participatory democracy than has been common in recent years. The growing feminist preoccupation with the mainstreaming mechanisms reveals a turn away from a focus on democratic participation and towards a focus on the implementation of gender-equality policy measures as mechanisms of governance. While the latter is clearly important, it is crucial to maintain a commitment to the former, for without inclusive deliberation as to what gender equality entails – and therefore what form gender-equality policies should take – the pursuit of gender equality can itself become an exclusionary process, undertaken for considerations of utility rather than justice and so privileging particular productive forms of gender identity over others (Mohammad 2005). To mainstream a gender equality perspective is not necessarily to democratize the state (Rai 2003). Future feminist political practices need to be attentive not only to fostering modes of governance that take the pursuit of gender equality as a policy goal, but also to ways of facilitating a more inclusive democratic debate as to what gender equality comprises.

There are various possible indicators of inequality, including life expectancy and physical health, bodily integrity and safety, educational access and attainment, access to paid work, rates of pay, political empowerment, and being treated with dignity (Robeyns 2003:76–86). Deciding what we measure is a political process with political consequences, such that access to the process by which the relative importance of these indicators is determined will correlate with the adoption of remedies that most directly reflect one's own particular egalitarian concerns (Okin 2003; Young 2001). In this way, conceptions of equality can be seen to be constitutive, generating equality policy frames that privilege certain concerns whilst obscuring others (Bacchi 1999). Pursuing one form of equality may serve to displace another from the political agenda. For this reason scholars have attempted not only to pluralize the measures of inequality (Sen 1992), but also to stress the importance of democratic deliberation in constructing these measures (Armstrong 2006; Robeyns 2003:69). This suggests that critical public discussion, or democratic deliberation, is vital to the conceptualization of gender equality.

Because the meaning of equality is contested, it is vital that marginalized groups are able to take part in the formulation of equality norms, rather than simply being the objects of policies thought by privileged minorities to be equitable. As a result, there is a strong normative presumption within much of the recent theoretical writing on marginalized groups that these groups need to be present in deliberative bodies in order that their perspectives can be voiced and taken into account when formulating public policies (Benhabib 1996; Young 2000; Phillips 1995; Williams 1998). This insight politicizes the formation of equality policies, and links it to the question of political inclusion. The demand for greater political participation is thus both a demand for greater political equality in its own right, and a demand for greater access to the process by which wider equality norms are determined. For this reason democratic participation needs to be understood as a constitutive part of the pursuit of equality itself. Moreover, this participation should not be viewed in an unduly narrow and restricted way in terms of parliamentary elections only, but should embrace the messy processes of participatory democracy (Sen 2004).

The concern, which underpins the more detailed interrogation of gender equality strategies in the following chapters, is that the growing focus on presence and process is being achieved at the expense of a commitment to voice, producing an increasingly de-politicized and technocratic approach to gender equality that marginalizes precisely this messy process of participatory democracy. While each of the three political equality mechanisms has strengths when considered as specific elements in a multi-faceted approach to political empowerment, what remains lacking from this package is a more deliberative engagement with citizens. Here gender equality advocates could usefully engage with other attempts to revitalize existing democratic practices, particularly deliberative innovations such as citizen's juries, deliberative opinion polling and consensus conferences, and direct-democracy innovations including referenda (Elster 1998; Fishkin 1991, 2000; Saward 1998, 2000; Smith 2005).

These innovations are motivated by a desire to increase and deepen citizen participation in the political decision-making process. They offer a potentially beneficial element of direct democratic engagement, currently lacking from the three political equality measures promoted by gender scholars and practitioners. Where both party politics and standard techniques of consultation tend to attract citizens who already have a strong political interest, deliberative approaches bring together a cross-section of the population so that all citizens have an equal opportunity to participate. The deliberations amongst diverse citizens may therefore generate conceptualizations of gender equality that are more sensitive to diversity amongst women and to the gender equality perspectives of subordinate men than has previously been the case. Such deliberative mechanisms could further complement feminist engagements with the state, addressing the recurrent concern regarding assimilation by unsettling the technocratic process of governance.

However, these mechanisms would entail relinquishing a focus on women as a group at a time when an exclusive gender equality focus is under threat. Feminist interventions in the state currently face a profound new challenge in the form of other equality considerations. The international institutions and national governments that have been relatively receptive to gender equality mechanisms are increasingly concerned to promote anti-discrimination in relation to other equality considerations also. Those state institutions that have proven willing to promote gender equality are now seeking to challenge discrimination on grounds of age, disability, religion and belief, ethnicity and sexual orientation and gender, and to do so in a more integrated manner than previously was the case (Squires 2007).

The emergence of multiple inequalities agendas presents new challenges for feminists. It has raised anxieties that gender equality considerations will be marginalized, and even undermined, by the pursuit of other equality claims, especially those of religion (Skjeie 2007). It is suggested that increased attention to the ways in which other structures of inequality intersect with those of gender (Crenshaw 1991) may incrementally lead to an undifferentiated celebration of diversity lacking in critical purchase *vis-à-vis* structural inequalities (Woodward 2005). On the other hand, this development may allow for greater sensitivity to intersectional or multiple discrimination issues (Hankivsky 2005; Squires 2005; Yuval-Davis 2005).

On a practical level the emergence of 'diversity' considerations on the policy agenda has led many states to merge women's policy agencies into generic equalities units, and to use mainstreaming as a process for considering multiple equality strands rather than gender alone (Squires 2006; Verloo 2006). The challenge posed by the recent embrace of diversity agendas requires feminists to engage more directly with theories and practices of intersectionality than has been common in recent years. If the twin-track endorsement of presence and process looks worryingly technocratic, a simple endorsement of greater voice for women via a robust defence of existing women's policy agencies will not suffice given the growing move to replace them with equality agencies. It may indeed be the case that the twin-track approach to the promotion of gender equality, in the form of the increased presence of women and the adoption of more gender-sensitive processes, has resulted in higher levels of assimilation than many advocates would have hoped, but the scope for bringing 'voice' back in will need to be re-conceived to acknowledge the differences among women and the intersections between multiple forms of inequality.

Conclusion

The new politics of gender equality is more state-oriented than the earlier forms of informal activism that characterized the women's movement in the

1970s. The pursuit of gender equality has become a mainstream rather than an anti-system project, and – in the process – has increasingly been framed in relation to utility-based concerns of efficiency in addition to (and sometimes rather than) rights-based concerns of social justice. Parity of political participation has gained a central place within gender equality projects, pursued by three distinct equality strategies which focus on presence, voice and process respectively. In recent years the emphasis on the importance of voice, secured by women's policy agencies, has dwindled, with a commitment to a twin-track policy that privileges presence and process increasingly coming to dominate. Each of the strategies is prone in various ways to the problems of essentialism or assimilation. The problem of assimilation is accentuated by the growth in increasingly technocratic modes of governance, while the problem of essentialism is unsettled by the growing concern with diversity and multiple equality agendas. The danger inherent in these developments is that gender equality becomes subsumed within, or marginalized by, a technocratic pursuit of equality conceived in a manner that lacks sensitivity to the specificity of gender inequalities. Yet, there are also opportunities to be grasped in relation to the greater access to policy-making processes created by new forms of governance coupled with a greater sensitivity in current policy frames to issues of intersectionality.

In order to address these issues, and to draw out the practical and theoretical contributions made by these political equality measures, this book documents the emergence, implementation and impact of quotas, women's policy agencies and gender mainstreaming (Chapters 1 and 2). It considers the relation between the mechanisms (Chapter 3), and the strengths and weaknesses of each of the political equality measures (Chapters 4, 5 and 6), focusing on the recurrent problems of assimilation and essentialism. It evaluates their potential for transforming political institutions and agendas rather than simply integrating women into them, and their ability to empower women politically without simultaneously reifying them. Finally, it reflects on the emerging challenges facing these gender equality measures, focusing on the likely impact of 'diversity' agendas for gender mainstreaming practices in particular (Chapter 7).

1
Equality Strategies: Quotas, Policy Agencies and Mainstreaming

Introduction

The commitment to promoting gender-balanced decision-making, currently espoused by international institutions and national assemblies around the globe, emerged in the face of the persistent under-representation of women globally (Karam 1998). Since 1788 when women first gained the right to stand for election in the United States of America, women's right to vote and be elected has slowly been recognized throughout the sovereign states of the world. Only a handful of countries continue to refuse women the right to vote and stand for election. Yet women's active participation in national parliaments is still notoriously low, rising from 3 per cent in 1945 to only 11.6 per cent in 1995. In July 2006 the world average for the percentage of women in national parliaments was still only 16.6 per cent. Increasingly aware of gender imbalances in political representation, political parties and national legislatures across the region have taken steps over the last twenty years to promote women's access to political decision-making, encouraged by a raft of declarations and directives from international bodies such as the United Nations and the European Union.

For example, the Universal Declaration of Human Rights affirms that everyone has the right to take part in the government of his or her country, and the UN Beijing Platform for Action states:

> Achieving the goal of equal participation of women and men in [d]ecision-making will provide a balance that more accurately

> reflects the composition of society and is needed in order to strengthen democracy and promote its proper functioning … Without the active participation of women and the incorporation of women's perspectives at all levels of decision-making, the goals of equality, development and peace cannot be achieved. (United Nations 1995:181)

It therefore calls on governments to:

> [c]ommit themselves to establishing the goal of gender balance in governmental bodies and committees, as well as in public administrative entities, and in the judiciary, including, *inter alia*, setting specific targets and implementing measures to substantially increase the number of women with a view to achieving equal representation of women and men, if necessary through positive action, in all governmental and public administration positions. (United Nations 1995:190)

Similarly, the Charter of Rome states that: 'The equal participation of women and men in decision-making processes is our major goal at European level' (Council of Europe 1996), and in its Recommendation of 2 December 1996 the Council of the European Union calls on the member states to develop suitable measures and strategies to correct the under-representation of women in decision-making positions.

It is therefore now widely acknowledged that women are under-represented politically around the world, and that this under-representation is problematic (Norris 1997; United Nations 1995). The most frequently articulated reasons within the gender politics literature focus on three issues: the development of a just and equal society is hindered; women's interests remain unfulfilled; and democracy is likely to become atrophied (Phillips 1995:62–83). The 'justice' argument implies that numerically equal representation of women and men in legislatures is itself an indication of parity, regardless of the beliefs of those present or the policies enacted (focusing attention on the importance of descriptive representation). The 'women's interests' argument holds that women need to enter formal politics to work for women's interests. Thus it is not presence alone, but the decisions made and policies formulated that matter (focusing attention on the importance of substantive representation). The 'democratic' argument proposes that women should enter into positions of power because they will engage in political activity differently – revitalizing democracy and thereby improving the nature of the public sphere (Phillips 1995). These arguments have underpinned feminist campaigns for the introduction of mechanisms and institutions that will better secure gender-balanced decision-making.

The introduction of political equality measures signals that the political demands of the women's movement have been influential. However, other explanations for their widespread recent adoption also exist. A second explanation for their adoption resides with the pragmatic concerns of political elites, concerned with the need to appeal to the female electorate and to conform to the norms of international organizations and more powerful states in order to gain legitimacy and secure development aid. A third explanation for their adoption focuses on the emergence of these international norms themselves, highlighting the role that international organizations, such as the United Nations, have played in promoting gender-balanced decision-making, by discursively equating modernization with feminization (Inglehart and Norris 2003:127–46). Evidence linking levels of gender equality to degrees of modernization (Inglehart and Norris 2003:127–46), coupled with effective feminist transnational activism (Walby 2002), has encouraged international organizations to adopt gender-balanced decision-making as an indicator of development. This in turn has provided political elites with strategic reasons to promote measures that promise to increase women's political participation, which in turn creates new political opportunities for the women's movement to argue for greater gender justice.

The pursuit of the equal participation of men and women in the political sphere has increasingly taken three distinct forms: the increased participation of women in national assemblies; the improved incorporation of women's policy concerns; and the introduction of a gender equality perspective into all policy-making areas. The desire to secure more gender-balanced decision-making and policy-making bodies has accordingly generated the widespread promotion of three particular political equality measures already mentioned. Each of these aims to facilitate women's empowerment by increasing their political representation in the expectation that this will lead to greater gender equality. The strategies clearly differ in their approach to facilitating women's democratic inclusion: whereas gender quotas focus on the composition of the legislature (descriptive representation), women's policy agencies focus on the pursuit of women's interests (substantive representation), and gender mainstreaming concentrates on the processes of policy formation and implementation across all issue areas, bringing gendered perspectives (rather than female bodies or women's interests) into the institutions of the state.

Nonetheless, these three distinct gender equality measures, which emerged at roughly the same time period to secure the same commitment to gender-balanced decision-making, are rarely considered explicitly in relation one to the other in terms of their relative merits, ideational coherence and material impact. This chapter outlines the key features of the three measures and briefly documents their adoption across the globe. The aim of the chapter is to demonstrate that gender equality is established as a high priority for international organizations and national governments, which now largely accept that indices on the political status of women are one key measure of development. The political inequality of women has come to be accepted as an ill that states seeks to cure (rhetorically if not substantively), with the pursuit of these three particular gender equality measures becoming part of the process by which states symbolize their commitment both to gender justice and to economic modernization.

Gender Quotas

Quotas are one particular mechanism for achieving gender balance in political institutions. They might more accurately be described as 'electoral candidate quotas' or 'legislature sex quotas', which aim to rectify the under-representation of women, not gender. Quotas entail various mechanisms that aim to secure sex-balanced decision-making, including party quotas that aim to increase the proportion of party candidates who are women and legislative quotas that require political parties to nominate a certain percentage of women among their candidates. They are a form of group representation, though a form that does not entail representatives referring back to or speaking for women in any direct way, for those elected as a result of quota policies are not directly accountable to women as a group. Nonetheless, those elected by quotas are argued to represent women by securing a more equitable distribution of representative positions, so bringing a wider range of perspectives into play (Phillips 1999:40–1), or via 'descriptive' representation, in which the representatives are 'in some sense typical of the larger class of persons whom they represent' as a result of shared experiences (Mansbridge 1999).

Although quotas provide a loose, unpredictable form of group representation (Phillips 2004), they have proven to be controversial, frequently perceived to undercut a normative commitment to fairness and equal opportunities, and, more concretely, to limit the political opportunities of incumbent candidates or potential male aspirants. Their primary aim is to increase the number of women in national legislatures, though it is widely hoped that they might also facilitate the improved representation of the female electorate, introducing new policy concerns and political styles into national legislatures.

Quotas were initially introduced at a party level in Western Europe in the 1970s, but increasingly also take the form of legislative quotas and are now present throughout the world, particularly in Latin America and Africa, causing some to suggest that 'quota fever' has affected the world (Dahlerup and Freidenvall 2005:32). Nearly every country has now pledged to promote gender-balanced decision-making, and more than 80 countries have adopted quotas for the selection of female candidates (either by constitutional amendment, by electoral law, or in major political parties' own statutes), each demanding that a certain minimum of the parties' candidates for election to the national parliament must be women (see Dahlerup and Freidenvall 2005; Krook 2004, 2005a). While this represents a significant uptake of gender quotas across the globe, quotas nonetheless remain less 'popular' than women's policy agencies (although they have gained much more theoretical and public attention): women's policy agencies have been adopted in 165 countries worldwide, as compared with the 80 countries that have adopted quotas to date, signalling that contestation continues to surround their adoption.

Quotas are widely viewed as the most effective means of increasing the representation of women. These quotas can take different forms: they can be set at different levels (for example, 20 per cent or 50 per cent) and can be applied at different stages of the selection process (for example, for shortlists or selections of parliamentary candidates). However, it is common to categorize them according to the nature of the institution that establishes the quota ruling (Dahlerup 2005). Constitutional quotas entail quota provisions mandated by the constitution of a country; legal quotas entail quota laws introduced by national legislatures; party quotas entail individual political parties introducing rules relating to the percentage of women nominated to stand as electoral candidates. Some scholars also use a category of 'soft quotas', which includes a range of measures that seek to increase women's representation, either indirectly through internal party quotas or more directly through informal targets and recommendations (see Krook *et al.* 2006).

As of 2006, 12 countries have adopted constitutional quotas for their national parliaments. Of these, 11 are non-OECD countries: Afghanistan, Argentina, Bangladesh, Burundi, Guyana, Iraq, Nepal, Rwanda, Taiwan, Tanzania and Uganda. France is the only OECD country to have adopted constitutional gender quotas. The earliest constitutional quotas were introduced in Nepal in 1990 and Argentina in 1991, with the remaining 10 countries introducing their constitutional quotas since 1995. Clause 114 of the 1990 Nepalese constitution states that at least 5 per cent of the total number of candidates seeking election to the lower house from any political party or organization must be women candidates, and cl. 46 states that at least 3 seats are reserved for women in the 60-member upper house (Rai *et al.* 2006). In Argentina, art. 37(2) states that 'real equality of opportunity between men and women for access to elective and political party office shall be guaranteed by positive actions in regulation of the political parties and the electoral regime', and art. 75(23) that no future law can lower the quota provisions (Araujo and Garcia 2006; Jones 1996, 1998). More recently, the newly adopted 2004 constitutions of Afghanistan and Iraq have both included quota provisions, following pressure from the international community to include gender equality considerations in post-conflict state-building (Ballington and Dahlerup 2006). In France, constitutional quotas were introduced in 1999, when the constitution was revised to include a commitment that 'the law favours the equal access of women and men to electoral mandates and elective functions' and that political parties were responsible for facilitating equal access.

As with constitutional quotas, legal quotas have been introduced since the early 1990s, with an increasing number of national legislatures introducing quotas since 2000. Legal quotas have been adopted in 38 countries (9 of which also have constitutional quotas). Again, most of the countries with legal quotas are outside the Organization for Economic Cooperation and Development (OECD) – Belgium, France and Mexico being the only countries within it to have legal quotas. For example countries in Latin America with legal quotas include Argentina, Bolivia, Brazil, Costa Rica, Ecuador, Honduras, Paraguay and Peru, in Africa Burundi, Eritrea, Liberia, Rwanda, Sudan, Tanzania and Uganda. Most of these quotas were introduced in the late 1990s and early 2000s. For instance, legal quotas were introduced in Mexico in 2002, requiring political parties to guarantee that women constitute at least 30 per cent of candidates to the Senate (upper house) and to the Chamber of Deputies (lower house), on both lists of candidates for the PR election and for the constituency elections. Legal quotas were also mandated by the Belgian parliament in 1994 through a law that specified that women would compose at least 25 per cent of all electoral lists until 1999, after which the quota requirement would be raised to 33.3 per cent. Following the passage of a new law on equality between women and men, parliament revisited the quota requirement and raised it to 50 per cent in 2002 (Meier 2004).

The pattern of adoption of constitutional and legal quotas suggests that their introduction is bound up with the process of democratization, where support for quota laws is framed as a commitment to democratization. Latin America has seen 11 out of 19 countries approving legal or constitutions quotas between 1996 and 2000 (with the exception of Argentina which introduced its quotas earlier in 1991), with the transition to democracy and the need for international legitimacy on the part of new democracies proving crucial in this region (Araujo and Garcia 2006). Countries deeming themselves to be democratic already, and subject to fewer pressures from international actors, are less likely to consider constitutional or legal quotas, but may have party quotas (Krook *et al.* 2006).

Whereas the adoption of constitutional or legal quotas tends to be a very recent phenomenon, the introduction of party quotas dates back to the 1980s in many European countries (1985 in Austria, 1987 in the Netherlands and Sweden). These are the most common type of formal quotas globally, including in OECD countries, and are currently in place in 163 political parties in 73 countries (Quota Project 2006). They are by far the most common type of quotas in Europe, with political parties in Austria, Denmark, Germany, Greece, Italy, Norway, Poland, Spain, Sweden and the United Kingdom all adopting party quotas. Left-wing parties have proven most likely to adopt gender quotas, though other parties sometimes follow their lead. In the overwhelming majority of countries in which party quotas operate, quotas remain publicly controversial and contested by many. For example, while all but two German parties (the Christian Social Union and the Free Democratic Party) apply gender quotas, stigma still tends to attach to those women who benefit from them (McKay 2004). Party quotas remain similarly controversial in the United Kingdom, with the Labour Party's 1993 policy requiring that all-women shortlists be used to select candidates in half of all vacant seats that the party was likely to win, including those seats where a Labour MP was retiring, proving highly contentious. Indeed, following a court ruling in 1996 that declared all women shortlists illegal (Russell 2000), Labour dropped the policy until it reformed the Sex Discrimination Act in 2002 to allow parties to pursue quotas to increase women's selection as candidates for political office (Childs 2002a). So while social-democratic or left political parties in many European countries were first to introduce gender quotas, quotas have nonetheless remained controversial, especially in countries with liberal citizenship models or among parties that espouse liberal values. For example, quotas remain deeply unpopular in New Zealand and the United States, where a liberal model of citizenship predominates (Krook *et al.* 2006). While political parties in New Zealand have debated the introduction of quotas, they have been rejected in favour of 'softer' measures (Catt 2003) and political parties in the United States also remain resolutely hostile to candidate quotas, which they perceive to work against the principle of meritocracy (Klausen and Maier 2001).

It is clear from the growing number of countries with party quotas, and the recent rapid increase in the number of countries with constitutional and/or legal quotas, that quotas are a global phenomenon, notwithstanding many normative anxieties about them. Accounts as to why quotas have emerged so swiftly onto the global political agenda tend to emphasize three explanations: the political activism of women, the strategic aims of political elites and the process of international norm transfusion (Krook 2004, 2005a).

The first explanation focuses on the political activism of women in grassroots women's movements, political parties and the state, and situates quotas in relation to arguments for greater gender justice. This account suggests that quotas are most likely to be adopted where women's increased political representation is a high-priority issue for the women's movement, and where the movement is relatively united in its support for quota policies. This approach finds support in the fact that quotas emerge earliest in countries with active women's movements. For instance, party quotas were first introduced in Denmark, Sweden and Norway in the 1980s, where women were active in both women's movements and the state, having secured 20–30 per cent of the seats in parliament (Dahlerup and Freidnevall 2005:27). Yet, as Krook notes,

> women as a group are frequently divided as to the desirability of quotas, with some of the strongest opposition coming from feminists, both inside and outside the political parties, who argue that quotas do not further the cause of female empowerment. (Krook 2004:60)

Given that quotas have not always been a high priority or consensual issue for the women's movement, the explanation for their widespread global adoption inevitably entails other factors.

The second explanation therefore looks to the role of political elites in ushering in the global embrace of gender quotas, focusing on the strategic advantages that might accrue to the elites from their introduction. This locates quotas within discourses of democratic legitimacy and economic development rather than gender justice. For instance, parties that have experienced long periods out of office or a dramatic decrease in popularity might seek to introduce party quotas as a means of appealing to the female electorate and so enhancing their electoral fortunes. This may be particularly relevant to OECD parties of the left experiencing declining support in a period of neo-liberalization. Other parties may then follow suit in order not to lose the electoral advantage. Democratic states have been shown to be more progressive in terms of their gender values (Inglehart and Norris 2003) and there may therefore be some political advantage in being seen to be promoting gender equality in the form of quotas (Matland 2005:277). On the other hand, political elites in non-OECD countries might give rhetorical support for legal or constitutional quotas (or perhaps introduce quotas without the sort of sanctions that might ensure their effectiveness) in order to demonstrate (most often to international funding bodies concerned to find indicators of modernization and democratization among potential recipients of development aid) a national commitment to women's rights (Htun and Jones 2002; Marques-Pereira 2001). This commitment is seen as particularly important in the context of international norms that associate gender equality with less corruption and good governance (Towns 2003). This explains the adoption of constitutional or legal quotas by post-conflict countries with high levels of international presence (such as Iraq and Rwanda) or countries in transition to democracy (such as in Latin America).

More generally, there appears to be a correlation between the level of democracy and the type of quota provisions adopted. Matland finds that among democratic countries only 14.8 per cent have adopted legal quotas, with 50 per cent having party quotas; among the semi-democratic countries 30.2 per cent have legal quotas and 24.5 percent party quotas; while among non-democratic states 14.3 per cent have legal quotas and 9.5 per cent party quotas (Matland 2005:277). He therefore surmises that semi-democratic countries will be inclined to adopt legal quotas 'because they perceive them as conferring legitimacy', making them appear more democratic, and the relative lack of power among political parties makes their legal adoption easier to introduce (Matland 2005:277).

The third explanation of the emergence of gender quotas focuses on the processes by which certain policy norms gain a privileged international status by being actively diffused transnationally. Most accounts of the emergence of gender quotas emphasize the role of transnational actors in establishing quotas as a policy deemed by international organizations to be particularly consistent with, and symbolic of, other widely held international norms such as political equality, democratization and sustainable development. Feminist transnational activists have successfully mobilized support for gender quotas, drawing on theories that link state development, from agrarian to industrial to post-industrial societies, to growing equality of sex roles (Inglehart and Norris 2003). Given the prevalence of developmental theories that posit that traditional societies are characterized by sharply differentiated gender roles, international organizations have been highly receptive to feminist demands that the promotion of gender-balanced decision-making should be viewed as a central part of the development process.

The role of the resultant recommendations that emerge from these international organizations, committing member states to improve women's access to decision-making, has been significant. For instance, the UN has played a central role in promoting gender-balanced decision-making and representation, stating that:

> The empowerment and autonomy of women and the improvement of women's social, economic and political status is essential for the achievement of both transparent and accountable government and administration and sustainable development in all areas of life. (United Nations 1995:181)

Surveys of the introduction of quotas in Latin America and sub-Saharan Africa stress the importance of transnational and regional norm diffusion following the UN-sponsored international conferences (Araujo and Garcia 2006; Tripp *et al.* 2006). From this perspective the global adoption of quotas reflects a growing commitment on the part of the international community to democratization and development, resulting in a 'fast track' to equal political representation (Dahlerup and Freidenvall 2005).

While many commentators have viewed this as a manifestation of the strength of the transnational women's movement (Dahlerup 2006:4), others fear that it indicates that a commitment to gender-balanced decision-making has been taken up either symbolically in a desire to appear modern, or as part of the neo-liberal project, facilitating other highly prized goals such as economic productivity that require a particular type of public gender regime (Towns 2003). Towns suggests that quotas should be understood as a means of constructing state institutions that are conducive to free markets and economic development, rather than as a means of securing greater democratic justice (Towns 2003), and therefore takes the adoption of gender quotas as an international norm associated with economic development to signal that women's movements are not in full control of the quotas agenda. Placing a more positive spin on this, Dahlerup argues that one of the under-acknowledged features of globalization has been the growing importance of a country's image in the international community, which creates new opportunities for women's movements to 'play the international card in their lobbying on the national level' (Dahlerup 2006:4). Both accept that globalization has made the diffusion of quotas around the globe more feasible by opening up new political opportunity structures within international organizations (Walby 2002), and by increasing the possibilities for transnational feminist 'leverage' (Hobson *et al.* 2007), given that gender equality has come to be discursively associated with other valued norms of democratization and development.

The international pressure to adopt gender quotas impacts differently on different states, however, given that pre-existing citizenship models shape both equality commitments and representative mechanisms. The uptake of gender quotas has not therefore been even, nor has their form been uniform. Ideas about the nature of citizenship frame quotas debates at both the party and the national levels, generating distinct political logics that influence the prospects and outcomes of quota campaigns (Krook *et al.* 2006). For example, the introduction of legal quotas in Belgium was facilitated by its consociational model of citizenship (Krook *et al.* 2006), which enabled advocates of gender quotas to appeal to existing representative practices in Belgium that guarantee the participation of a range of different groups based on linguistic, religious, and class cleavages (Meier 2000), and use these to argue for their extension to women (Mateo-Diaz 2002). On the other hand, the introduction of constitutional quotas in France was shaped by the republican citizenship model, in that parity stressed the equitable sharing of power between women and men, the two halves of the human race, in order to ensure normative consistency with the dominant republican discourse (Agacinski 2001; Gaspard *et al.* 1992). This meant that the constitutional amendment was called 'the parity reform', with the term 'parity' used in preference to quotas in order to distinguish it from arguments for special representation rights for minorities, which were perceived in France to be American (and therefore problematic), notwithstanding America's actual hostility to quotas. Meanwhile, polities operating with liberal, rather than republican or corporatist, models of citizenship have frequently rejected or resisted quotas as a means of bringing more women into political office, privileging strategies that facilitate access rather than mandating outcomes, as this fits better with the dominant equality discourse that privileges equality of opportunity rather than equality of outcome (Phillips 2004). This means, for instance, that quotas of all forms are both unpopular and illegal in the United States (Stephanopoulos and Edley 1995), and attempts to increase women's descriptive representation there operate indirectly through internal party quotas or more directly through informal targets and recommendations (Krook *et al.* 2006).

So, although the emergence of gender quotas is clearly a global phenomenon, the national specificity of quota campaigns is such that national quota campaigns rarely engage the same groups of actors in the same way (Krook 2004:62). The focus on national citizenship models is most pertinent in countries where domestic rather than international norms remain influential, such that quotas emerge in an 'incremental' fashion within the logic of existing citizenship models (Dahlerup and Freidenvall 2005). Where international norms have a greater impact, quotas are often introduced from 'above' rather than 'below', transforming rather than extending existing citizenship norms and practices.

The rapid adoption of gender quotas internationally therefore needs to be understood in relation to a range of factors, including feminist mobilization, the strategic interests of political elites and international pressure, which will play themselves out differently in different contexts. Overall, it seems that gender quotas are most likely to be adopted where there is a cohesive women's movement that mobilizes in favour of quotas; where this women's movement has established alliances with political elites who see strategic advantages in supporting quota campaigns; where international organizations also put pressure on political elites to act; and where transnational actors supply information about how best to act. This scenario suggests that domestic women's movements work with international organizations and transnational actors to convince political elites of the strategic advantages of supporting quota campaigns notwithstanding normative controversies that frequently accompany their introduction.

Women's Policy Agencies

Where quotas focus attention on the composition and decision-making of national legislatures, policy agencies address the problem of gender and political inequality by focusing attention on the under-representation of both women and women's issues within state bureaucracies, and by developing mechanisms by which their substantive representation within state bureaucracies can be improved. These agencies, which are sometimes also referred to as 'national machineries for the advancement of women', or 'gender machinery', are institutional arrangements within state bureaucracies devoted to women's policy questions (Stetson and Mazur 1995:1), defined by the UN as any bodies 'recognised by the Government as the institutions dealing with the promotion of the status of women' (E/CN.6/1988/3, para. 21).

The emergence of these agencies as one of the central mechanisms for realizing women's substantive political representation created what is often called 'state feminism' and women working within women's policy agencies have come to be referred to as 'femocrats', a term coined in Australia and New Zealand in the 1980s (Franzway *et al.* 1989:133; Sawer 1990; Watson 1990). These femocrats are argued to have the potential to act as important agents for women's increased representation by facilitating the creation of a 'triangle of empowerment' between women in elected office, women's movements and appointed officials within the policy agencies (Mazur 2002; Vargas and Wieringa 1998; Weldon 2002).

The first women's policy agencies emerged following the United Nations World Conference on Women in Mexico City in 1975, which recommended that governments establish agencies dedicated to promoting gender equality and improving the status and conditions of women. The need for state-based institutions charged formally with furthering women's status and gender equality has been mentioned systematically at every women's conference since and has figured prominently in UN official policy directives (Mazur 2005:2). Following the lead given by the 1975 United Nations conference on women, policy agencies were actively promoted by transnational women's groups and widely adopted by national governments throughout the late 1970s and 1980s (Chappell 2002). By the mid 1980s 127 states had created women's policy agencies (Mazur 2005:2). The trend to establish such agencies continued throughout the 1990s, with 165 countries operating women's policy agencies of some form by 2004 (Directory of National Machineries for the Advancement of Women, DAW, March 2004). This represented a dramatic response to the 1975 recommendation, and has been widely viewed by gender equality advocates as a significant indicator of success. Yet the emergence of these agencies also marked a 'bureaucratization of feminism', about which many feminists retain a lingering suspicion, given the women's movement's earlier tendency to focus on informal political activism. Both the feminist embrace of bureaucratization and the state embrace of women's policy concerns was as swift as it was surprising. As True and Mintrom note, 'This rapid global diffusion of a state-level bureaucratic innovation is unprecedented in the post-war era' (True and

Mintrom 2001:30). Why these agencies have been adopted so widely, and to what effect, remain interesting – and profoundly important – issues for gender equality advocates.

The form that policy agencies take varies widely. They can, for instance, include stand-alone government ministries, offices within the head of state's department, quasi-autonomous state agencies such as national commissions or divisions for gender equality within ministries of labour, social welfare or national development, parliamentary commissions and delegations (Mazur 2002; Stetson and Mazur 1995; True and Mintrom 2001:31). One way of categorizing women's policy agencies is to distinguish them by location and function, generating three broad categories, namely: units within governments with advisory, monitoring or implementation responsibilities; statutory commissions; and advisory and consultative bodies (Goetz 2005:2–3; Sawer 2005:2–7).

Units within government comprise those bodies within the state's bureaucracy that are centrally located in a cabinet office, a central planning body or a government department, such that they can both advocate gender issues and monitor policy-making from a gender equality perspective, and may also be involved in policy implementation. A successful unit of this type will have a central location, high-level political support, access to professional gender equality expertise, and be well resourced. It is unlikely to have strong links with women in civil society. It may well foster the substantive representation of women, but is not directly accountable to women.

Statutory commissions comprise those gender equality bodies that are state-funded but enjoy relative independence from the state; they have 'oversight' and investigative power and are able to put pressure on the government, and to receive and investigate complaints by the public regarding gender-based rights violations. A successful unit of this type will have a high public profile and effective alliances with international bodies and access to new policy ideas.

Advisory and consultative bodies comprise those bodies that liaise with women's organizations, canvass their opinions in relation to new policy proposals, commission research into women's experiences and perspectives, and filter the views of civil society actors into governmental structures (usually via the women's units within government). A successful unit of this type will have a peripheral location, high-level movement support, access to women's organizations and be well networked into civil society. In practice, many women's policy agencies have a vague mandate, which covers all three of these functions, rendering their location subject to continual revision and criteria for the evaluation of their impact complex.

Explanations as to why women's policy agencies were so widely adopted focus, as with the explanations regarding quota adoption, on women's political mobilization, the strategic interests of political elites, and the process of international norm transfusion. While each of these explanations clearly has merit, the rapid emergence of the agencies globally remains something of a surprise: women have mobilized in favour of the creation of women's policy agencies notwithstanding the women's movement's earlier hostility to working within the state; political elites have created the agencies notwithstanding a pervasive lack of understanding of or interest in women's empowerment; and international organizations have advocated the creation of these agencies and monitored their effectiveness notwithstanding their commitment to other goals, such as neo-liberal economics, frequently held to be antithetical to gender equality. The feminist literature tends to privilege the role of women's political mobilization, generally framing the emergence of women's policy agencies as a matter of gender justice; however the role of international organizations and political elites in the adoption of women's policy agencies suggests that other strategic interests may have been at stake.

The emergence of women's policy agencies marked a sea change in feminist political relations with the state, given that the women's movement in the 1970s and 1980s had frequently been expressly hostile to the state and repudiated formal political engagement in favour of autonomous movement activism. Nonetheless, while early second-wave feminists focused on extending the boundaries of the 'political' by exploring heterogeneous political processes rather than formal political institutions (Squires 2002), the apparent receptiveness of many liberal democratic states to demands for women's increased participation led many feminists to believe that engagement with the state should not be viewed entirely cynically as inevitably entailing co-option. However, not all feminists supported this goal. Within advanced industrial democracies socialist feminists lobbied throughout the 1970s and 1980s within political parties for the inclusion of women's demands in their policy agendas, while radical feminists placed women's issues high on the political agenda via social movement activism. It was liberal feminists in particular who embraced the idea that women's policy agencies might pursue the interests of women within the state.

The women's movement in all its diverse manifestations remained ambivalent about the desirability of women's policy agencies, which seemed to signify an alignment between feminist demands and a liberal pluralist view of the state, in which women are understood to constitute a potentially unitary group whose interests can be extended through the state (Franzway *et al.* 1989:140). The bureaucratization of feminism was therefore viewed from the outset as both a significant achievement and a source of concern: providing greater access to decision-making, but potentially entailing co-option and depoliticization. Sensitive to these tensions, many liberal and socialist feminists nonetheless decided to push for the increased representation of women's affairs in decision-making, aiming to gain access to policy-making power structures (Franzway *et al.* 1989). While this has at times been viewed as a capitulation to reformist politics in developed countries, women's movement demands for women's policy agencies within developing countries have usually been framed by wider demands for regime change and democratization, with women's entry into the state being represented as a means of securing greater transparency and good governance (Alvarez 1999; Baldez 2002; Honculada and Ofreneo 2003).

The decision by states to respond to feminist demands by creating women's policy agencies appears to have been motivated by a range of factors. These include: normative consistency – with women's absence from state institutions coming to be seen as challenging the legitimacy of the state in liberal terms (Franzway *et al.* 1989:135); electoral concerns – with a concern about feminist activism and the female vote encouraging many states to introduce women's policy agencies as a means of appealing to a female electorate (Stetson and Mazur 1995:3); and international pressure – with states succumbing to pressure from international organizations, such as the Commission on the Status on Women in the UN in order to conform to international norms and secure international aid (Alvarez 1999; Gopal Baidya 2005). The relative significance of these factors naturally varies between states: within advanced industrial democracies the creation of women's policy agencies enabled elite politicians to respond to the various forms of women's movement demands in a way that brought them into alignment with the state, enabling them to be seen to be responding to certain liberal feminist demands while simultaneously diverting attention away from more radical challenges. Meanwhile, in many developing countries, the strategic aims of political elites have focused on meeting the demands, directives and goals of international organizations, which lobbied actively for the creation of women's policy agencies (Goetz 2003; Rai 2003; Waylen 2000).

This suggests that women's transnational political mobilization has been highly effective in shaping the strategic interests of political elites. One cannot understand the creation of women's policy agencies by nearly every democratic state around the globe within the space of just three decades without reference to the transnational networking among feminist actors, facilitated by the preparations for the four UN women's conferences. These conferences, held in Mexico City (1975), Copenhagen (1980), Nairobi (1985) and Beijing (1995), brought thousands of women together from around the world (Tinker and Jaquette 1987:419; True 2003:377), fostering a rapid increase in the number of women's international non-governmental organizations and facilitating the development of new gender-equality policy networks. The activities of women's transnational social movements, coupled with the work of the UN's own women's policy agencies, the Commission on the Status of Women (CSW) and the Division of the Advancement of Women (DAW), have secured the global creation of women's policy agencies on a state level (Beijing Platform of Action, cited in Rai 2003:2). The key achievement here was the ability of women's transnational social movements to secure a commitment to the creation of women's policy agencies as an international norm associated with good governance.

In their 2001 study of 157 countries, True and Mintrom found that presence at UN women's conferences and linkages to international women's NGOs were strongly associated with the adoption of national institutional mechanisms for the advancement of women. Although True and Mintrom do not distinguish between the women's policy agencies and the mainstreaming practices these agencies increasingly adopt, their data relates to the creation of women's policy agencies, not all of which adopt mainstreaming practices, even rhetorically, showing that the transnational networking of women's organizations provided the political momentum and societal pressure for the establishment of women's policy agencies (True and Mintrom 2001). The International Year of Women and the UN international conference system is therefore regarded as having spawned a transnational gender-equality policy network, which has used intergovernmental and non-governmental institutions to support the creation of women's policy agencies within national governments. Women's policy agencies were therefore created largely as a response to the demands of international organizations such as the UN's Commission on the Status of Women that national governments create bodies capable of pursuing and reporting on the growing number of international resolutions and directives on equality for women that these international organizations were issuing. The issuing of so many gender equality resolutions and directions was in large part a response to the mobilization of transnational feminist policy networks.

Many of the 134 countries reporting to the UN Division for the Advancement of Women on their policy agency activities reported drawing on international and regional agreements and bodies to 'bolster national efforts', using international agreements such as CEDAW as leverage for reforming national laws to conform to global standards, and using monitoring reports submitted to various UN bodies as a means of securing progress. International conferences appeared therefore to be enabling mechanisms for feminists, even in the context of 'the intensification of international forces inimical to feminist goals and sustainable living' (Pettman 2005:622, see also Ackerly and Moller Okin 1999; Carney 2003, 2004, Stienstra 2000). Notably, this focus on the creation of new state institutions occurred at a time when most analyses emphasized the 'rolling back' of the state in the wake of a neo-liberal commitment to market governance.

Opinions differ however as to whether this dynamic represented the positive development of new transnational forms of feminist activism, or a more negative displacement of national feminist agendas by international organizations. While some view these networks as facilitating the goals of local women's movements in circumstances where they faced a hostile national government, others suggest that they simply impose an international agenda that creates dissonance with local agendas. How the emergence of women's policy agencies is viewed depends to some extent on the degree to which civil society actors are subsequently included in the activities of the agency. This in turn depends on whether the agencies take the form of units within government with monitoring or implementation responsibilities, or whether they are primarily consultative bodies: whether they simply monitor policy-making from a gender equality perspective or whether they also liaise with women's organizations and filter the views of civil society actors into governmental structures.

Gender Mainstreaming

During the 1990s many policy agencies began to define their remit in terms of the promotion of gender equality rather than the advancement of women and were increasingly made responsible for gender mainstreaming (Rai 2003; True 2003). For example, the 1995 Beijing Platform for Action defined their main task as supporting government-wide 'mainstreaming of a gender-equality perspective in all policy areas' (para. 201). For some commentators the introduction of mainstreaming represented a consolidation and extension of the policy agency's role (Mazur, 2005; Staudt, 2003), but for others it created ambiguity and confusion (Kardam, 2005:3), representing a profound challenge to the work of women's policy agencies.

Gender mainstreaming entails a set of tools and processes designed to integrate a gender perspective into all policies at the planning stage by considering the likely effects of policies on the respective situation of women and men, and then revising the policies if necessary such that they promote gender equality rather than reproduce gender inequality. Adopted by the UN at the 1995 conference on women in Beijing and then taken up by the EU and its member states and by international development agencies, gender mainstreaming is now – like quotas and women's policy agencies – 'an international phenomenon' (Walby 2004:2).

As with women's policy agencies, gender mainstreaming focuses on the policy-making process, but aims to integrate a gendered perspective into all policy-making arenas, rather than to promote women's interests in specific policy areas conventionally associated with women. Where the United Nations World Conference on Women in Mexico City in 1975 had recommended that governments establish agencies dedicated to promoting gender equality and improving the status and conditions of women, the 1995 conference recommended gender mainstreaming as an additional mechanism for pursuing gender equality, intended to complement the positive action measures that women's policy agencies and gender quotas entailed.

Gender mainstreaming is a process that seeks to engage with and transform the policy-making process such that it better represents the substantive interests of women, and thereby aims to produce policies that are more conducive to gender equality than has previously been the case. Unlike women's policy agencies, mainstreaming claims to offer a way of anticipating the future consequences of existing inequalities and seeks to prevent their future reproduction. In this way mainstreaming is a process that questions the presumed neutrality of all bureaucratic policy-making, highlighting the way in which apparently impartial policies might reproduce existing inequalities by failing to address their structural impact. While frequently implemented by women's policy agencies, gender mainstreaming represents a call for the diffusion of gender issues beyond the remits of women's policy agencies to the full range of policy-making departments within institutions and governments.

There are numerous definitions of gender mainstreaming, many of which offer a slightly different conceptualization of what the strategy entails. The most frequently cited are those that emerge from the international organizations that have been central to its formulation and implementation. The UN defines it as the promotion of a

> strategy for making women's as well as men's concerns and experiences an integral dimension of the design, implementation, monitoring and

> evaluation of policies and programmes in all political, economic and societal spheres so that women and men benefit equally and inequality is not perpetuated. The ultimate goal is to achieve gender equality. (United Nations 2002:2)

The Council of Europe views it as a strategy that aims to 'reorganize, improve, develop and evaluate policy processes in order to incorporate a gender equality perspective' (Council of Europe 1998:2–3). The Commission defines it as

> the systemic integration of the respective situations, priorities and needs of women and men in all policies and with a view to promoting equality between women and men and mobilizing all general policies and measures specifically for the purpose of achieving equality by actively and openly taking into account, at the planning stage, their effects on the respective situation of women and men in implementation, monitoring and evaluation. (Commission of the European Communities 1996:2)

These definitions all share an emphasis on the policy process (across all issue areas) as the site of mainstreaming, the adoption of a gender equality perspective in the policy process as the key feature of mainstreaming, and the pursuit of gender equality as the key aim of mainstreaming.

Gender mainstreaming therefore represents a departure from the strategy initially pursued by those women's policy agencies that focused on promoting distinctive 'women's issues' within the context of social policy only, by aiming to make gender equality into an integral part of all public policy-making (McCrudden 2001:75), bringing 'a gender-equality perspective' into the mainstream of all policy-making (True and Mintrom 2001:28). However, variations emerge in relation to what 'a gender-equality perspective' entails and so what it is precisely that is being 'mainstreamed'. This is evidenced by the fact that while some people talk of 'mainstreaming equal opportunities' (Booth and Bennett 2002:431), others speak of 'mainstreaming gender' (Pollack and Hafner-Burton 2000:432), rendering the concept somewhat vague in practice (Beveridge and Nott 2002:299). The 'gender' in gender mainstreaming frequently gets interpreted in a number of different ways, reflecting deeper normative debates about the nature of both 'gender' and 'gender equality', but at the conceptual level it does signal a desire to move away from the focus on 'women' (as embodied in women's policy agencies and 'gender' quotas) and to take gender relations as the object of concern.

The mainstreaming literature frequently distinguishes between 'expert-bureaucratic' and 'participative-democratic' models of mainstreaming (Donaghy 2004a; Nott 2000), or between 'integrationist', and 'agenda-setting' approaches (Jahan 1995:126). This distinction echoes and accentuates the divergent responsibilities attributed to women's policy agencies, which include both monitoring and consultative functions. The tension between these functions is accentuated in the mainstreaming literature, with Jahan's integrationist and agenda-setting models intersecting with Nott's expert-bureaucratic and participative-democratic models, highlighting the correlation between processes and outcomes.

The expert-bureaucratic (or integrationist) approach entails a focus on gender experts and the bureaucratic creation of evidence-based knowledge in policy-making, where the gender experts usually aim to integrate a gender perspective into existing policy paradigms without questioning them. The participative-democratic (or agenda-setting) approach focuses on the participation, presence and empowerment of disadvantaged groups (usually women in this context) via consultation with civil society organizations, thought to facilitate a rethinking of existing policy paradigms from gendered perspectives (see Beveridge and Nott 2002:301; Lombardo 2005; Shaw 2002). The participative-democratic approach to mainstreaming therefore shares many of the features and concerns of consultative women's policy agencies, in that both aim to facilitate the substantive representation of women's interests by liasing with women's organizations, canvassing their opinions in relation to new policy proposals, commissioning research into women's experiences and perspective, and filtering the views of civil society actors into governmental structures. The expert-bureaucratic approach to mainstreaming, on the other hand, shares many of the features and concerns of those women's policy agencies that are units within governments with advisory, monitoring or implementation responsibilities, in that both aim to monitor policy-making from 'a gender equality perspective' (which is taken to be a known quantity rather than a subject of political contestation), by drawing on professional gender equality expertise. While the feminist literature has generally viewed the participative-democratic model of mainstreaming to be the more desirable one, it is the expert-bureaucratic model that has been more actively promoted by states across the globe (Beveridge and Nott 2002; Donaghy 2004; Lombardo 2005).

The concept of gender mainstreaming emerged in the early 1990s (True 2003:369) in the context of the work of the World Bank and in decision-making by the United Nations Development Programme, and was established as a global strategy for achieving gender equality in the 1995 Beijing Platform for Action ratified by all United Nations member states. Not only did international organizations submit themselves to the technique of mainstreaming, they also bound their member organizations through treaties, accords and funding programmes. Since 1995, global governance institutions such as the UN, the OECD and the World Bank have all adopted mainstreaming, as have the majority of 'northern' international development agencies, including bilaterals, such as the Canadian International Developments Agency (CIDA) and the Swedish Internal development Cooperation Agency (Sida), and multilaterals, such as the World Bank and Inter-American Development Bank (IDB) (Moser 2005; Organization for Economic Cooperation and Development 2004; Ravens-Roberts, 2005). These organizations have also 'supported' 'Southern' governments in the implementation of gender mainstreaming (Kabeer 2003; Moser 2005).

Within Europe, 'much of the reflective work' on gender mainstreaming took place in the context of the Council of Europe (Shaw 2005:4, see also Beveridge and Shaw 2002). Gender mainstreaming was endorsed in the Treaty of Amsterdam (1997) as the official policy approach to gender equality of the European Union (EU) and its member states (Rees 2005:555). The EU, for instance, adopted a new guideline in 1999 that requires member states to implement gender mainstreaming in relation to the four pillars of the employment guidelines (equal opportunities, employability, adaptability and entrepreneurship) (Rubery 2002:500). The EU thereby provided the catalyst role in getting EU member states to introduce mainstreaming, putting gender mainstreaming on the agenda as an issue to be used within the internal political process (Rubery 2002:503), and – more coercively – requiring that all requests for grants from the European Social Fund incorporate a prior gender impact assessment (Woodward 2001). As a result, by 2001 almost every EU member state had put in place some formal mechanism for gender mainstreaming (Rubery 2002:503; for a review see Mackay and Bilton 2000).

As with women's policy agencies a couple of decades earlier and gender quotas in the same period, there was a swift and widespread adoption of gender mainstreaming, representing what many commentators view as an example of 'inspirational policy-transfer' (Beveridge and Nott 2002:299). Unlike the accounts of the adoption of women's policy agencies and gender quotas, which attempt to account for the adoption of new gender equality strategies with reference to the political mobilization of women, international influence and the strategic aims of political elites, the explanations of the global adoption of gender mainstreaming usually present it as a more incremental process, developing from prior equality policies. While its advocates believe it to be a more transformatory strategy than the group representation strategies it seeks to improve upon, many of those committed to the value of group representation have viewed its emergence with scepticism, perceiving it to be technocratic rather than transformatory, co-opting feminist achievements rather than developing them. This scepticism relates to the fact that elite technocratic experts appear to have had such a key role in introducing mainstreaming into supranational bodies such as the EU, UN and World Bank (Booth and Bennett 2002:440).

This locates the emergence of gender mainstreaming, not in relation to social movement activism, but in relation to policy learning within supra-state institutions. Jacquot, for instance, suggests that mainstreaming emerged within the EU in response to the recognition of the persistence of gender inequalities after fifteen years of public policies aimed at eliminating it (Jacquot 2003:2–6, see also Lombardo 2003). Given that these policies had taken the form of equal treatment and positive action policies, a new approach was called for. The first 'equal treatment' phase, which took the form of art. 119 adopted in 1957 and the directives based on that article, generated an individualized rights-based approach to gender equality, which aimed to bring women's rights into line with those of men by eradicating discrimination. It resulted in a number of high-profile legal challenges concerning the equal treatment of women and men in pay and employment coming to the European Court of Justice (Hoskyns 1996; Rees 2005). However, it was deemed problematic on a practical level because member states often failed to implement EC legislative norms and on a more theoretical level because it took the experiences, preferences and rights of men as its starting-point and so systematically privileged male over female perspectives. Positive action, which took the form of action programmes designed by the Commission (1982–5 and 1986–90) that focused on flexible work practices and the reorganization of family responsibilities, aimed to recognize the specificity of women's experiences and to take women's needs as their starting point, focusing on issues such as childcare. These positive action policies were also deemed to be problematic by policy-makers because they are a very costly instrument and appear to privilege women rather than men, while some feminists argued that women's differences were being depicted as a 'problem' of women's special needs, which needed to be dealt with if women were to compete with men 'in races where rules have not been designed with them in mind' (Rees 2005:559). The limited impact of equal treatment and positive action policies was increasingly perceived as an indication that a more 'systemic' solution was called for, which should ideally entail 'soft' measures that are cheap to implement (though as Woodward points out (2005), political commitment, expertise, dedicated staff, organizational restructuring and cultural change are all expensive). Gender mainstreaming therefore emerged as a third equality strategy to complement and improve upon these two prior approaches. This approach aimed to focus on the systems that created structural inequalities, rather than reacting to its results via an assertion of either individual or group rights, and was about 'embedding gender equality in systems, processes, policies and institutions' (Rees 2005:558).

This suggests that the EU developed mainstreaming in response to the limitations of earlier gender-equality policies. Its initial formulation was shaped by the policy sequencing in each institutional setting, in which actors responded to the perceived weaknesses of previous policies while incorporating traces of these frames within the new proposed approach. Thus, responding to the perceived weaknesses of the equal treatment and positive action policies, the EU initially focused on 'equal opportunities mainstreaming'. However, there are other accounts that locate the emergence of mainstreaming in relation to the limitations of previous women-in-development policies, emphasizing the importance of the shift from 'women in development' (WID) to 'gender and development' (GAD) within the multilateral and bilateral development agencies.

Development scholars suggest that mainstreaming is a 'logical extension of "women in development" efforts to promote gender equality in the economic development work of state institutions and international agencies' (True 2003:369–70; see also Goetz 1998). The WID approach, which emerged in the late 1960s, addressed the exclusion of women from development processes and institutions (Boserup 1970) and argued for the creation of development projects that focused on women. This approach was gradually criticized by feminist development scholars and activists for integrating women into existing institutions and structures. These critics accordingly developed a GAD approach, which aimed to transform the social and institutional context rather than ease women's integration into it. This shifted the focus from women-specific development studies and strategies to one that examined the ways in which development affected gender relations. As Moser points out:

> [U]nderlying this fundamental shift from WID to GAD has been the recognition of the importance of focusing less on the biological differences between women and men – termed sexual – and more in terms

of gender – the socially defined aspects of being male and female. (Moser 2002:2)

Whereas the focus on sex depicted women as the problem, the concept of gender allowed policy initiates to consider gender relations, including male roles and responsibilities. Advocates of this GAD approach focused their attention on transforming multilateral agencies such as the World Bank and the International Monetary Fund, rather than individual governments or regional supra-state bodies such as the EU. On this account mainstreaming developed within the institutional context of the UN (including the United Nations Development Programme (UNDP) and the United Nations Development Fund for Women (UNIFEM)) and the World Bank as a response to the limitations of previous development policies and the political mobilization of transnational feminist policy networks.

The World Bank, the world's largest and most influential development institution, lending more money to more countries than any other development body, and giving extensive policy advice to governments, embraced gender mainstreaming in the mid 1990s as part of the series of measures introduced in recognition that neo-liberal imperatives embraced in the 1980s, which focused on free-market economic reform that entailed open trade, reduced social spending, deregulation and privatization, needed to be tempered by social development concerns (Bedford 2006). As the benefits promised by this approach proved elusive, the Bank adopted a 'limited, but significant ideological shift' (O'Brien *et al.* 2000:9). This ideological shift, marked by the appointment in 1995 of James Wolfensohn as president, entailed the increased acceptance of policy intervention to temper market excesses and heightened emphasis on participation, empowerment and poverty alleviation. The embrace of gender mainstreaming in the mid 1990s can be seen as part of this shift.

The early developmental focus on 'women' reflected the prior existence of WID units, just as the EU focus on 'equal opportunities' reflected the prior existence of equal treatment and positive action policies. The nature of these policy developments shape current discourses, with the EU continuing to conceive of mainstreaming in relation to equal opportunities and development discourses continuing to conceive of mainstreaming in relation to women's empowerment. So, where EU scholars focus on mainstreaming as a response to the perceived limitations of equal treatment and positive action policies, development scholars perceive it to be a response to the limitations of the WID approach used to target women as a group with economic potential by many development agencies during the 1970s and 1980s (Anderson 1993). Early articulations of mainstreaming were therefore formulated as 'equal opportunities mainstreaming' within the EU and as 'mainstreaming women' in development agencies, only becoming 'gender mainstreaming' following the 1995 Beijing Conference. Indeed, development debates about mainstreaming still tend to focus on the concept of gender (Baden and Goetz 1997), where the EU accounts still tend to emphasize the concept of equality (Rees 1998). However, accounts of the emergence of mainstreaming in the EU do acknowledge the central influence of the Beijing Conference in addition to the internal dynamics within the institution, signalling the intermeshing of development and European policy debates. Significantly, while mainstreaming was first introduced in the EU in the 3rd Action Programme, drafted in 1989 and adopted in 1990, and while the mainstreaming principle was approved by the Commission in 1990 and by the Council in 1991, the diffusion of mainstreaming within Europe only really occurred following the 1995 Beijing Conference, suggesting that the pressure from international actors was key.

Another influence in the emergence of mainstreaming worth mentioning is that of the Nordic model of gender equality. 1995 also marked the admission of Sweden, Finland and Austria to the EU, and the concerns of these particular member states can also be seen to have shaped the policy shift to mainstreaming. Indeed, the systematic incorporation of the word 'mainstreaming' in documents by the EU at Beijing was at the insistence of the Nordic delegations, who were particularly committed to pursuing gender equality measures within the EU given that the female populations of the Nordic countries were fearful that EU membership would entail the lowering of their existing gender equality standards (Jacquot 2003:13). As one Swedish government communication on gender equality stated: 'In Sweden, we have come far by international comparison; in fact, we have come the farthest in the world. We gladly share our experiences, we readily export our Swedish model for gender equality' (1999/2000:24, p. 6). Indeed in 1996 gender equality became an explicit aim of all Swedish international development cooperation (Towns 2002:162) and when Sweden assumed the presidency of the Council of Ministers of the European Union, it declared gender equality a prioritized goal to permeate all other issue areas (Towns 2002:157). In this way Swedish international advocacy for gender mainstreaming was also significant.

This suggests that the narrow legislative basis of art. 119, and the resistance among many member states to extending gender-equality policies, coupled with the impact of the UN Beijing Conference and the influence of the Nordic countries in the EU, combined to bring mainstreaming onto to the European political agenda. Yet, while it has been and remains an extremely high-profile concern among certain state feminists and transnational feminist activists, it would be misleading to imply that mainstreaming was placed on the political agenda as a result of the activism of national women's movements. As Woodward notes:

> The impetus for the articulation and insertion of mainstreaming in public policy came primarily for highly placed actors in the policy process and academic feminists … It would be hard to argue that in the first years of mainstreaming, it was a top priority for grass roots European women's movements in most countries. Indeed, the first five years in Belgium were dedicated to educational programs informing women's organizations how they could use mainstreaming. (Woodward 2005:3–4)

As a result mainstreaming was widely perceived, both by policy-makers and women's movement actors, to derive in a top-down manner from international organizations rather than from local or national pressure.

The emergence of gender mainstreaming, as with gender quotas, is associated with the growing role of transnational networks and international non-governmental organizations (Pollack and Hafner-Burton 2000:434; True and Mintrom 2001:28–9). The UN Beijing Conference was particularly significant because the process of preparing for the conference allowed for the circulation of ideas and favoured the formalization of emerging ideas. As True suggests, transnational networks of women's organizations have increasingly served as

> conduits not only of information about differing policy models and gender mainstreaming initiatives at the local and national levels but also – and crucially – of knowledge concerning alternative political strategies and how they may be applied to further promote gender policy change. (True 2003:377)

In this way various complex national, regional and international developments led to the emergence of gender mainstreaming as a significant equality strategy in the mid 1990s, with the adoption of gender mainstreaming influenced by key experts present within the state (including femocrats and female parliamentarians) and transnational women's networks effective at an international level, ensuring that the strategic aims of political elites included gender mainstreaming.

However, governments across the globe did not adopt gender mainstreaming simply because feminists convinced them that it represented a transformative new approach to gender equality. As with gender quotas and women's policy agencies, gender mainstreaming has also come to be associated with favoured international norms such as modernization and good governance, such that there is international pressure on national governments to adopt mainstreaming in order to be seen to be conforming to the norms of modern statecraft. For example, in her EU-funded cross-national comparison of how mainstreaming is conceived by policy-makers in Belgium, France, Greece, Ireland, Lithuania, Spain, Sweden and the UK (2002–4), Daly finds that the primary incentive for countries to engage within gender mainstreaming is to 'modernize' their gender equality approach and architecture, stemming from a concern with 'policy-making exigencies or current styles or fashions' rather than 'a new philosophy of gender inequality' (Daly 2005:441). Mainstreaming is 'a symbol of modernity', which serves to construct policy problems in relation to the modernity of politics. This means that there is a 'funnelling effect' in which agencies adopt some of the tools of mainstreaming in the absence of an overall gender equality framework, rendering mainstreaming as a mode of delivery rather than a policy agenda (Daly 2005:436). This, in turn, may indicate that the widespread adoption of mainstreaming needs to be accounted for in relation to more than simply the pursuit of gender justice.

Conclusion

The emergence of these three equality strategies suggests that there has been a growing concern with gender inequality internationally, with a series of measures being promoted by international organizations and adopted by states that aim to promote gender equality. Women's policy agencies and gender mainstreaming have generally proven to be less controversial than quotas and have generated less public debate, though the extent to which they have been adopted and implemented nonetheless varies from country to country according to the women's political mobilization, the strategic interests of political elites, national normative frameworks, and international influence (Stetson and Mazur 1995:2–4; Rai 2003). Despite these important variations, the most striking thing about these three strategies is the speed and extent of their adoption globally.

The widespread dissemination of the three strategies around the globe suggests that these policies 'spread virus-like across policy sectors' (Richardson 2000:1019). The speed and extent of their uptake is quite striking, especially as it is generally thought to be unusual for a 'new normative concept' to gain cross-national acceptance, 'not just as a term of art deployed by international negotiators, or a specialist term accepted by a particular disciplinary or professional group – but as an idea that is absorbed into domestic political interchange across a variety of national polities' (Meadowcroft 2000:159). Interestingly, the dissemination of quotas, women's policy agencies and gender mainstreaming indicate that ideas can, as political scientists have suggested, be a motor of change (Dolowitz and Marsh 1996; John 1999), with 'an ability to disrupt existing policy systems, power relationships and policies' (Richardson 2000:1017). But why the three strategies in particular should have proven so amenable to policy transfer requires further thought.

Reflecting on the successful policy transfer of the idea of sustainable development, Meadowcroft suggests that one possible explanation for this rapid absorption lies in the fact that this is an idea that was explicitly formulated by an international body, on the basis of ideas that were already rooted in national contexts and discursive communities, which then filtered downwards through transnational channels into national and sub-national politics. He also suggests that the rather open texture of the idea, which draws together key concerns about environment and development, 'while leaving ample room for different interests to contest their implications', may be significant (Meadowcroft 2000:160). This is relevant, given that the policies of the three strategies were all largely formulated in and around the UN Conferences for Women, drawing on the local concerns and commitments of diverse women's organizations (as the focus on women's mobilization in the accounts surveyed above emphasizes), and were subsequently endorsed in the 1975 and 1995 Platforms for Action (as the focus on international influence suggests) (Ackerly and Moller Okin 1999). Moreover, the concepts appear to be sufficiently open in texture to allow for different interests to contest their implications (making normative consistency more readily achievable in diverse contexts).

The international adoption of these three equality strategies therefore needs to be understood in relation to a model of leverage politics (Hobson *et al.* 2007), made possible by the emergence of multi-level governance, which decentres the state as the primary site for brokerage among social groups. While much of the work on multi-level governance has focused on the flow of policy-making upwards and downwards to the regional or local level, the explanations of the emergence of these three gender equality measures emphasize another dynamic of multi-level governance, namely the ways in which movement actors transform and translate ideas into their local and national settings, using legal or moral leverage to exert pressure on their governments (Hobson *et al.* 2007). The widespread dissemination of gender equality strategies has entailed women's movement actors leapfrogging their national governments, working in transnational networks and organizations to create legal or moral leverage on recalcitrant governments to follow international norms. Moral leverage has frequently been used to put pressure on national governments to conform to international protocols, and codes of good practice, which advocate the adoption of the three gender equality mechanisms. So while these take the state as their object (implying that they work with a national governmental focus that might be increasingly anachronistic in an era of global governance), they emerge onto the global agenda via processes of transnational networking and moral leverage that constitute a prime example of social movements successfully making use of the political possibilities opened up by the emergence of multi-level governance.

Feminist activists and women's organizations have not always mobilized at a transnational level, but generally follow a supranational strategy when they meet solid opposition at the national level or where there are positive incentives to operate at the supranational level in terms of funding, training, status or access. The growth of transnational feminist activism therefore suggests that the political opportunity structures have been more favourable at the international level than at the national level for many feminists. The interesting question that arises from this account of the emergence of these three equality measures is why this should have been so: why have international organizations offered feminists the political opportunities to promote their demands for greater gender equality? One possibility is that the pursuit of gender equality has been conceived by global governance and development organizations as a means of constructing state institutions that are 'conducive for "modern" free markets', facilitating both development and economic growth (Towns 2003:1). As Towns argues, the pursuit of gender equality, and the commitment to gender-balanced decision-making and gender mainstreaming in particular, has become a privileged indicator of the movement from traditional statehood to modern capitalist democracy.

The three strategies each focus on the formal institutions of the state aiming to secure women's increased participation in decision-making and policy-making processes and have been advocated by various complex alliances of women's organizations (national and transnational) and elite political actors in national and international organizations. Women have organized at an international level to ensure that gender equality becomes a strategic interest of political elites, thereby bringing the aims of women's movements and political elites into alliance via the use of international organizations to disseminate international norms that equate gender equality with democratic governance. While the feminist literature has generally viewed these strategies as a measure to ensure women's political emowerment, the institutions of global governance have more frequently viewed them as a means to enhance the market character of modern democratic states (Towns 2003). Recognition of these differential framings of the three mechanisms – one located in debates of gender justice, the other in terms of economic utility – has led some to argue that their global dissemination represents an inspiring example of feminist activism and democratic innovation, while others argue that their dominance represents a depressing example of neo-liberal co-optation and technocratic delimitation.

It is, of course, possible to square these two accounts, given that neo-liberalism is not in fact a monolithic project, but is rather a confluence of a plethora of discrete political struggles (Larner 2005:1–2). Given this, it is possible to view these three gender equality mechanisms as a product of both neo-liberal governance and other more oppositional social movement aims and achievements, with different values and goals attached. The important issue for consideration is not whether these three measures emerged as a result of women's political mobilization or as a result of the strategic interests of political elites – for it is clearly both – but to explore the ways in which the attempt to strategically frame the pursuit of gender equality in terms of the dominant political rationalities of states impacts upon the formulation and implementation of the measures. Specifically, the key consideration is whether arguments that emphasize the utility of gender equality for economic growth and good governance facilitate the recognition of women's potential contribution and thereby promote transformative strategies of displacement, or whether they undermine the radical potential of the three strategies, such that they become limited strategies of inclusion. One way of establishing which of these scenarios is most compelling is to explore the impact the three mechanisms have actually had to date.

2
Making a Difference? Evaluating Impact

Introduction

Have women's policy agencies, gender quotas and gender mainstreaming made a difference? And if so, what sort of impact have they had? Although the literature on the emergence of these strategies acknowledges the role of the strategic interests of political elites as well as women's political mobilization to be central, all three measures are generally judged, in the political science literature at least, in relation to the normative aims of the women's movement rather than in relation to the strategic interests of political elites. Most of the relevant scholarship starts from the premise that they are essentially a means to greater democratic justice (Towns 2003:2). Accordingly, the most commonly adopted criteria of evaluation for women's policy agencies and gender quotas focus on democratic participation and gender equality, seeking to determine whether the mechanisms increase women's participation in and access to political decision-making (descriptive representation), and/or transform the policy agenda such that it better represents women and promotes gender equality (substantive representation).

This gives two basic indicators of success, with descriptive representation most commonly invoked in relation to gender quotas, substantive representation invoked in relation to gender mainstreaming, and a combination of the two in relation to women's policy agencies. For example, the criteria used to evaluate women's policy agencies usually take the form of the extent to which women's policy agencies 'bring more women, and the women's movement actors that speak for them, into the affairs of government – descriptive representation – and introduce feminist ideas into policy discussion and outcomes – substantive representation'

(Stetson and Mazur 2003:2). Gender quotas are usually evaluated in terms of whether they increase the numbers of women in legislatures, but are also considered in relation to whether they influence what it is that gets represented (Mateo Diaz 2005:3), whereas gender mainstreaming is more commonly evaluated in relation to its ability to facilitate gender-sensitive policy-making (Daly 2005), though reference is sometimes made to both policy and personnel change (Rees 2002).

The three measures have therefore tended to be evaluated in terms of their representative functions, both descriptive and substantive. It is widely assumed that the three strategies will each increase women's representation and thereby facilitate gender equality. The mode of representation adopted by each is quite distinct, however. Conceptually, women's policy agencies aspire to promote both descriptive and substantive representation (by bringing femocrats into the state bureaucracy to work for women's advancement); gender quotas are a means of securing women's descriptive representation (by increasing the number of women in legislatures), though advocates hope that they will also increase women's substantive representation (if female parliamentarians act for women); and gender mainstreaming is a means of facilitating women's substantive representation (by introducing a gender perspective – rather than women – into the policy-making process), though some advocates hope that it will also increase women's descriptive representation (by institutionalizing consultation with women's civil society organizations and briefings from gender experts).

Evaluations of the success of these three mechanisms therefore tend to use the descriptive/substantive representation schema, considering how effective they have been in relation to each. Do quotas, women's policy agencies and gender mainstreaming bring more women into the affairs of government? Do they introduce new ideas into policy discussion and outcomes, which better represent women's interests and/or perspectives? Do they result in policy-making that promotes greater gender equality?

Evaluating the Success of Gender Quotas

Given that gender quotas are a relatively recent phenomenon and are controversial in many countries, most of the research on quotas has tended to focus on their adoption rather than their implementation (Dahlerup 2006:10). In many countries quotas have simply not yet been in operation long enough to gauge their effectiveness (Krook 2005:19; Peschard 2005:23). However, there are a growing number of national case-studies that evaluate the impact of quotas, taking women's increased descriptive representation as the key indicator of success. In this they focus primarily on quantitative rather than qualitative indicators of impact, measuring the number of women in parliament rather than wider measures of female empowerment (Dahlerup 2006), taking democratic participation – rather than the gender equality that this participation might lead to – as the relevant indicator of impact. However, there is also a rich stream of research (both qualitative and quantitative) that seeks to establish whether increasing the descriptive representation of women in national legislatures results in the improved substantive representation of the female electorate (Chaney and Fevre 2002; Childs 2004, 2004a; Edwards and Chapman 2003; Lovenduski 2005; Mateo Diaz 2005; Wängnerud 2000).

The factors most frequently pinpointed as determining the level of female representation are the length of time since enfranchisement, the socio-economic, cultural and political context, and the electoral system, with many studies finding that the date at which women obtained the right to vote and to stand for election is significantly related to the current sex-balance of national assemblies, that socio-economic empowerment is a necessary but insufficient condition to ensure women's equal representation, and that the degree of proportionality of electoral systems is also influential (Caul 1999; Mateo Diaz 2005; Norris 2004; Norris and Lovenduski 1995). The focus on the importance of electoral systems has been significant in that it has challenged the assumption that the level of women's political representation will reflect their socio-economic status, and that an improvement in women's overall socio-economic position will be required to improve their political presence. While macro socio-economic conditions clearly do affect the presence of women in parliaments, specific institutional reforms have also been proven to be significant (Mateo-Diaz 2005:50–88). Emphasizing the 'relative autonomy of politics', gender scholars suggest that 'gender quotas may emerge and play a role in altering existing patterns of political representation, regardless of supposed social and economic prerequisites, in any number of different contexts in countries around the world' (Krook 2004:44). Thus, while differences in education and employment, which are products of prior inequalities, create structural constraints on women's availability for political office, the introduction of quotas may ameliorate their operation, without the resource implications entailed in tackling occupational segregation by gender or making good quality childcare available to all (Phillips 2004:8). The introduction of gender quotas is therefore thought to offer a 'fast track' to women's increased representation, offering an institutional mechanism that circumvents the need to wait for greater socio-economic empowerment and electoral reform (Dahlerup and Freidenvall 2005).

However, while some of the studies that have been conducted to date find that quotas are extremely effective in terms of increasing the proportion of women in national legislatures (Caul 2001; Matland and Studlar 1996), it is also the case that high levels of female representation can be achieved without quotas (Peschard 2005:24), and that many studies have found quotas to be highly ineffective (Htun 2002; Matland 2005). A quota provision does not automatically lead to a rapid or considerable increase in women's representation (Dahlerup 2006:10). Indeed, Matland argues that: 'the adoption of quotas has not, on the whole, led to dramatic increases in women's representation' (Matland 2005:278). The explanations as to the varying impact of quotas usually focus on the nature of the quota measures themselves, coupled with the nature of the institutional framework into which they are introduced (Krook 2005:31).

Given that constitutional and legal quotas bind all parties and are enforced by courts and state bureaucracies, this form of quota might be expected to have greater impact than party quotas, which bind only particular parties and are enforced by party leadership. However legislative quotas produce a diverse proportion of women representatives internationally, ranging between 4.6 per cent and 35.3 per cent, while party quotas produce a similar – and similarly diverse – proportion, varying from 5 per cent to 45.3 per cent (Krook 2005:33). This suggests that neither the adoption of quotas nor the type of quota adopted is decisive in determining the proportion of women elected. Simply having a quota law or rule is no guarantee that the law or rule will have a significant impact: the provisions must be drawn up such that they ensure equitable representation. Norris finds that: 'in general, ceteris paribus, the higher the level of the specified quota, the closer the quota is applied to the final stages of election, and more binding the formal regulation, the more effective its impact' (Norris 2000:3). This has led many individual case-studies to focus on the detail of the electoral systems, the wording of the quota policies and the political will of parties in implementing the quota provisions.

In relation to electoral systems, quotas are found to have the greatest impact under proportional-representation electoral systems with closed lists, high district magnitude and a placement mandate (requiring parties to ensure that women have an equitable representation throughout the whole electoral list) (Caul 1999; Htun 2002; Htun and Jones 2002; Krook 2005). In their evaluation of the effectiveness of legal quotas in

Latin America, Htun and Jones argue that closed lists and placement mandate are vital (Htun and Jones 2004). For instance, Argentina has a 30 per cent quota and 30.7 per cent women representatives, while Brazil also has a 30 per cent quota and yet has only 6.8 per cent women representatives (Sacchet 2003). Significantly, Argentina's quota law specifies a placement mandate, requiring that women be positioned on lists in proportions sufficient to get elected, while Brazil operates with open lists, leaving it to voters to determine the placement of voters (Peschard 2005; Sacchet 2003). However, open lists do not appear to have disadvantaged women in either Peru (Schmidt and Saunders 2004) or Poland (Matland 2005) which suggests that closed lists are not required for quotas to be effective. Moreover, quotas can have a strong impact in first-past-the-post electoral systems, as for instance when the British Labour Party adopted party quotas between 1993 and 1996 in the form of 'all-women shortlists' and women's representation at Westminster increased from 9.2 to 18.2 per cent (Squires 2004). This suggests that PR electoral systems are also not required for quotas to be effective.

Political parties are generally thought to play a crucial role in implementing or undermining the effective implementation of gender quotas (Meier 2000; Murray 2004). Much of the literature assumes that parties of the left will be more likely to implement quotas than will parties of the right (Htun 2002), but this pattern is again undercut by cases which show parties of the right to be more compliant in obeying quotas laws than parties of the left. For instance, in France, the National Front implemented the French Parity law more rigorously than did the Socialist Party, even though it had been the Socialist government that had introduced the law (Murray 2004). Moreover, while much of the literature finds that political elites within parties frequently fail to enforce quotas (Sacchet 2003; Peschard 2003), some studies have found that party elites can implement quotas despite public opposition (Meier 2000). Notwithstanding the complexity of these findings, it is clear that 'good faith compliance' with quota provisions on the part of political parties is crucial if quotas are to be implemented effectively.

Overall, quotas have been shown to be most effective in increasing women's descriptive representation where there is a proportional representation electoral system and political parties are supportive (either as a result of genuine political will or out of a desire to comply with effective regulations and avoid real sanctions). More broadly, these findings suggest that while the adoption of gender quotas has been dramatic, the implementation of quotas has been erratic, and the impact frequently less dramatic than one might have expected. Where the introduction of quotas has not resulted in increased levels of female representation, scholars have generally pointed either to non-implementation or else to adequate implementation of an inadequate provision as the explanation.

There is clearly a concern that emerges with respect to the dramatic increase in the rate of adoption of gender quotas, coupled with their erratic impact on the level of descriptive representation. Given that gender quotas have been so controversial in many countries, their adoption is frequently held by feminists to represent an important victory, with data about the global adoption of quotas being taken as an important manifestation of greater gender equality. Yet the celebration of this achievement may obscure the difficulties entailed in the effective implementation of quotas, and may mask the low levels of representation that result. For instance, the introduction of the French parity law generated widespread public debate (Lovenduski 2005:132), but its implementation resulted in 12.3 per cent women in the 2002 National Assembly rather than the previous 10.2 per cent in 1997 (Murray 2004): hardly dramatic progress.

In addition, it is important to note that measuring impact in terms of the numbers of women present in the national legislature (descriptive representation) alone may delimit our horizons unduly. For instance, Matland notes that non-democratic states have high levels of compliance with quota provisions: in 2005 North Korea had a quota provision of 20 per cent and precisely 20.1 per cent women in its national parliament (Matland 2005:278). Here quotas have clearly been implemented with great effectiveness and have certainly had an impact on the descriptive representation of women. Whether they have also improved the substantive representation of women must be questioned however, given that the national assembly exercises no real political power. This suggests that, even where they are effective in terms of descriptive representation, gender quotas may be functioning as a symbol of democratization without actually improving the substantive representation of women or securing greater gender equality.

This raises the more general long-standing concern about assimilation and co-optation, indicating that the preoccupation with gender quotas may serve to focus feminist attention on women's formal inclusion in the existing order rather than on wider social transformation. This preoccupation with political inclusion – focusing on descriptive representation rather than the gender equality outcomes this representation may facilitate – may work to marginalize concerns about economic injustices (Fraser 1995) and result in a 'parting of the ways between political and economic concerns' (Phillips 1999:1) and broader gender equality considerations. Certainly, as long as the measure of the success of gender quotas is taken to be descriptive representation alone this strategy cannot be shown to be engaging with the deepening socio-economic inequalities that result from neo-liberal policy commitments (Murphy 2003). The success of quotas may therefore act to legitimate and perpetuate women's absence of power, rather than being an effective remedy (L. Vincent 2004). On the other hand, it could be argued that gender quotas are a necessary, but not sufficient, measure towards securing greater substantive representation and wider social transformation (Dahlerup 1998). To determine which is most likely the link between descriptive and substantive representation needs to be explored in order to ascertain whether quotas displace a concern with a transformative political agenda or facilitate its pursuit.

In order to evaluate the extent to which gender quotas might lead to the improved substantive representation of women, scholars have tried to go 'beyond numbers' and establish whether women's increased presence in parliaments does 'make a difference' (Carroll 2001; Childs 2004a; Lovenduski 2005; Mateo Diaz 2005; Sacchet 2003; Swers 2002; Wängnerud 2000). Testing for substantive representation is a more complex task than is testing for descriptive representation, and studies have variously focused on the differences between male and female representatives in terms of attitudes and parliamentary activities. This has been tested by trying to establish differential attitudes (Childs 2004), voting behaviour (Carroll 2001; Mateo Diaz 2005) and issue specialization (Wängnerud 2000), in order to determine whether female parliamentarians 'act for women' in some way (Celis 2005). Most of the work in this area has argued that the sex of the representative does make a difference to their issue priorities and political behaviour, with women giving more support for feminist values, expressing a stronger concern with social policy issues and giving a higher priority to constituency work (Norris and Lovenduski 1995:224). For instance, Wängnerud finds that in the Sweden parliament 'female politicians have consistently been the group that has pursued social welfare policy issues to the greatest extent in their parliamentary work' (Wängnerud 2005:17). Childs also finds a sex difference among Labour's MPs in Westminster in terms of their voting behaviour in that women were less likely to rebel against the party whip than were the rest of the Labour Party parliamentarians (Childs 2004a).

However, there are two limitations to these indicators of impact: first, it is recognized that this focus on sex differences in attitudes and behaviours may downplay the extent to which the increased presence of women in parliaments may change the attitudes and behaviour of male representatives such that there is issue convergence in gender roles (Swers 2002:10; Mateo Diaz 2005:180). For instance, Wängnerud and Mateo Diaz both find that the pattern in which women privilege social welfare policy more than men has become weaker over time (Mateo Diaz 2005:137; Wängnerud 2005:18), suggesting that convergence around new policy priorities, rather than sex difference with regard to existing ones, may be the better indicator of impact. Second, one may establish that female parliamentarians act differently from male ones, without thereby proving that they are acting for the female electorate in a representative manner. In order to test for this, one needs to test for the level of congruence between female voters' opinions and legislators' behaviour. Interestingly, research in Western European parliaments indicates that female parliamentarians may be less representative of female voters than male parliamentarians are of male voters (Mateo Diaz 2005:201).

This may be explained by the fact that female parliamentarians have compensated for their sex disadvantage by acquiring disproportionately high levels of education and cultural capital, rendering them unrepresentative and more interested in transforming public opinion than in reflecting it (Mateo Diaz 2005:233–4). It may simply indicate that there are limits to the extent to which individual parliamentarians can act as spokespersons for marginalized groups (Weldon 2002a:1155). Either way, it suggests that feminist advocacy may be a third possible indicator of success, in addition to descriptive and substantive representation. In order to operationalize this indicator, there would need to be some agreement as to the nature of feminist goals. Yet while much of the difficulty in trying to determine whether and to what extent quotas impact on the substantive representation of women resides in the fact that substantive representation entails women's interests being articulated within the policy process and influencing policy outcomes, there is very little agreement as to what constitutes women's interests, how these are to be determined, who is best placed to discern their content, and whether they can really be thought to be homogeneous.

Overall, it appears that attempts to establish the effectiveness of quotas in relation to descriptive representation alone are subject to charges that quotas introduce only symbolic change, failing to address wider socio-economic inequalities (Vincent 2004). This suggests that quota mechanisms may be open to the charge of assimilation. Meanwhile, attempts to establish their effectiveness in relation to substantive representation are subject to difficulties in determining what women's interests comprise, and frequently invoke, assumptions about women's perspectives and attitudes that fail to recognize intra-group diversity. This suggests that quota mechanisms may also be open to the charge of essentialism.

Evaluating the Success of Women's Policy Agencies

Evaluations of the impact of women's policy agencies also tend to use both descriptive and substantive representation as indicators of success, measuring their impact in terms of their ability to 'bring more women, and the women's movement actors that speak for them, into the affairs of government – descriptive representation – and introduce feminist ideas into policy discussion and outcomes – substantive representation' (Stetson and Mazur 2003:2). Descriptive representation does not here refer simply to an increased number of women employed within state bureaucracies, but also incorporates a concern with the greater inclusion of women's movement actors in the policy-making process via consultative mechanisms. For this reason some scholars also take accountability and institutional power as measures of the effectiveness of women's policy agencies (Weldon 2002), evaluating both the relation between the agency and the women's movement (accountability) and the relation between the policy agency and the government (institutional power).

There is now a substantial literature that evaluates the impact of women's policy agencies on the policy-making process in relation both to Western post-industrial democracies (see Sawer 1996 and Chappell 2002; Stetson and Mazur 1995) and to developing countries (see Alvarez 1999; Baldez 2001, 2002; Kardam and Acuner 2003; Rai 2003; Roseau 2005; Vargas and Wieringa 1998). These are generally national-level case-studies with a few cross-national comparisons examining two or more countries (Chappell 2002; Hausmann and Sauer 2007; Lovenduski 2005; Outshoorn 2004; Rai 2003; Sawer 1996; Stetson and Mazur 1995; Teghtsoonian 2005) and very few international comparative studies (True and Mintrom 2001). There has as yet been no research that 'systematically studies whether women's policy agencies make a difference in women's representation in all regions of the world' (Mazur 2005:5), but the large number of individual studies is making this process increasingly possible.

The largest comparative study to date, conducted by scholars in the Research Network on Gender Politics and the State (RNGS), focuses on women's policy agencies in Western post-industrial democracies (Stetson and Mazur 1995). The study focuses on 14 countries – Australia, Austria, Belgium, Canada, Finland, France, Germany, Ireland,

Italy, Netherlands, Spain, Sweden, UK and USA – with teams in each country collecting data since 1997 (Mazur 2005:6). This project aims to discover

> the degree to which women's policy agencies bring more women, and the women's movement actors that speak for them, into the affairs of government – descriptive representation – and introduce feminist ideas into policy discussion and outcomes – substantive representation. (Stetson and Mazur 2003:2)

This research therefore aims to explore the extent to which women's policy agencies facilitate both women's descriptive and substantive representation, by helping the actors 'that speak for women and gender equality' to enter government policy-making arenas, and by bringing 'women's interests and gender equality issues into public policy discussion, formulation and implementation' (Mazur 2005:3).

In order to evaluate the success of women's policy agencies in relation to these two aims, RNGS scholars studied individual policy debates within various liberal democracies that led to some sort of state action in relation to job training, abortion, prostitution, political representation, and a top-priority issue specific to each country being studied. They aimed to establish the effectiveness of the agencies in assisting the movement in reaching its goals, and the characteristics of agencies associated with that effectiveness. This research departs from previous studies of social movement impact (Gamson 1975) in taking into account procedural goals in the form of the increased participation of women (who were actively advancing some aspect of women's interests) in the policy-making arena, showing that this literature is particularly concerned with democratic participation in equality norm formation rather than with social justice outcomes defined in advance of this process.

In trying to determine the extent to which, and the circumstances in which, different kinds of women's policy agencies provided effective linkages for women's movements to achieve substantive and procedural responses from the state, the RNGS researchers used four categories of classification for the state responses to women's movement actors: dual response, where the state both accepts individual women, groups and/or constituencies representing gender interests into the process and changes policy to coincide with feminist goals; co-optation, where the state accepts the individual women, groups and/or constituencies into the process but does not give policy satisfaction; pre-emption, where the state gives policy satisfaction, but does not allow women, as individuals, groups or constituencies into the process; and no response, where the state has no procedural or substantive response to movement demands.

The researchers used a further four categories of classification to measure the women's policy agencies' effectiveness in representing women's movement claims: insider, where the women's policy agency incorporates women's movement goals into its own positions on the policy issues and is successful in gendering the dominant frame of the public debates on the issue; marginal, where the women's policy agency asserts movement goals, but is not successful in gendering the policy debate; non-feminist, where the women's policy agency is not an advocate for movement goals but genders or degenders policy debates in some other way or ways; and symbolic, where women's policy agencies neither advocate movement goals nor gender policy definitions on the issue (Mazur 2005:7). Using these two variables, the researchers aimed to establish the impact of the agencies, with success being defined as an insider agency generating a dual response from the state and failure being defined as a symbolic agency failing to produce any response either descriptive or substantive.

Lovenduski, Mazur, Ousthoorn and Stetson all argue that the comparative longitudinal research suggests that many of these agencies were important in realizing women's movements' demands in policy-making and in gaining access for women to decision-making arenas (Lovenduski 2005; Mazur 2001; Oustshoorn 2004; Stetson 2001; Stetson and Mazur 1995). On the basis of studying 132 policy debates they find that women's policy agencies produced successful alliances, enhancing women's representation both descriptively and substantively, in 40 per cent of cases. In 16 per cent of the time the result was failure. Within this, they find that the degree of success varies by policy debate, with the highest rate of success being achieved in relation to political representation (40 per cent success) and the lowest in relation to the top-priority issue (8 per cent success).

However, trying to identify the factors that led to success proved fairly complex. Mazur and Stetson considered three sets of factors: features of the women's movement, of the wider policy environment, and of the women's policy agencies themselves. In relation to the first of these, they suggest that success is most likely where the women's movement is cohesive in relation to their demands (movement unity) and considers the issue a high priority (issue priority). However, they also argue that women's movements need to be understood as taking more diverse forms than simply autonomous feminist movements, including any fluid groupings that take a public stance that is explicitly gendered and affirms the representation of women as women in public life, which suggests that movement unity will be difficult to achieve. In relation to the second, they suggest that success is most likely where there is a left-wing government and a good 'fit' between the approach of the mainstream policy actors of the given policy area and the women's movement actors (see McBride 2005 on the lack of success in hostile policy environments). However, this correlation didn't apply in all cases, and with certain policy issues 'there is virtually no difference in the policy environment characteristics between the cases of successful alliances compared with the failed alliances' (Mazur 2005:11).

In relation to the third factor, namely the features of the women's policy agencies themselves, the researchers found it much harder to determine which of these were most likely to lead to success. The group considered a wide range of possible factors, including scope, type, proximity, administrative capacity, leadership and policy mandate, but found no clear agency characteristics across all policy issues (Mazur 2005:10). For instance, in relation to abortion, successful agencies tended to have separate budgets and staff and be led by feminists; in relation to job training and political representation, they found no single profile of women's policy agency for either successful or failed alliances; in relation to the top-priority issue, resources did not appear to be significant, but closeness of the agencies to power and feminist leadership was. With respect to political representation, successful agencies tended to be cross-sectional, close to party leaders, led by feminists and with small or no separate budgets, though Lovenduski *et al.* found that the success of the women's policy agencies could be determined most effectively with reference to their relation to the women's movement and wider policy environment, rather than with reference to their internal characteristics (such as resources and administrative capacity) alone (Lovenduski *et al.* 2005:271). In other words a 'dual response' was most likely where the women's movement was cohesive and prioritized political representation, and where the left was in power and the arguments for women's political representation fitted with wider governmental policy frames.

This suggests that the policy agency itself may not be central to the process of increasing women's descriptive and substantive representation in these debates: their activities 'may not be necessary to successful policy outcomes if issue priority and movement cohesion are high' (Lovenduski 2005:283). While they 'provided a boost' to movement changes of policy success in favourable conditions, they are 'unable to compensate' when conditions were unfavourable (where the women's movement did not prioritize the issue of political representation and/or were not cohesive, and where the issue did not fit with wider governmental policy frames). Women's policy agencies assisted, but were not essential, to gendering (in terms of both presence and outcome) political representation debates. This, in turn, suggests that while policy agencies do largely act as 'state feminists', supporting women's movement goals within state bureaucracies, these agencies do only support the women's movement, and are generally unable to realize policy success in the absence of a strong and cohesive women's movement. Women's policy agencies, whatever their status and resources, cannot substitute for an active women's movement.

Cumulatively these studies suggest that the success of policy agencies will depend on the characteristics of the women's movement and the policy environment as well as the features of the agency itself, with accountability being more likely where the women's movement is cohesive and institutional power more likely when the policy environment is favourable. However, most of the discussions concerning the obstacles to the effectiveness of women's policy agencies have tended to focus on the features of the agencies and the policy environment rather than those of the women's movement. The preoccupation with institutional power inevitably raises concern about the tendency of policy agencies to co-opt feminist activism, assimilating women's movement demands into the pre-existing confines of the policy environment. Meanwhile, the tendency to assume that the women's movement is cohesive, coupled with the lack of systematic attention to the diversity among women's organizations within the state feminist literature, suggests that women's policy agencies may be working with essentialist notions of women's interests.

Emphasizing the importance of institutional power in relation to the pursuit of substantive representation, many studies find that high-level machineries operating close to the centre are effective and that a free-standing ministry is an asset (Sawer 1996; Squires and Wickham-Jones 2002:63). Accordingly, the UN Division for the Advancement of Women (DAW) Expert Group on National Machineries for Gender Equality recommend that women's policy agencies 'should be at the highest level of government falling under the responsibility of the President, Prime Minister or Cabinet Minister … and be located in the central planning or policy coordination area of government' (UN DAW 1998). However, while institutional power may facilitate feminist advocacy, it frequently distances the agencies from women's movement actors.

There may be a structural tension between the representative and advocacy functions of women's policy agencies. For example, some case-studies suggest that the weak and under-resourced nature of the policy agency, coupled with the need to prepare national reports to the

CEDAW committee, increased collaboration between the agencies and civil society actors, such that the report reflected the views of women rather than the government institution (Kardam 2005:4–5). This indicates that a lack of resources and marginal location may encourage collaboration with civil society actors. More generally, it may imply that there is a tradeoff between women's movement accountability and institutional power. Accordingly, the limitations of both high- and low-level machineries have been recognized: for while a location on the periphery of the public service allows for limited access to decision-making and a minimal impact of policy, a central location may blunt their capacity to advocate clear feminist policy (Franzway *et al.* 1989:139–40).

Perhaps as result of the competing perceptions as to the agencies' primary function, a lack of clarity as to their mandate, which results in frequent changes in location, personnel and policy brief, has frequently been cited as an obstacle to success. The UN Commission on the Status of Women note that women's policy agencies have often been 'understaffed and under-funded, with unclear mandates, frequent shifts in structural location and weak capacity to perform the myriad functions assigned to them' (DAW 2005:3). The ever-changing structure, location and remit of policy agencies have been widely documented, and noted as an obstacle to their success in both developing and OECD countries. For example, agencies were developed in Uganda in the context of democratization and economic reform under structural adjustment policies, first taking the form of a Ministry of Women and Development (1988), then becoming a part of a wider Ministry of Women in Development, Culture and Youth (1992), which was renamed the Ministry of Gender and Community Development (1994) (Kwesiga 2003:206). Similarly, in the UK a Women's Unit (WU) was established in 1997, charged with scrutinizing legislation to promote sexual equality and with promoting female-friendly policies. It was then restructured as the Women and Equality Unit in 2001, taking responsibility for policy on gender equality issues ('coordinating policy on women and gender equality issues') (Cabinet Office 12 July 2001), including sex discrimination and equal pay, and dropping its focus on consultation. More recently, in light of a governmental equality review and the proposed creation of a single equality commission, the unit looks likely to become an Equalities Unit.

This pattern is common among women's policy agencies, such that the twenty-third special session of the General Assembly on 'Beijing +5: Women 2000' noted obstacles to the effectiveness of these agencies as including inadequate financial and human resources, unclear mandates, and communication problems within and among government agencies

(United Nations, 16 November 2000). Similarly, the UN Division for the Advancement of Women details constraints as including: mandate, location and leadership; resources (including funds and staff); statistics and data; monitoring and accountability; co-ordination and collaboration among the national mechanisms (Division for the Advancement of Women 2005:21). Accordingly, the UN Division for the Advancement of Women suggests that the effectiveness of women's policy agencies would be improved by a number of bureaucratic changes, including: enhanced resources (including staff and budgets); improved co-ordination and collaboration among different women's policy agencies; and strengthened monitoring and accountability (including collecting better statistics). While these measures all focus on increasing the institutional power of the agencies, the DAW does also recommend mobilizing political will by working with women parliamentarians and civil society groups, complementing the more narrowly bureaucratic measures with more directly representative considerations. It does not address the ways of dealing with the issue of unclear mandate however, although this appears to be a central obstacle to success.

The issue of unclear mandate arises in part because of competing expectations as to what women's policy agencies should be striving to achieve. Some argue that they should be contributing to a process of democratization by collaborating with women's movement actors and women in public office (Vargas and Wieringa 1998), while others suggest that they be understood as 'advocacy bureaucracies' only, focusing on gaining institutional power and achieving substantive representation (Goetz 2005). These differing perceptions of the appropriate function of women's policy agencies map onto, and prefigure, two central models of gender mainstreaming that have emerged, namely the participatory-democratic and the expert-bureaucratic. In the case of women's policy agencies, this tension is partially resolved by the distinct forms that women's policy agencies take.

Government units, with their central location, access to professional gender equality expertise and resources tend to focus on the expert-bureaucratic pursuit of institutional power, while consultative bodies, with their peripheral location and access to women's organizations, will focus on the participative-democratic pursuit of accountability. Government units may find it difficult to remain open to civil society actors, while consultative bodies may have little influence over the policy-making process: the greater the institutional power, the weaker the accountability and vice versa. One way of dealing with these competing agendas is to acknowledge that different types of women's policy agencies are more likely to gain institutional power or to be accountable, and that a really successful strategy would be to ensure that different types of women's policy agency worked together, developing clear strategies for supporting the work of the others and counter-balancing their weaknesses (as for example, the Women's National Commission and the Women and Equality Unit do in the UK). In this way a vibrant consultative body will balance the technocratic tendencies of the machinery within government. However, most studies of women's policy agencies to date have not distinguished between agencies by type, tending to evaluate the success of agencies *per se*.

Overall, it appears that women's policy agencies can help to give voice to women's movement goals and to frame the public debates on policy issues in a way consonant with these goals, where the women's movement is cohesive and its goals fit with wider governmental policy frames. Advocates of policy agencies argue that they should therefore be seen to play a crucial role in enhancing women's representation. However, their research has also shown that where the women's movement is cohesive and the policy environment favourable, women's movement actors can gain access to the state without such agencies, which cannot therefore be deemed to play a definitive role. Moreover, no single profile of women's policy agencies has been identified with success, which renders attempts to make agencies more successful by changing their institutional profile a questionable strategy. Nonetheless, there is a clear tendency to argue for the strengthening of these agencies in terms of their resources and location such that they can articulate women's movement demands more effectively. To date there has been relatively little attention paid to the question of the appropriate role and profile of the agencies in circumstances where the women's movement is not cohesive and where its demands are contested.

Evaluating the Success of Gender Mainstreaming

Gender mainstreaming has been described as a 'deceptively simple concept that is likely to be extremely difficult to operationalize' (Mazey 2000:343). Indeed, simplicity does not appear to be a common feature of mainstreaming, either conceptually or operationally. At a conceptual level it requires reflection about the meaning of gender (in relation to women and men), of equality (in relation to opportunities and outcomes, redistribution and recognition) and of mainstreaming itself (in relation to the processes of policy-making). At an operational level mainstreaming also appears to demand rather a lot, requiring 'the identification of gender issues in the process of design, implementation and evaluation of all policies', aiming to 'provide a means of taking into account the gender effects of politics from the start and to provide a new and potentially transformatory perspective on policy approaches and on the organisation of society' (Rubery 2002:502). As a result, notwithstanding the rapid diffusion of mainstreaming as a new approach to gender equality, there is continued debate about both its conceptualization and its operationalization.

Gender mainstreaming combines 'the potentially radical concept of gender' with a 'technique of mainstreaming' (Wank 2003:2). By invoking the concept of gender, the strategy appears to shift the focus away from women's interests and perspectives, to the socially constructed nature of gender relations and the structures and processes that reproduce inequalities between different genders, facilitating a transformative 'frame of analysis' that enables gender relations to be understood as changeable by policy interventions.

Where the adoption of gender mainstreaming has entailed the introduction of a new approach to gender equality, it has usually entailed institutional change in the form of the introduction of new mainstreaming tools and new mainstreaming units, and has sometimes also embraced wider cultural and personnel change, altering the way policy is made (Daly 2005:442). The tools most frequently adopted as part of the implementation of gender mainstreaming are 'analytic' and 'educational', rather than consultative or participatory (see Council of Europe 2003; Verloo 2005:351), with gender disaggregated statistics and gender impact assessments being adopted in an '*a-la-carte*' fashion (Daly 2005:436). 'Gender-disaggregated statistics' produce data on things such as labour force participation, life expectancy, educational attainment and literacy rates by sex (not gender) (see for example, the World Bank GenderStats electronic database), while gender impact analysis involves assessing 'the direct and indirect impact of any budget measures on existing gender inequalities, and using that assessment as a factor in deciding whether those measures should proceed' (Himmelweit 2002:50). Gender budgeting in particular has become a central feature of mainstreaming practices (Elson 2000; Sharp and Broomhill 2002).

The effective production of sex-disaggregated statistics and implementation of gender impact assessments are most frequently taken to be indications that mainstreaming is being implemented, though institutional change and the adoption of consultation practices can also indicate that mainstreaming is being implemented. Where women's policy agencies already exist they may be made responsible for the implementation of gender mainstreaming; where they do not, dedicated gender mainstreaming units may be set up to provide training to policy-makers in the techniques of gender mainstreaming. Additionally, where the tools of mainstreaming are taken to include consultation and participation a relevant indicator of effective implementation would entail 'the institutionalization of consultation practices, the creation or consolidation of advisory bodies representing women's groups, and an increase in government investment with a view to equipping women's representatives with the necessary skills to participate in policy-making' (Daly 2005:443).

Whether these latter indicators are used or not tends to depend on whether the expert-bureaucratic or the participative-democratic model of mainstreaming is in play. If the former, the impact of mainstreaming is judged by the degree to which mainstreaming practices are embedded within organizational practices, through the adoption of mainstreaming structures and instruments such as mainstreaming units, gender disaggregated statistics and gender impact assessments (see Elgstrom 2000; Pollack and Hafner-Burton 2000; Verloo 2000). If the latter, the impact of mainstreaming is judged in relation to the extent to which there is a broadening out of the range of actors involved in the policy-making process, via a visible increase in social dialogue through the institutionalization of consultation practices, the creation or consolidation of advisory bodies representing women's groups or an increase in government investment with a view to equipping women's representatives with the necessary skills to participate in policy-making (Beveridge *et al.* 2000; Daly 2005:442–3; Kelly and Donaghy 2001; Lovecy 2002; Mackay and Bilton 2000; Mazey 2002; Squires and Wickham-Jones 2001). Policy change, the most concrete measure of success, has as yet been little employed in relation to mainstreaming strategies to date, perhaps because evaluation of the outcome of mainstreaming is still premature given that many of the relevant policies have not yet been implemented.

In practice, the strategy has generally focused attention on 'a set of techniques of policy praxis' (Daly 2005:448), which can be implemented without a significant engagement with the transformative potential of the analytic frame. The suggestion that it is important to distinguish between mainstreaming as 'a philosophy or frame of analysis' and as 'a set of techniques of policy praxis' signals the perceived disjuncture between the transformatory potential held out for mainstreaming in theory, and the array of processes implemented under the name of mainstreaming in practice. The complexities involved in taking gender as a frame of analysis, coupled with the linguistic difficulties inherent in translating 'gender mainstreaming' into a wide range of languages, has meant that many organizations have adopted some of the mainstreaming tools in the absence of an overall gender framework (Daly 2005:436). As a result, evaluations of the success of gender mainstreaming tend to focus on the effective implementation of these specific techniques of policy praxis, bracketing larger questions about social transformation.

Given that gender mainstreaming aims to introduce a gender equality perspective rather than women into the policy-making process, it has not generally been evaluated in relation to the criteria of descriptive representation. Although it could be argued that substantive representation is a relevant criterion of evaluation (especially in relation to the participative-democratic forms), there has been surprisingly little attention paid to the process by which the 'gender equality perspective' to be mainstreamed is determined, with most of the literature assuming that this will be determined by 'gender experts' and 'gender-disaggregated statistics' rather than by participatory democratic processes. The impact of mainstreaming has therefore tended to be judged with reference to the extent to which technical gender equality processes are adopted, with representative criteria taking a low profile.

While it is generally agreed that the pace at which mainstreaming has been adopted as a policy commitment has been dramatic (Rubery 2002:516), it is also widely suspected that the extent to which mainstreaming has been effectively implemented even in the narrow technical sense has been much less impressive. This remains a suspicion, largely because there are so few systematic studies of the implementation of mainstreaming, but also because the nature of the mainstreaming process means that it is rather difficult to determine clear indicators of impact even when the studies are conducted. As Breitenbach points out: 'It is still very hard to find specific case study examples of how this approach is successfully applied, and what difference it makes, and it will be some time before there is any substantial evidence of impact in reducing inequalities' (Breitenbach 2004:13). As a result, Rees notes, it 'remains difficult to assess accurately what is going on globally' (Rees 2005:561), not least because, as Rubery rightly points out, 'there are severe difficulties in distinguishing both between the rhetoric and reality of gender mainstreaming and between what are general statements of intent, including future commitments to new initiatives, and actual real policy change' (Rubery 2002:511).

Most evaluations of mainstreaming within international organizations find that mainstreaming practices have not resulted in the articulated goal of gender equality, and have also fallen short of declared policy (Bretherton 2001; Riley 2004). Because international organizations bound their members to introducing gender mainstreaming through treaties, accords and funding programmes, many a national government has formally committed to mainstreaming, yet remains fairly reluctant to undertake the internal institutional changes required to implement it in practice. The studies of the implementation of mainstreaming that are emerging suggest that many countries and organizations adopt mainstreaming in name only, using the term to describe pre-existing equality policies. For instance, in a recent review of mainstreaming, Mosesdottir and Erlingsdottir suggest that the 7 countries in their study (Austria, Denmark, Finland, Hungary, Iceland, Netherlands and Spain) 'had to adopt gender mainstreaming because of their EU membership or their associated status to the EU' (Mosesdottir and Erlingsdottir 2005:526). As a result mainstreaming is adopted in name only, and these countries continue to 'rely more on special action measures based on the perspectives of equal treatment and the women's perspective (difference) than on gender mainstreaming' (Mosesdottir and Erlingsdottir 2005:526).

In these circumstances the impact of mainstreaming is therefore limited to rhetorical change only, with its formal adoption hiding the continuation of 'business as usual' (Arranz *et al.* 2000; Casqueira Cardoso 2000). Comparative research into the implementation of mainstreaming strategies offers some support for these claims, finding that different definitions of mainstreaming are used according to institutional context (see Yeandle *et al.* 1998). There is a continued confusion about what mainstreaming entails, with many practitioners continuing to believe that it involves adding 'women's projects' onto the policy agenda, even where these projects sustain unequal-gendered power relations (True 2003: 384).

Moreover, comparative research suggests that the focus on mainstreaming continues to come largely from pressure from international organizations, such as the UN, the Council for Europe and the EU, and that were this to diminish, mainstreaming would lose its appeal at a national level (Facon *et al.* 2004). Rubery notes that while most EU member states have put in place some formal mechanism of gender mainstreaming, there is wide variation in the effectiveness of these mechanisms, with both uptake and effectiveness depending on the political interests of the parties (see Rubery 2002:511–16 for detailed evaluation of impact in specific policy areas). This suggests that the adoption of mainstreaming at national level may have occurred in many states as a result of external legal and financial pressures, with little internal commitment to the process, inevitably resulting in a disjunction between adoption and effective implementation.

There are some studies that depict mainstreaming as having a positive impact. A UN expert consultation with representatives from Asia/Pacific, East and Central Europe, the Middle East and Latin America/Caribbean identified seven principal achievements of mainstreaming in the South: women's policy agencies now firmly in place; considerable improvement in sex-disaggregated data at an international and national level; a significant strengthening of women's organizations with an important advocacy role; far greater public awareness of gender inequality than a decade ago; resource allocation to social sectors having improved the status of women; legal reforms now in place in countries across the globe; and women's human rights now providing the women's movement with a framework for advocacy (Moser 2005). These seven achievements relate to each of the four key indicators, with the creation of women's policy agencies and the improvement in sex-disaggregated data signalling embeddedness, the strengthening of women's organizations signalling presence, greater public awareness of gender inequality signalling cultural change, and resource allocation to social sectors and legal reforms signalling policy change. A survey of mainstreaming in the World Bank also found that campaigns such as 'Women's Eyes on the Bank' resulted in significant mainstreaming initiatives, including the establishment of an External Consultative Gender Group, a Gender Analysis and Policy section and an increase in the number of Bank gender specialists (O'Brien *et al.* 2000:43).

Other examples of the effective implementation of mainstreaming include the devolved governments of Scotland, Northern Ireland and Wales, where the institutional culture is presumably less entrenched and so more amenable to change (Brown, *et al.* 2002; Chaney 2002; Donaghy and Kelly 2001; Mackay and Bilton 2000). Studies suggest that 'constitutional change and the government's modernization agenda are seen as an important enabling context within which equalities work can develop' (Mackay and Bilton 2000:109; see also Dobrowolsky 2002). Accordingly, the devolved governments of Scotland, Northern Ireland and Wales are deemed to 'have made much stronger commitments to mainstreaming than the central United Kingdom government' (Rubery 2002:504). Chaney finds that while 'thoroughgoing gender mainstreaming is not presently a reality in the political decision-making of the new Welsh government', 'progress has certainly been made', in which devolution provided an important enabling context (Chaney 2003:14). Yet even here, the progress made is in relation to institutional and personnel change, rather than cultural or policy changes, where Chaney notes that little progress has been made in determining objectives and targets relating to equality or in monitoring progress towards objectives (Chaney 2003:15).

However, research into the impact of mainstreaming has also indicated that it has actually had a detrimental effect on the pursuit of gender equality, legitimating the dismantling of women's policy agencies and reducing the commitment to equality goals (Sauer 2005; Sawer 2005; Squires 2006). In Canada, for instance, Teghtsoonian notes that under the National Government of 1996–9 mainstreaming comprised only the training of policy staff; and while the election of a Labour-led coalition government in 1999 promised a more systematic approach to mainstreaming, by 2002 it was clear that 'most departments' had not 'engaged with gender analysis'(Teghtsoonian 2003). This experience is symptomatic of a wider trend in which mainstreaming has been phenomenally successful in terms of its widespread international adoption, but much less so in terms of consistent and committed implementation at the national or state level.

The inconsistent and unenthusiastic application of mainstreaming may be symptomatic of its derivation in institutions beyond the nation-state, meaning that the strategy lacks the necessary internal advocates, fails to mesh with existing policy priorities or institutional structures, or becomes interpreted in ways which resonate with national priorities, norms and structures, but which limit its envisaged potential. As True rightly argues, this suggests that 'gender mainstreaming efforts from above will not change institutional practices and norms unless they are supported by social movement activism on gender equity and subject to the ongoing critical scrutiny of a gender perspective by feminist scholars and activists' (True 2003:384). Therefore, while at a conceptual level gender mainstreaming shifts the focus away from the descriptive representation of women by aiming to introduce a gender perspective – rather than women – into the policy-making process, its impact is frequently argued to be greatest where feminist actors are engaged in the process.

Conclusion

A striking thing about the evaluations of the impacts of these three strategies is the relative paucity of evidence of their success, according to the criteria most generally adopted within the political science literature. This is due partly to the fact that these strategies are relatively recent phenomena that have been implemented only recently in many states and may require a longer period of implementation before their full impact can be evaluated. But it is also due to the fact that the indicators of success themselves are normative, which means that they are both contested and difficult to quantify. While descriptive representation is a relatively straightforward empirical indicator, which is quantifiable, substantive representation and gender equality are both more complex normative indicators. Given that gender quotas are primarily conceived as a means of securing women's descriptive representation (by increasing the number of women in legislatures), it has been easiest to evaluate the impact of gender quotas in relation to quantitative measures of the numbers of women in national legislatures. However, even here most commentators have hoped that quotas will do more than increase the descriptive representation of women alone, frequently arguing that women are more likely to act for women and that quotas will therefore result in the improved substantive representation of women. Evaluations of the impact of women's policy agencies take the substantive representation of women as a more central measure of success, given that these agencies are designed specifically to promote women's interests, though here it tends to be the representation of the women's movement by femocrats rather than the representation of the female electorate by female parliamentarians that is being judged. The representative process tends to figure less centrally in evaluations of the impact of gender mainstreaming, with the focus shifting to ideas rather than actors in that gender mainstreaming aims to introduce a gender perspective into the policy-making process and offers a series of tools which equally enable all policy-makers to adopt this perspective, thereby uncoupling the link between descriptive representation and the pursuit of gender equality. While some manifestations of gender mainstreaming do aspire to institutionalize consultation with women's civil society organizations and briefings from gender experts, it is the knowledge of the gender perspectives that is primarily sought rather than the presence of female actors.

One can broadly conclude that all three strategies do bring more women into the affairs of government, with gender quotas facilitating the greater inclusion of female candidates in state decision-making via candidate quota mechanisms, women's policy agencies facilitating the greater inclusion of women's movement actors in the policy-making process via consultative mechanisms, and gender mainstreaming facilitating the greater inclusion of gender experts in state policy-making as producers of gender-disaggregated statistics and advisers of gender impact assessments. The three strategies therefore bring different types of women into the affairs of government: social movement activists, state femocrats, party candidates, and feminist academics. In this way each of the strategies increases women's political presence, with gender quotas securing the most high-profile presence of women, while women's policy agencies and gender mainstreaming secure presence in the less public spheres of state bureaucracies. Whether this increased presence leads to the greater substantive representation of women is more contested, both empirically and normatively: empirically contested because there are still relatively few studies that show these strategies to lead to greater gender equality beyond the more equal inclusion of women in the affairs of government; and normatively contested because the suggestion that women are likely to act for women appears to entail essentialist claims about women's identities and reductive claims about women's interests. So, while campaigns for greater political equality for women have proven to be far more successful than many early second-wave feminists thought possible, the link between these political successes and the pursuit of wider socio-economic and cultural equality concerns is still highly contested.

3

Working Together? Analysing Interrelations*

Judith Squires and Mona Lena Krook

Introduction

While gender quotas, women's policy agencies and gender mainstreaming have emerged as three significant political equality measures in recent years, the three are clearly quite distinct. Women's policy agencies, promoted as a global strategy roughly twenty years prior to the focus on quotas and mainstreaming, aim to promote both the substantive and descriptive representation of women, giving individual women greater access to policy-making arenas and promoting women's group interests in specific policy fields. These functions appear to be disentangled somewhat in gender quotas and gender mainstreaming, with quotas focusing on presence but offering no guarantees in terms of formal mechanisms that this will result in the substantive representation of women, and gender mainstreaming focusing on integrating 'a gender perspective' into the policy-making process but offering no commitment regarding the increased participation of women.

Intriguingly, while quotas and mainstreaming are increasingly treated as partner measures for the empowerment of women through politics (United Nations 1995, 2002), it is not actually very clear that they are in

---

* This chapter draws substantially on a paper co-authored with Mona Lena Krook entitled 'Gender Quotas and Gender Mainstreaming: Competing or Complementary Representational Strategies?', presented at the Political Studies Association Women and Politics Conference, held at the University of Edinburgh, 11 February 2006.

fact complementary, nor is it clear that women's policy agencies fit into this twin-track schema. Mainstreaming requires that policy-makers take gendered effects into account when drafting legislation, but does not require that policy-makers be women, while quotas promote women to the ranks of policy-makers, but do not compel them to consider gender when proposing public policy. As such, quotas and mainstreaming engage separate groups of actors and pursue different types of goals. Although the 1995 Beijing Platform for Action advocated both gender quotas and gender mainstreaming, several features of quotas and mainstreaming indicate – at least at the conceptual level – that these approaches may in fact constitute competing approaches to gender equality.

The apparent disjuncture between the two approaches is compounded by the fact that, although quotas and mainstreaming appeared as global strategies at roughly the same time, research on quotas and on mainstreaming have developed largely in isolation from one another. Those who investigate quotas focus on electoral politics and similarly track their diffusion around the world (Dahlerup 2006; Krook 2006), but also seek to identify reasons for their adoption and non-adoption (Baldez 2004; Krook 2007; Krook *et al.* 2006), as well as for variations in their implementation and impact (Jones 2004; Krook 2005; Murray 2004; Schmidt and Saunders 2004). Those who study women's policy agencies, in contrast, focus on the advocacy of women's movement demands inside the state (Lovenduski *et al.* 2005; Stetson and Mazur 1995), seeking to identify the conditions in which feminists can exert pressure on the state (Chappell 2002; Goetz 2004; Rai 2003), and evaluate the challenges posed by state reconfiguration (Banaszak *et al.* 2003; Oustshoorn and Kantola 2007). Those who study mainstreaming focus on public policy and examine its spread across countries (Hafner-Burton and Pollack 2002; Mosesdottir and Erlingsdottir 2005; True and Mintrom 2001), tensions and contradictions in its theory and practice (Eveline and Bacchi 2005; Squires 2005; Verloo 2005; Walby 2005), and limits encountered in its implementation (Hoskyns 1992; Lombardo 2005; Rees 1998; Rees 2005; Squires and Wickham-Jones 2004). Very little work, however, has theorized the conceptual foundations of these strategies in a way that reveals how they converge or diverge in their attempts to promote women's political representation. This chapter considers these differences as a basis for exploring the ways in which the three strategies conflict and may undermine each other, as well as ways in which they combine and may complement one another.

Competing Strategies

Women's policy agencies and gender quotas employ targeted positive action policies in order to increase women's descriptive and substantive representation in the policy-making and decision-making arenas of government respectively. As such they complement one another by offering two modes of group representation for women. Similarly, although women's policy agencies are increasingly referred to as 'gender machinery' and while quotas are generally misleadingly referred to as 'gender quotas', in practice both focus on women rather than gender, aiming to secure women's advancement via these distinct forms of group representation. Women's policy agencies and gender quotas might therefore be viewed as similar, with gender mainstreaming as distinct, in that both focus on women (rather than gender), employ positive action (rather than equal treatment or mainstreaming) measures, and aspire to secure a form of group representation that links descriptive and substantive concerns. Gender mainstreaming can be viewed as distinct from these two approaches, in that it focuses on gender, aims to supersede previous positive discrimination frameworks, and aims to secure a gender equality perspective rather than women's representation. As a result, advocates of women's policy agencies and gender quotas often express fears that mainstreaming is being introduced as a way of repudiating and abandoning positive action measures, and used to justify the closure of women's policy agencies and to argue against the introduction of gender quotas (Teghtsoonian 2003).

Indeed, it is clear that the emergence of gender mainstreaming has been used to marginalize women's policy agencies in some instances (Rai 2003) and to change the remit of the agencies in others, shifting their focus away from women-specific policies towards gender-equality policies – often reflected in a change in denomination from a women's unit to a gender or equality unit (see Squires 2006). In these circumstances mainstreaming is considered to have provided a 'rationale for abolishing or downgrading women's units, services and policies at various government levels', as has been documented in Australia, Canada and New Zealand (Mackay and Bilton 2000:62; Teghtsoonian 2003). This has led critics to argue that 'far from creating the necessary conditions for substantive equality, mainstreaming can serve to silence women and remove gender from the political agenda' (Guerrina 2003:104). Many gender practitioners therefore fear that gender mainstreaming will be used as a strategy to undermine support for specific targeted actions for women.

There are also tensions between quotas and mainstreaming. Quotas take on a number of different forms, but all provisions privilege the increased presence of female legislators rather than the promotion of wider gender equality agendas. As such, they seek only to improve women's access to political office, rather than to enact a dramatic shift in policy priorities. In some ways, these features make quotas an 'easier' strategy to defend and mobilize than gender mainstreaming, precisely because they seek not to transform public policy, but rather to promote a broader degree of political inclusion. At the same time, however, presumed links between the descriptive and substantive representation of women mean that quotas implicitly place the responsibility for pursuing gender equality on female elected officials, whether or not they are interested in promoting the interests of women as a group (Childs and Krook 2005; Goetz and Hassim 2003). Where advocates of quota policies frequently endorse the link between descriptive and substantive representation, arguing that women-friendly policy originates with female legislators (Schwindt-Bayer 2004; Swers 2004), gender mainstreaming unravels the link, building on studies which show that not all women in politics aim to represent women's concerns (Carroll 2001; Childs 2004), while some men in politics are strong advocates of women's issues (Celis 2004; Flammang 1985), in order to prioritize the pursuit of gender equality rather than the representation of women.

These patterns are further complicated by the fact that quotas and mainstreaming address fundamentally different structures within the political process: quotas focus on the vertical distribution of power within party and parliamentary structures, while mainstreaming entails the horizontal flow of initiatives across departmental boundaries, meaning that a precise mapping of descriptive features onto substantive elements of political representation will be imperfect at best. Moreover, the distance between these two facets of representation is compounded by the notion of equality that informs quota policies, which seeks to address the lack of parity within elected assemblies rather than systemic patterns of exclusion across civil society. As a result, quotas focus exclusively on political participation as the primary indicator of gender equality, dramatically reducing and restricting the broad gender equality remit of mainstreaming policies.

Although individual policy-makers understand and apply mainstreaming in a variety of different ways (Booth and Bennett 2002), all versions of mainstreaming undermine the need for more women in politics, as policy-makers – whether or not they are women or men – are expected to consider the gendered implications of all public policies. Indeed, the focus on 'gender', rather than 'women', acknowledges the relevance of men's lives to gender-equality policies, thus empowering male bureaucrats and legislators in mainstreaming debates. While this turn to gender has the potential to make the strategy more transformative (Rees 1998), it also removes the 'epistemic privilege' of female policy-makers, who are no longer seen as the only ones capable of drafting gender equality legislation.

These tendencies are exacerbated by the policy frames of economic efficiency – as opposed to principles of democratic fairness – that were drawn upon initially to legitimize mainstreaming within international circles (Hancock 1999; Kenner 2000; True 2003). In the process, mainstreaming reduces the need to focus on electoral politics as a way to promote women's status, as it not only removes the onus on political parties to respond to women's movement demands, but also ostensibly replaces the need for women's movement mobilization itself. In their place, it elevates experts and bureaucrats as the central political actors, who may be put in charge of mainstreaming public policy with or without any specific background in gender issues (Razavi and Miller 1995; Kardam 2000). The most common strategy involves simply retraining the actors who are already part of the policy-making process, rather than incorporating new actors – specifically women inside the political parties – who were previously the main source of information on ways to combat gender inequalities (Lovecy 2002; Teghtsoonian 2003; Woodward 2001). Mainstreaming thus entails a firm shift away from a 'politics of presence' to a 'politics of ideas' (Phillips 1995), or a move away from women's descriptive representation, which requires an increased number of women in political office, towards their substantive representation, which mandates only increased attention to gender in the making of public policy. As a result, mainstreaming may erode support for 'women-only' policies – the staple of the early gender equality strategies of equal treatment and positive action – by framing them as 'old-fashioned' and focused solely on ameliorating women's conditions to the exclusion of men.

For example, Rees labels equal treatment, positive action and gender mainstreaming 'tinkering', 'tailoring' and 'transforming' respectively, where tailoring entails 'legal redress to treat men and women the same' but continues to take men as the norm; tinkering recognizes that there are differences between men and women and that specific measures are required to address disadvantages experienced by women as a consequence of those differences; transforming, by contrast, 'ideally should involve identifying how existing systems and structures cause indirect discrimination and altering or redesigning them as appropriate' (Rees 2002:46–8). On this account, as Bacchi points out, there is an apparent tension between the two strategies, with mainstreaming representing an improvement on positive action programmes, which presumably includes both gender quotas (Bacchi 2004:1) and women's policy agencies.

In addition, there is a fairly widespread fear that gender mainstreaming not only will hinder positive action being taken, but also will allow the specificity of gender itself to gradually disappear such that mainstreaming becomes a synonym for diversity policy more generally (Woodward 2005:3). Given the decoupling of gender equality from female presence, there is an anxiety that, without women the feminist commitment to 'gender' will dissipate, making mainstreaming a tool for pursuing diversity policies more generally. This 'spectre' is raised precisely because gender mainstreaming is in principle more open to negotiating the complex demands of equality and diversity than are the dedicated politics action policies of women's policy agencies and gender quotas. Much of the anxiety that surrounds gender mainstreaming among feminists emerges from the concern that equality policies which attend exclusively to gender will be eclipsed by policies that attempt to engage with other forms of inequality. For instance Woodward asks whether 'gender will fall out of mainstreaming', noting that 'to mainstream' is a policy verb now frequently used without the prefix 'gender' as a technique for inserting a policy theme horizontally (Woodward 2005:2). While this may bring dividends in allowing diversity considerations to be included within feminist equality strategies in a more systematic fashion than has been the case to date, it clearly puts mainstreaming at odds with the other two political equality measures, which continue to focus explicitly on women.

The existence of mainstreaming practices is being used as a rationale for closing down women's policy agencies, and inevitably erodes female parliamentarians' distinctive claim to represent women by giving 'gender-sensitive' bureaucrats greater responsibility for consulting directly with women's movement organizations and gender experts. This suggests that positive action and gender mainstreaming strategies can and do compete.

Complementary Strategies

Notwithstanding the theoretical and practical tensions detailed above, international organizations and national governments have generally viewed quotas, women's policy agencies and mainstreaming as distinct but complementary strategies, insisting that gender mainstreaming does not replace the need for targeted policies and positive action (UN 1997). For instance, the Council of Europe (2003) states that:

> [E]quality between women and men can only be reached by using the dual and complementary strategies of specific gender-equality policies [including the balanced participation of women and men in political and public decision-making] and gender mainstreaming.

Many of those who drafted the original mainstreaming statements argued explicitly that positive action programmes would still be needed: 'mainstreaming is not about diminishing the importance of specific actions, but giving them a fresh boost' (Maria Tavares da Silva cited in Jacquot 2003:8).

Where mainstreaming is depicted as complementing quotas and policy agencies, it tends to be viewed as a broadly conceived strategy that actually embraces positive action programmes, with specific group representation strategies as one element of a wider mainstreaming process. This approach has been widely adopted by development agencies, with many including support for women's participation in decision-making within their mainstreaming policies rather than as complements to them (Moser 2005, 578–9). For example, the mainstreaming strategy of UK's Department for International Development comprises two strands: one that aims at equality via integration of women's and men's concerns in all policies and projects; and a second that aims at empowerment via specific activities (DFID 2002). Similarly, the current position of the EU is that it is pursuing positive action and gender mainstreaming as a twin-track approach to gender equality, while also issuing directives aimed to ensure that national legislation delivers on the principle of equal treatment as enshrined in the Treaty of Rome (Rees 2005:559).

Accordingly, many advocates of gender mainstreaming argue that it should not be viewed as a practical alternative or theoretical challenge to the logic of positive action policies (Stratigaki 2005). In some articulations, the distinction between the two is simply skirted over. For instance the Beijing Platform for Action states that:

> The equitable distribution of power and decision-making at all levels is dependent on Governments and other actors undertaking statistical gender analysis and mainstreaming a gender perspective in policy development and the implementation of programmes. Equality in decision-making is essential to the empowerment of women. In some

countries, affirmative action has led to 33.3 per cent or larger representation in local and national Governments. (United Nations 1995:187)

This obfuscates the theoretical tensions between mainstreaming and positive action by juxtaposing the first sentence with the second two.

Others explicitly argue that positive action has a role to play within mainstreaming practices. For instance, Rees – who has been a strong advocate of gender mainstreaming – argues that 'equal treatment legislation and positive action measures can … be seen as both approaches to gender equality in their own right, but also as tools in the delivery of gender mainstreaming' (Rees 2005:559–60). In other words, mainstreaming is at times depicted as representing an improvement on earlier gender equality strategies, which may be interpreted as complementing or replacing the earlier strategies, and at other times it is depicted as incorporating these earlier strategies within its wider remit.

Indeed, the common depiction of mainstreaming as going beyond the opposition between equal treatment and positive action measures is complicated by the existence of different models of mainstreaming itself. As outlined in the previous chapter, the literature on mainstreaming distinguishes between integrationist and agenda-setting approaches (Jahan 1995:126), where the first focuses on experts and the bureaucratic creation of evidence-based knowledge in policy-making, the second on the participation, presence and empowerment of disadvantaged groups via consultation with civil society organizations (see Beveridge and Nott 2002:301; Lombardo 2005). In certain integrationist manifestations, mainstreaming can invoke the logic of equal treatment while in other agenda-setting manifestations it comes closer to embracing positive action (Squires 2005). Given that integrationist forms of mainstreaming aim to be implemented by the regular actors in the policy-making process, they therefore seek to 'resonate' with the existing frames within which regular actors operate (Verloo 2001:9) and are therefore likely to aspire to treating women equally in relation to the existing norms of politicians and civil servants. By contrast, certain agenda-setting manifestations of mainstreaming aim to recognize the perspectives and concerns of women outside the policy-making elite, privileging women's 'different' voice (Donaghy 2003). This suggests that while Rees's transformative vision of mainstreaming may 'go beyond' equal treatment and positive action in principle, many practical manifestations of the strategy tend to fall back into one or other of these approaches (Squires 2005).

Moreover, at a practical level there is evidence that women's policy agencies continue to play an important role in gender mainstreaming, providing the expertise and training necessary to help government actors understand and implement gender mainstreaming tools effectively (Staudt 2003; Woodward 2003). A recent French gender audit, for example, was instituted and has been overseen by femocrats in the women's rights service (Mazur 2005). Meanwhile the UN states that in the UN system itself, 'gender mainstreaming does not replace the need for targeted, women-specific policies and programmes or positive legislation, nor does it substitute for gender units or focal points' (UN 1997). Similarly, Verloo stresses that mainstreaming cannot fully develop, cannot thrive in a climate that does not allow the articulation of feminist organization, be it inside institutions or autonomous. Gender equality units are a valuable asset for gender mainstreaming. They do not become redundant (Verloo 2002:4). This suggests a complementarity between positive action measures in the form of women's policy agencies and mainstreaming processes.

It is also worth noting that, while mainstreaming has been represented by many international organizations, development agencies and national governments as a complement to – or sometimes a frame for – positive action, it has not generated the high levels of public debate that quotas have, and has 'no ready popular resonance' (Daly 2005:433). Thus, while gender equality professionals and academics have devoted much attention to mainstreaming in recent years, the popular imagination still tends to focus on equal treatment and positive action policies, where important new developments continue to take place. Most countries adopt a mix of gender equality approaches rather than using mainstreaming to supplant other approaches and many states have recently witnessed not only the introduction of mainstreaming, but also significant changes to equal treatment and positive action approaches. For instance, although the UK government has formally endorsed gender mainstreaming, in practice it has done relatively little to implement it (Veitch 2005), while equal treatment legislation is being reformed to apply to wider spheres of application (such as public services and facilities) and positive action programmes are being reformed to apply to men as well as women (such as targets for boys' educational development). Daly suggests that these findings 'challenge those parts of the literature that have tended to represent the three approaches rather schematically, in terms, for instance, of three generations' (Daly 2005:437), arguing that Rees's chronological typology 'freezes' each approach and in so doing precludes the possibility that each may develop and change over time. By contrast to this chronological periodization, Daly suggests that 'approaches to gender equality are living entities, enduring over time and also subject to change and capable of showing dynamism' (Daly 2005:438). The widespread adoption of gender mainstreaming should not therefore divert our attention away from important developments in relation to equal treatment and positive action policies.

This suggests that while there may be theoretical tensions between the three strategies, they may all be being implemented and developed in ways that accentuate, rather than erode, their complementarity. Notably, evidence suggests that the presence of feminist actors makes a difference to the extent to which mainstreaming is implemented. Rees suggests that the prerequisites for mainstreaming include appropriate institutional arrangements, awareness training, expertise, commitment from the top, resources, representation and culture (Rees 2002). While quotas and women's policy agencies rarely deliver on all of these prerequisites, they do increase the levels of female representation in the decision-making and policy-making arenas of government and may change the culture of the institution. They may also facilitate the development of awareness training and expertise; as Veitch notes, 'the development of gender expertise within government is dependent on political patronage of the mainstreaming process, and that still largely rests with women politicians' (Veitch 2005:605).

This suggests that the effective use of quotas to increase the number of female parliamentarians may be a precondition for the effective implementation of a mainstreaming strategy. The fact that mainstreaming is perceived to be more effective in Northern Ireland, Scotland and Wales than in the central UK administration for instance lends support to this possibility, given that these assemblies have significantly higher levels of female representation. Research suggests that the high levels of female representation in these new administrations has transformed women's political roles and the nature of politics in these polities, and is argued to have had a 'significant enabling effect on the promotion of gender mainstreaming' (Chaney 2003:10).

Despite the conceptual tensions noted above, quotas, women's policy agencies and mainstreaming share substantial continuities and complementarities in terms of their ultimate goals of promoting gender equality. Indeed, analysing them as potential partners reveals a number of important theoretical and practical advantages for pursuing them in conjunction with one another. First, treating women as both objects and subjects of politics allows for a more flexible and sophisticated conception of gender, while also retaining a focus on women as a group. More specifically, it creates greater fluidity among the categories of policy actor and policy recipient by recognizing that these are not absolute, but frequently overlap with and even contradict one another with regard to the preferences of individual women. Second, operating with a wider definition of politics that includes both parliamentary and policy arenas points to numerous ways in which different sites of representation may, and often do, reinforce one another. In many cases, for example, female politicians and bureaucrats work together to propose, pass and implement mainstreaming policies (Eschle 2001; True 2003). Third, focusing on a broader range of political actors – rather than simply one set in isolation from another – sheds light on how the concerns of a politics of presence may intersect with a politics of ideas. In certain instances, the numbers of women in parliament may play a crucial role in influencing the precise form of mainstreaming – namely, integrationist or agenda-setting – that is ultimately adopted, depending both on policy-making procedures and on the preferences of individual female legislators (Kardam 2000; Razavi and Miller 1995; True 2003). Fourth, exploring the links between the descriptive and substantive representation of women exposes the issue to empirical scrutiny, rather than simply assuming that they overlap completely or not at all. The available evidence is mixed, but suggests that while these two facets of representation may not directly correspond to one another, they may nonetheless be mutually reinforcing (Veitch 2005), and some view the increased representation of women as an essential component of mainstreaming (Bacchi 2004:3). Finally, incorporating multiple definitions of equality uncovers a range of possibilities regarding interventions to change the means and ends of the political process. Indeed, separating them analytically points to a variety of ways in which particular policy reforms may pursue and meet wider normative goals of inclusion and fair treatment. Thus, a number of theoretical and practical considerations indicate the ultimate compatibility between mainstreaming, women's policy agencies and quotas as gender equality strategies.

Conclusions

There are clearly both conceptual and practical differences between the three strategies. Conceptually, these differences focus around the distinct conceptions of gender, politics, representation and equality deployed in each strategy. Quotas and women's policy agencies focus on women, thereby entailing a risk of essentialism; whereas mainstreaming privileges gender, thereby entailing a risk of marginalizing the policy focus on women. Quotas focus on parties and parliament, thereby embracing a fairly narrow institutional vision of politics; whereas women's policy agencies and mainstreaming traverse a wider terrain aiming to establish links between civil society actors, politicians, bureaucrats and experts. Quotas focus on descriptive representation while mainstreaming draws our attention to issues of substantive representation, and women's policy agencies promote both descriptive and substantive representation. Quotas and women's policy agencies are forms of positive action, while mainstreaming is held to represent a third equality approach, distinct from the equal treatment and positive action approaches. The three strategies therefore seem to stand in tension with one another on the conceptual level. Women's policy agencies appear to straddle the divisions between quotas and mainstreaming, focusing on women, gender or wider equality concerns depending on their remit; operating either at the heart of government or on the peripheries with civil society actors depending on their location; pursuing both descriptive and substantive representation by bringing both women and their policy concerns into government; and pursing equal treatment, positive action or gender mainstreaming approaches to equality, again depending on their remit. Yet, in practice, it remains an open question as to whether these differences render the strategies competing or complementary, for each of the strategies can be implemented in numerous ways, which may 'limit or undermine the potential for change' (Bacchi 2004:6).

There are important limits to each of the strategies, but there remains the potential for them to reinforce rather than undermine one another: quotas and policy agencies provide important resources in facilitating the effective implementation of mainstreaming, while mainstreaming can diversify and develop new forms of inclusive political engagement, particularly when the norms of the political system themselves are being scrutinized from a gender perspective. Where they are broadly conceived as a means of unsettling the apparent impartiality of existing institutional norms these strategies can become complementary strategies. The narrower and more limiting the interpretation of quotas, women's policy agencies and mainstreaming, the more likely they are to conflict.

4
Fair Representation? Quotas

Introduction

Women's right to participate in public life on an equal basis with men is inscribed in numerous human rights documents, including art. 25 of the International Covenant on Civil and Political Rights and art. 7 of the Convention on the Elimination of All Forms of Discrimination against Women (CEDAW). Given that equal treatment laws have generally failed to address the manifest inequality of outcome in relation to men and women's political participation rates, affirmative action strategies in the form of gender quotas have emerged as a central mechanism for securing this right, with advocates arguing that a recognition of the special needs of women as a group may be a 'precondition to the realization of the "universal" human rights of that group' (Lacey 2004:49). However, while art. 4 of CEDAW specifies that 'temporary special measures aimed at accelerating *de facto* equality between men and women shall not be considered discrimination', much of the controversy surrounding the adoption of gender quotas relates to their perceived repudiation of the principle of equal treatment with respect to equal merit.

Critics of quotas are not generally persuaded that the principles of universal human rights and equal treatment are best secured via a strategy that privileges a particular group, while advocates of quotas frequently defend the use of such measures with reference not to the principle of human rights but to the practical benefits of recognizing group differences in terms of representation and democratic engagement – thereby widening the apparent gulf between the two perspectives, with critics focusing on issues of justice and equality and advocates focusing on issues of utility and difference.

This chapter focuses on the controversies surrounding the principle of gender quotas, exploring the relative merits of three arguments for quotas, based on the claims of justice, representation and democracy respectively, each of which has been used to justify a concern with women's increased participation in formal politics in general (Phillips 1995:62–3; Phillips 1998:229–38), and the introduction of gender quotas in particular. Where the justice argument suggests that candidate selection should be characterized by equality of opportunity and that women have an equal right to positions of political influence, the representation argument holds that women have distinctive interests or experiences that are best appreciated and represented by women and that their substantive representation is therefore best secured by women's increased descriptive representation, while the democracy argument proposes that, because of their different natures or experiences, women are likely to participate in political processes in distinctive ways and that their increased participation in formal politics will enhance democratic procedures by embracing new approaches to political engagement. While the first of these arguments is rights-based and makes appeals to equality norms, the second and third are more consequentialist, utility-based arguments that appeal to women's difference, arguing for group recognition on the basis both that women are different and that they will make a difference. Where the first tries to establish prejudice, the second and third try to establish worthiness (Skjeie 2001:174). The justice argument frames gender quotas within a strategy of inclusion, whereas the representation and democracy arguments frame them within a strategy of reversal.

Each of these three arguments for quotas has generated debate (Klausen and Maier 2001; Mansbridge 2005; Squires 1996), with arguments against quotas also being made on the basis of their role in relation to the pursuit of justice, representation and democracy. The debate regarding the justice argument hinges on whether quotas undermine the normative commitment to equality of opportunity by employing selection criteria other than merit, or whether they facilitate the realization of equality, using inequality of outcome as an indicator that inequality of opportunity is not currently a reality and that positive action measures are therefore needed in order to help unsettle the institutional discrimination at work. Meanwhile, controversy regarding the representation argument hinges on whether quotas should be viewed as a means of securing the female electorate's improved substantive representation, or whether this expectation invokes essentialist notions of female identity which should be repudiated. Consequentialist arguments about substantive representation, which are used to augment more formal rights-based arguments, therefore generate anxieties about the nature of the proposed link between descriptive and substantive representation, leading to discussion as to whether women should be conceived as a 'group' defined by a shared set of experiences or interests, and how such an approach might remain sensitive to the diversity among women. Finally, the controversy regarding the democracy argument hinges on whether the preoccupation with gender quotas signals a determination to reform the institutions of government, bringing new political actors into the heart of the state and thereby transforming its nature, or whether it signals a worrying institutionalization and narrowing of feminist political horizons, which ultimately marginalize more transformative concerns and projects.

While non-feminist critics of quotas have generally focused on the equality debate, it is the debates about representation and democracy that have tended to preoccupy feminists, with sceptics exploring the extent to which quotas manifest the problems of essentialism and assimilation identified as endemic to group-based demands for recognition. For, given that quotas are frequently justified by claims that female representatives will represent the interests and identities of women, there appears to be an inevitable tendency to depict women as having unified interests and homogeneous identities which works against the explicit recognition of the differences among women and antagonism between their plural interests. They operate with a homogeneous category of women, which is neither sensitive to the diversity among women nor open to the claims for representative inclusion issued by other marginalized social collectivities. Meanwhile, given that they focus on securing gender equality in relation to the narrow institutions of parliament alone, quotas may well delimit wider concerns about gender equality, co-opting women into existing institutions rather than seeking to transform the nature of political engagement more profoundly.

This chapter will suggest that it is normatively preferable to argue for gender quotas from an equality perspective, rather than a difference one. While the first justice argument can be used to justify gender quota strategies on the basis of women's rights, the second and third arguments are unhelpful because in their attempt to establish women's worthiness they inevitably tend to depict the 'different' features of women as a group that, once asserted, work to constitute that group in particular regulatory ways. Rather than unsettling existing gendered practices and norms, the representation argument for quotas generally reinscribes conventional notions of women as particularly concerned with those 'feminine' areas of specialization that are primarily a product of the oppressive gender regimes that feminists generally seek to challenge (Randall 1982:102–6).

However, if we endorse the justice argument but not the representation argument, suggesting that quotas are 'simply' a legitimate means of ensuring that a fair number of female candidates get integrated into the existing political structures, rather than as a means of securing the female electorate's improved substantive representation, we are confronted with the charge raised in relation to the democracy argument, namely that quotas symbolize an institutionalization and narrowing of feminist political horizons. However, rather than attempting to defend the claim that women's presence alone will lead to the greater democratization of existing political practices, the desire to enhance democratic procedures and embrace new approaches to political engagement would be better pursued by exploring proposals for democratic innovation directly, rather than elliptically via the presence of female MPs. In other words, the justice argument provides the best grounds for defending quota provisions, the appeal to the consequentialist representation argument is misplaced, and accepting this highlights the need to consider strategies for democratization explicitly rather than hoping that quotas will do this work for us.

Quotas as Positive Action

Quotas are a form of positive or affirmative action. Positive action is frequently used to describe a variety of measures designed to increase the educational, employment or political outcomes of 'under-represented minorities'. Many advocates of positive action view these measures as a means to eliminate discrimination and to remedy the effects of past discrimination against designated groups. Positive action policies can take many forms, including policies such as extra points added on to some rubric for evaluating candidates, extra recruiting money allocated for the expressed purpose of obtaining representation from individuals who are members of a disadvantaged group, or special training so that people from a disadvantaged group might be able to compete equally with those from advantaged groups (Boylan 2002:117). Quotas are a particularly strong form of positive action, which have proven to be especially controversial. Indeed, there have been concerns that quotas might contravene equal treatment legislation (for example, in the United Kingdom, in 1996, the Labour Party's all-women shortlists were ruled to be in breach of fair employment practices) or breach constitutional principles of universality and of equality of citizenship (for example, in France and Italy).

The general principle of quotas is criticized on the grounds that they 'unjustifiably elevate the opportunities of members of targeted groups, discriminate against equally qualified or even more qualified members of majorities, and perpetuate racial and sexual paternalism' (Beauchamp 1998:143). There are concerns about what should count as 'morally relevant' characteristics for redress and special consideration through positive action (Nickel 1995); about aiming preferential treatment at groups rather than individuals (see Sunstein 1991:281–310); and about the assumption that past discrimination justifies preferential treatment for a group's current members. As a result of the concern that quotas undercut the commitment to individualism and meritocracy, so revered within liberal democracies, many countries have shied away from the use of quotas in general. For example, the use of quotas has been legally suspect in the United States since a 1978 Supreme Court ruling against 'preferential hiring' (*Regents of the University of California* v. *Bakke*, 1978), and a review of affirmative action programmes in the United States in 1995 sought to establish whether these programmes were fair by asking whether the programme effectively avoided quotas (Stephanopoulos and Edley 1995). Critics of positive action generally tend to argue that educational attainment, test scores, school grades, years of experience and so on are our best measure of skills and talents. This suggests that the hiring or promotion of those with weaker measures along these dimensions over those with stronger ones constitutes 'reverse discrimination'.

On the other hand, proponents of positive action in relation to the employment and educational spheres frequently distinguish between 'credentials' and 'performance', arguing that credentials are a weak predictor of performance in many cases and so individuals with weak credentials might nonetheless turn out to have high levels of productivity (see Holzer and Neumark 2000). This suggests that the indicators generally taken to evaluate merit may be inappropriate, and highlights the complexity of defining 'merit' in a manner that is both relevant and culturally neutral (Swift and Marshall 1997:36). Merit is not, as Fredman points out, 'an objective and quantifiable property' (Fredman 1997:599), and prejudice and stereotyping will frequently feature in selection criteria. This unsettles justice claims based on an endorsement of equality of opportunity and meritocracy, for as Young points out: 'if objective, value-neutral merit evaluation is difficult or impossible, the legitimacy of a hierarchical division of labour is called seriously into question' (Young 1990:193).

Translating this to the political arena, it is argued that women currently have to be 'better than men to be selected' (Elgood *et al.* 2001), given the level of unwitting prejudice and sexist stereotyping that characterizes many selection procedures (Edwards and McAllister 2002; Shepherd-Robinson and Lovenduski 2002). One might argue that the skills conventionally used by selection committees and political parties to determine which candidate is most meritorious in relation to the representative role, are rather poor indicators of the representative's ability to effectively represent all of their constituents. Thus, advocates of electoral quotas can retain a concern with merit and equality of opportunity by arguing that the current (masculine) understanding of merit is too narrow (Bacchi 2006:34). Far from lacking the necessary skills required of politicians, female candidates may actually bring valuable, though generally unrecognized, skills to the job of representing the electorate (Shepherd-Robinson and Lovenduski 2002). This is significant given that much of the controversy surrounding the use of quotas hinges on whether group identities should be used to determine the allocation of social resources rather than skills and talents. If female candidates can be shown to have particular skills in relation to the representative functions of parliamentarians, which are not being rewarded by current selection procedures, then quotas can be justified even on a minimal conception of equality of opportunity (Swift 2001:99).

Where the criteria of merit are drawn too narrowly in a manner that institutionally discriminates against marginalized groups, the principle of meritocracy inevitably entrenches a hierarchical division of labour. Genuine equality of opportunity will therefore require some mechanism for unsettling those institutional conventions that systematically reproduce inequalities of outcomes for certain groups. Yet anti-discrimination laws' focus on individuals is argued to obscure 'the essence of discrimination' whereby opportunities available to an individual seeking parliamentary selection 'are determined according to assumptions based on her membership of a group rather than her individual needs or talents' (Fredman 1992:132).

Positive action, by contrast, recognizes and attempts to eradicate structural disadvantage, on the assumption that where the norms of merit perpetuate institutional sexism, an 'equality conditional on merit may well be a false promise' (Fredman 2001:156). In this context gender quotas represent a form of positive action that is introduced to remedy the structural inequality that results from the institutional discrimination that characterizes political structures. Inequality of outcome can be taken as a key measure here of whether equality of opportunity is being conceived in a structurally discriminatory manner, for when outcomes are not equal, 'we can be reasonably certain that the opportunities were not so' (Phillips 2004:8). The fact that the formal right of women to stand for election continues to result in such low levels of female representation suggests that structural constraints (which may include overt discrimination but which also entails institutional discrimination) still operate in candidate selection processes. Where anti-discrimination laws can address overt discrimination, positive action is needed to address the more structural forms of discrimination. Equality of opportunity, rather than recognition of difference, remains the primary objective here, with inequality of outcome being used to test for its realization and quotas introduced where this test suggests that equality of opportunity is not currently a reality due to structural discrimination. The justice argument for equality of opportunity therefore translates into a defence of gender quotas if one can establish structural discrimination (Phillips 1995:64).

However, the limitation of this positive action strategy is that the quotas do not address the norms and rules that generated the discrimination directly, but rather seek to redress the inequalities that result from them. This particular defence of gender quotas invokes a strategy of inclusion, seeking to add women into existing political structures, rather than to transform them. A more transformative approach to political equality would entail a revisioning of the norms and rules themselves. For the existence of structural discrimination, measured by the fact of inequality of outcome, suggests that equality can be meaningfully advanced only if practices and structures are altered proactively by those in a position to bring about real change, which will entail reshaping the existing structures rather than simply changing the sex of those who inhabit them (Fredman 2001). This suggests that one could usefully consider a mainstreaming strategy in relation to political representation itself. Here the aim would not be to ensure that women are treated equally in the selection and election process as currently framed (as with an equal treatment approach), nor to ensure that women's disadvantage be addressed via quota policies (as with a positive action approach). Rather, the aim would be to consider gender in relation to the design, implementation, monitoring and evaluation of political practices so that women and men benefit equally and inequality is not perpetuated. The argument would not be that women might 'do' politics differently and so should be present in greater numbers, but that politics should be conceived otherwise in order that women as well as men can participate equally.

Examples of this approach can be found in attempts by women to seize the political opportunities created by constitutional reform to pursue gender equality given that the making, or remaking, of constitutional agreements generates significant possibilities for transforming those political structures that cause indirect discrimination and thereby perpetuate structural inequality. For instance, constitutional change in Britain has facilitated higher levels of female representation in the new administrations than in Westminster, ensuring that the process of devolution resulted 'not only in the renegotiation of powers between centre and sub-state nation or region, but also in the redistribution of political power between the sexes' (Mackay *et al.* 2003:84). While the use of gender quotas in the elections to the Welsh Assembly and the Scottish Parliament provide one clear explanation for the high levels of female representation, the active role that women played in influencing both the electoral systems and the nature of representation itself was also central: 'a coalition of women's organizations, grassroots activists, female trade unionists, party women, key insiders and gender experts' lobbied for a role in shaping a 'women-friendly' Scottish Parliament that would 'counteract the traditional masculinist biases of political institutions' (Mackay *et al.* 2003:85). Constitutional change enabled actors to move beyond a rule-and-exemption approach (Barry 2001:40–50), allowing them to transform the norms of representation such that they might become gender neutral rather than institutionally gendered. For instance, the Scottish Parliament meets at times that acknowledge the demands of family life and the timetable of school holidays (Mackay *et al.* 2003:88). Mainstreaming here entailed the various values, interests and life experiences of different groups of women being taken into account when mechanisms for political participation were devised and practised.

Given that policy-making generally takes place within the confines of entrenched constitutions rather than with respect to the creation of constitutions, the opportunities for mainstreaming in relation to political structures have generally been rather limited, leaving feminists to negotiate the resources offered by positive action approaches, 'tailoring' their political systems rather than transforming them. However, the concern about this approach is that it may distract from a more transformative approach to political change. It is therefore clearly worth exploring the potential for mainstreaming equality considerations into our political structures where possible, especially as 'permanent quotas are both static and highly essentializing' (Mansbridge 2001:30).

Quotas as Group Recognition

It is frequently suggested that in relation to political representation equality of outcome is not just a means of testing for equality of opportunity but is also a desirable goal in its own right (Phillips 2004:8). This is because representatives are chosen not simply on the basis of their political abilities such as verbal skills, but also on their ability to represent voter's experiences, interests and views. This ability is likely to be enhanced, Phillips suggests, by a representative's 'closeness of fit' with the electorate in terms of identity (Phillips 2004:9). This closeness of fit matters, this argument suggests, precisely because there is structural inequality between men and women in relation to levels of political participation, which suggests that men and women have structurally different interests to be represented: interests most likely to be understood and articulated by those with a shared identity. These arguments lead to the depiction of quotas as a form of group representation, where the group in question is variously conceived as an interest, identity or social group. Rather than focusing on the discrimination experienced by women and making a justice-based claim for equality, this argument focuses on the worthiness of women and makes a utility-based claim for presence. This shifts the justification for quotas away from a principled equality-of-opportunity frame to one of consequentialist 'recognition-of-difference'.

The notion that women might represent an 'interest group' entails the claim both that women have an 'objective situation' different from that of men and that they are conscious of their own interests as distinct (Sapiro 1998:167). Many feminists have expressed scepticism about basing claims for increased political representation on the notion of women's interests, arguing that this demands too much, given that many of the problems affecting the lives of women are currently largely 'invisible' (Diamond and Hartsock 1998:193–8). Indeed, the idea that women have interests that are best represented by women has been 'fiercely contested by feminists, their sympathisers and their opponents in a continuing and sometimes acrimonious debate' (Lovenduski 1996:1). However, it is also common to find feminist theorists arguing that it is precisely the fact that women's interests remain 'uncrystallized' (Mansbridge 1999:628) that makes their representation by women – who share their identity – so important. Where interests are clearly established and easily represented, the identity of the representative is of little import, as long as the issues are conveyed effectively. However, in circumstances where interests are uncrystallized descriptive representation can enhance substantive representation where shared experiences give the representatives a tacit understanding of the issues of concern to their 'identity group'. This suggests that where the interests in question are not clear and preformed, but are still in the process of being uncovered via processes of consciousness-raising, the identity of the representative becomes particularly significant, especially if the representation takes a deliberative rather than an aggregative form, where the open-ended quality of deliberation 'gives informational and communicative advantages to representatives who are existentially close to the issues' (Mansbridge 1999:635–6).

Many advocates of gender quotas therefore work with an assumption that quotas will improve not only the descriptive representation of women, but also their substantive representation: that they will result not only in higher levels of female representatives, but also in a more 'woman-friendly' policy agenda. The presumption that 'women are often best represented by other women, as they have an understanding of what equality means for them that is not available to men' (Williams 1998:13), is reinforced by research that suggests that female constituents demand a greater responsiveness from women MPs (Childs 2002; Sawer 2002), based on the belief that they share a different perspective on political issues (Lovenduski 1997). Indeed, the assumption that there is a distinctive female approach to politics, in both its style and content (Ross 2002), motivates numerous studies with the aim of establishing that an increased proportion of women in parliaments leads to the 'feminisation of the political agenda' (Grey 2002:28; Chappell 2002), promoting 'women's rights issues such as child care, sexual harassment and employment' (Fredman 2002:186). These studies generally rely on the notion of 'critical mass', which is based on the assumption that if a sufficient proportion of female politicians are secured, usually thought to be 30 per cent, they will be able to 'shape the processes and policies of that organisation', which will 'result in governance more responsive to women' (Grey 2002:19). However, while frequently cited, the theory of 'critical mass' remains underdeveloped (Studlar and McAllister 2002) and many scholars are becoming uneasy about the role it has come to play in current research, arguing that it is a 'limited, if not redundant, concept' (Childs and Withey 2006:20).

Studies designed to establish the utility of securing a critical mass of women in legislatures often reveal that the correlation between descriptive and substantive representation is not always clear-cut, with increased numbers of female representatives frequently failing to translate into either the improved representation of the female electorate or the improved advocacy of feminist issues (Mateo Diaz 2005).

Far from transforming the political agenda by their presence, evidence seems to suggest that women are generally assimilated into the existing political culture and share its priorities, meaning that 'their collective presence has thus far failed to produce major shifts in policy and practice' (Htun 2004:445). For instance, British research has been ambivalent on the connection between descriptive and substantive representation, with some studies of the 101 Labour women MPs elected to Westminster in 1997, following the use of all-women shortlists, finding that the female MPs themselves consider that they have substantively represented women since their election, enabling the articulation of a feminized agenda in parliamentary debates, in select committees and in the Parliamentary Labour Party's women's group (Childs 2004), with others finding these same female MPs to have been more loyal to the Blair government than their male counterparts, with the voting records of the new intake Labour women MPs demonstrating that they voted disproportionately with the government, rather than putting specifically female concerns on the political agenda (Cowley and Childs 2003). Similarly, taking South Africa, where the African National Congress has a 30 per cent quota that resulted in 30 per cent of MPs who were returned in the 1999 election being women (a figure which rose to 32.8 per cent in 2004), Vincent suggests that the power of these women to influence that overall agenda of social policy is 'as difficult to measure as it is to discern' (L. Vincent 2004:91). Meanwhile in Argentina, Htun and Jones' study of quotas found that a third of the female legislators introduced bills in the area of women's rights, and 11 per cent bills relating to children and families (Htun and Jones 2002:45–7), which suggests that a proportion of women actively promoted women's substantive representation, but that the majority did not. As Htun and Jones note: 'The vast majority of women who enter politics in Latin America do not campaign on women's issues … nor do they make such issues the central focus of their legislative careers' (Htun and Jones 2002:48).

The group representation argument for quotas is therefore problematic, both empirically and theoretically. Not only does it appear that in practice women do not consistently represent women, but it is also evident that the appeal to group recognition arguments serves to discursively entrench stereotypical notions of female identity in ways that may perpetuate rather than unsettle existing gendered practices. As Skjeie rightly argues: 'utility arguments are themselves degrading, and contribute to the continued definition of "woman" as "the other", the sex with "special interests" or "experiences"' (Skjeie 2001:174). However, even though the assumed relationship between the two is repeatedly criticized as wrongly premised upon a link between representatives' characteristics and their actions (Pitkin 1967:66–72), and notwithstanding evidence that women do not consistently act for women, many contemporary feminist theorists continue to maintain that there are theoretically coherent grounds for presuming a relationship between the numbers of women elected to political office and the passage of legislation beneficial to women as a group (Mansbridge 1999; Phillips 2004). Also, many feminist political scientists continue to make appeal to the notion of 'critical mass' to suggest that higher levels of descriptive representation (more women in parliaments) will generate better levels of substantive representation (greater legislative attention to women's issues).

But critical mass is a conceptually weak tool. The assumption that the percentage of women in a particular political institution is the key to understanding women representatives' behaviour and effects fails to consider why women might seek to act for women, even though studies reveal that the differences that follow from the presence of women representatives are contingent and mediated (Childs and Krook 2005). The problem with the notion of 'critical mass' is its tendency to collapse the analytic distinction between descriptive and substantive representation, such that the 'contention that women representatives seek the substantive representation of women is too often simply "read" off from their bodies in a manner that is both essentialist and reductive' (Childs and Krook 2005). Once the assumption that the latter can be read off the former is problematized, conceptual space opens up between the two, allowing one to scrutinize the processes by which they interact.

This suggests that the conceptual distinction between substantive and descriptive representation, whereby substantive representation engages with 'what' is represented, while descriptive representation details 'who' is representing whom (Pitkin 1967), needs to be augmented by a more explicit consideration of 'how' and 'where' representation unfolds. For this reason, Childs and Krook suggest that:

> [b]ecause the likelihood that female representatives act for women depends on a range of different factors, gender and politics scholars would do better to investigate not *when* women make a difference but *how* the substantive representation of women occurs. (Childs and Krook 2005)

While simply counting the numbers of women present in national legislatures will give us a clear indication as to whether affirmative action has been effective in addressing women's previous political exclusion, it will tell us very little about the likelihood that feminist policy concerns will be placed on the political agenda. For this we need to focus on process rather than presence.

In order to avoid this 'logic of identity', feminist theorists have attempted to open up the conceptual space between the descriptive and substantive representation of women by focusing on the processes of political engagement and the quality of the communicative relations between represented and representative (Squires 2001). For example, Young depicts representation as participation in activities of authorization and accountability (Young 2000:125). In characterizing representation 'as a process involving a mediated relation of constituents to one another and to a representative' (Young 2000:127), she focuses our attention on the processes involved in representation rather than simply the identity of the person making the representative claim. If representation is understood as a cycle of anticipation and recollection between constituents and representative, involving both authorization and accountability, the quality of the representation depends on the scope for 'citizens to discuss with one another and with representatives their evaluation of policies representatives have supported' (Young 2000:132). This casts representation in a more deliberative light than is generally the case in debates that focus on the link between descriptive and substantive representation as well as opening up the possibility of conceiving representation as occurring in numerous distinct ways, each with their own appropriate form of communication.

For instance, Mansbridge distinguishes between various processes by which representation takes place, which she labels as promissory, anticipatory, introspective and surrogate (Mansbridge 2003), and argues that 'the appropriate normative criteria for judging these newly identified forms of representation are systemic ... The criteria are almost all deliberative rather than aggregative' (Mansbridge 2003:515). Where representation by promising assumes a power relation between voter and representative that runs forward in linear fashion, in anticipatory representation the power relation works not forward but backward, through anticipated reactions: the voter looks back to the past behaviour of a representative in deciding how to vote in the next election. This model is more deliberative because it requires communication between the represented and representative and depicts the represented as 'educable' by representatives, the media, opposition candidates and others, who all seek to offer 'explanations' of the representatives votes (Mansbridge 2003:520). While detailing these distinct forms of representation, Mansbridge draws our attention to the fact that all require good deliberation among citizens, though she notes that there is little sustained discussion on what the criteria of good deliberation should be (Mansbridge 2003:525). Significantly, the continued sway of critical mass hinders such discussion. The pursuit of the substantive representation of women would be better served by a more nuanced exploration of the various communicative processes by which the female electorate, and women's organizations and feminist groups, each engage with the representative system – which should include a sustained consideration of women's policy agencies and gender mainstreaming, as well as gender quotas, as representative mechanisms.

These theoretical reflections focus on the process of representation, which contrasts with the focus of most quota debates that concentrate on who the representatives are and what they represent. Rather than simply reading representation off from female bodies, these approaches explore the communicative processes by which representative claims are established. They rightly focus our attention on the dynamics of authorization and accountability rather than simply the presence of sexed bodies. If quota debates are to move beyond the use of critical mass to explain the relation between descriptive and substantive representation, they will need to draw on these theoretical insights and explore 'how' the process of representation takes place, paying particular attention to the quality of communication and the sharing of knowledge between representatives and their constituents. The resulting engagement with temporality, plurality and deliberation would enrich existing scholarship by offering a more differentiated and relational understanding of representation.

So, whereas debates about quotas as a form of positive action focus attention on whether it is just to increase the 'descriptive representation' of women in order to redress structural discrimination within the political system, debates about quotas as a form of substantive representation focus attention on the correlation between descriptive and substantive representation, trying to establish whether there is a democratic argument for having increased numbers of female legislatures because this is a guaranteed means of improving the representation of the female electorate. Where the concern in relation to quotas as a form of affirmative action is that their implementation may undermine merit – unfairly disadvantaging other aspirant candidates – the concern in relation to quotas as a means of securing the improved substantive representation of women is that their conceptualization may conflate female bodies with feminist minds – unrealistically assuming homogeneity among women in relation to their interests and identities.

Quotas as Democratic Innovation

A third, democracy-based, argument for gender quotas proposes that, because of their different natures or experiences, women are likely to participate in political processes in distinctive ways and that their increased participation in formal politics will enhance democratic procedures by embracing new approaches to political engagement. This argument posits that quotas, rather than being viewed as a means of ensuring that women's interests are better represented, will facilitate a feminist repudiation of narrow, interest-based political contestation and usher in a less competitive style of political practice (Phillips 1995:73).

Many articulations of this argument draw on Gilligan's claim that women's experience of interconnection shapes their moral domain and gives rise to a different moral voice (Gilligan 1982:151–76) that privileges an 'ethic of caring' over an 'ethic of justice', which celebrates a contextuality, narrativity and specificity not valued in the latter. The claim that women's experiences as mothers within the private sphere provides them with distinctive ways of thinking about the world that can 'offer a powerful critique of "politics as usual"' has been used as a compelling set of reasons why those who care should have a political voice (Mackay 2001:123). It is suggested that women, who have traditionally been associated with caring practices, might 'humanize politics' by promoting a care perspective (Mackay 2001; Sevenhuijsen 1998). This focuses attention on the possibility of feminine styles of behaviour (Childs 2004), where women make a difference in relation to the modes of acceptable political interaction (Puwar 2004). This argument for quotas proposes that women are particularly worthy of increased presence, given that they are likely to transform the gendered practices of political institutions, which are currently suffused by the norms of masculinity (Brown 1988).

However, this 'democracy argument' can be criticized, both because it rhetorically entrenches essentialist notions of femininity, and because there is simply little empirical evidence that quotas lead to democratic innovation in practice – indeed given that they tend to institutionalize earlier feminist engagements with the political, which had previously been characterized by informal prefigurative politics, they could be thought to reduce the potential for democratic innovation. To focus attention on gender quotas is to focus one's attention squarely on the existing institutions of representative liberal democracy, framing gender equality in relation to existing institutions of politics, thereby operating within a narrow and possibility impoverished and male-defined conception of the political. There is of course a strong rationale for being concerned with institutional political presence. While emphasizing the importance of recognizing the worth of women's informal political activism, Lister rightly notes that 'it can only be part of the full citizenship equation for, on its own, a *different* politics runs the risk of being marginalised as an *unequal* politics' (Lister 1997:154). She suggests that political empowerment through informal politics is not synonymous with gaining power in the wider society; that both are needed; and that any citizenship that promotes women's equality, as well as their difference, will need to engage with the formal political system, as well as the informal (Lister 1997:155). Nonetheless, the concern remains that to focus on quotas is to remain bound within a discourse of institutional politics that propagates individualism and adversarialism.

The aim of quota policies is to secure gender parity in upper echelons of political parties, ensuring that half the parliamentary or legislative body is female. This ambition may be challenging and woefully difficult to achieve in practice, but some critics charge that it still does not go far enough. It revolves around current institutional political and liberal democratic constructs at a time when citizens are calling increasingly for something more than the traditional institutions of democratic governance. One particular concern is that the implementation of gender quotas may secure increased numbers of women in national legislatures in a manner that delimits rather than facilitates a wider feminist agenda of transformation.

As noted in Chapter 2, quotas have been found to have the greatest impact under proportional-representation electoral systems with closed lists, high district magnitude and a placement mandate (Caul 1999; Htun 2002; Htun and Jones 2004; Krook 2005). However, while this may secure the greatest number of women, it also hands the party power over which women it selects, ensuring that 'all politicians must remain popular with (mostly male) party bosses to survive' (Vos 1999:108), given that it is they that select which women are promoted within party structures. While considered positive in relation to the implementation of a quota system, the list system therefore ensures women's quiescence to the existing political party and its political priorities, because these women owe their primary allegiance to the political party that placed them high on its list, rather than to the voter (L. Vincent 2004). The absence of close links between an MP and a specific constituency to which the MP is responsible means that women cannot claim to have a power base independent of the male party hierarchy. This means that although they gain their political status by virtue of their womanhood, they are under little constraint to 'act in ways that are empathetic or sensitive to the needs of the majority of women' (L. Vincent 2004).

The concern is that quota strategies allow political elites to accommodate women into the present structures of politics, thereby appearing to take the demands of gender equality seriously, without having to change their substantive political priorities to any significant extent. Any differences in gendered styles that do exist are likely to be modified by the norms and conventions of political parties and parliamentary procedures such that the common experiences of being politicians may well come to outweigh those of gender (Phillips 1995:75). If this is so, then 'increasing the representation of women in institutions designed by men' will do little to address 'the disadvantages experienced by so many women' (Lovenduski 1996:15). Although many of those who advocate quotas believe that the increased presence of women will make a meaningful contribution to changing the social inequalities that are responsible for the imbalance in the representative structure in the first place, there is little evidence that tinkering with who is present in national legislature will achieve the desired change. Indeed it may make matters worse by legitimizing fundamentally undemocratic processes and masking actual inequality.

Quotas are a means of integrating women into existing political structures, which may be counter-productive in relation to the broader goal of increasing the substantive representation of women. Where increased presence is achieved in isolation from other substantive changes it can give rise to complacency and shift the emphasis away from other radical challenges to existing social and cultural norms. Thus the proportion of women in a parliament may rise while the government ignores or is hostile to women's issues. Examples of this include the Mulroney government in Canada during the 1980s and early 1990s. As Young notes, Canada has witnessed massive cuts to an array of women's organizations: 'In substantive terms, issues of importance to women have all but disappeared from the policy agenda of government' (Young 2000:182). Meanwhile Dobrowolsky argues that: 'At a time in Canadian history when there are more women than ever in prominent political positions, inequalities are growing rather than subsiding …' (Dobrowolsky 2000:242). For this reason she questions whether the substantive representation of all women will ever really be secured through better access to existing structures of representative politics, arguing that this aim actually requires a 'sizeable infusion of radical democracy' (Dobrowolsky 2000:243).

Many of the responses to the problems of institutionalism entail focusing on the importance of participation. For instance, Phillips' defence of group representation, which modifies the mechanisms of representative democracy in order to secure a greater parity of presence for women, moves 'in close parallel with arguments for more participatory democracy' (Phillips 1995:190). Theorists grounded in a tradition of participatory democracy are, Phillips feels, best placed to develop arguments for a politics of presence and for group representation, which avoid the pitfalls of the overly narrow arguments for group representation based on the traditions of interest-group pluralism or identity-based politics. Notably, Phillips thinks that Young's particular vision of group representation

> avoids most of the pitfalls in appealing to shared experience as an automatic guarantee … it makes no claims to essential unities or characteristics; it recognises the potential diversity and disagreement within any social group; and it provides some basis for the accountability of representatives to those they might claim to represent. (Phillips 1995:54)

Young claims that those social groups that have suffered oppression need guaranteed representation in order that their distinct voice can be heard, but proposes mechanisms that are closer to a form of agenda-setting mainstreaming than to a quota strategy: the provision of public resources to support the self-organization of group members, the provision of further public resources to enable the group to analyse and generate policy proposals in institutionalized contexts, and group veto power regarding specific policies that affect a group directly (Young 1990:184). Groups are to be 'represented' in the 'democratic public' by being given formal and financial recognition by the state and veto power of specific policy proposals. The proposal is not that they are given directly elected representatives within the national legislature itself, but that links between state decision-making and group organizations are institutionalized. Significantly, this proposal suggests that democratic innovation and group representation are more likely to be negotiated via a strategy of women's policy agencies and/or gender mainstreaming rather than gender quotas.

Given this, it becomes central to consider why it is that candidate quotas in particular have been adopted so widely in relation to gender, but so rarely as a means of addressing the political under-representation of other sorts of collectivities. Htun notes, for instance, that

> institutional remedies for the under-representation of women and ethnic minorities (or majorities) assume distinct forms: women tend to receive candidate quotas in political parties, which require that political parties field a minimum number of certain group members, whereas ethnic groups tend to be granted reserved seats in legislatures. (Htun 2004:439)

She suggests that, where mobilized, ethnicity tends to become the central consideration in political behaviour, while gender 'almost never defines how individuals vote and what parties they affiliate with' (Htun 2004:439), and that the differential use of quotas and reserved seats can be explained functionally with reference to the different natures of the groups themselves: quotas suit groups whose boundaries cross-cut partisan divisions where reserved seats suit groups whose boundaries coincide with political cleavages (Htun 2004:429). On this account quotas provide a means of integration into already existing political institutions while reserved seats guarantee groups' members a 'share of power independently, if need be, of existing parties' (Htun 2004:442). By contrast to reserved seats, the problem that quotas are intended to address is one of descriptive, not substantive, under-representation, so the solution they offer entails helping women to integrate into mainstream parties rather than as a way of changing what parties do. Quotas are therefore structurally unlikely to result in significant substantive transformation.

This argument reinforces concerns about quotas' ability to usher in democratic innovation, but – interestingly – appears to reduce the anxiety about group recognition. Cast in this light, quotas become positive action strategies that don't entrench group identities because the group dissipates once the wrong of under-representation has been addressed. Where reserved seats are conceived as a group recognition mechanism, quotas are 'self cancelling' (Htun 2004:451), in that they attempt to address a wrong suffered by a group, which unites 'to contest common experiences of political exclusion and discrimination' but which will disappear once this goal is achieved. That is, once women have entered political office in representative numbers the motivation for 'acting' as women will disappear and female parliamentarians will realign themselves in relation to party agendas once they have secured their presence: the 'logic of the quota is to put the group out of business as a group' (Htun 2004:451). Htun's suggestion that 'women seeking quotas aim to have their different position absorbed by universalistic institutions' (Htun 2004:451) stands in stark contrast to the group recognition argument in that it holds out no particular expectation that women's increased descriptive representation will correlate with increased substantive representation. While this will be a cause for concern for those interested in using quotas as a means of increasing the recognition of women's interests or identities (however conceived), and for those interested in using quotas as a means of making political practices more democratic and deliberative, it does have the virtue of reducing concerns about critical mass and essentialism.

Quotas as (Strategic) Essentialism?

A key concern underpinning the above debates relates to the fact that the category of 'women' is rarely interrogated in these studies, with few indications as to whether quotas facilitate the representation of a cross-section of all women or privilege that of a few. The literature on gender quotas tends to assume women to be a cohesive group, which makes it susceptible to the charge that it obscures the differences between women. Gender quotas, which are actually sex quotas, are not sensitive to the contradictions and antagonisms between women, nor are they concerned to address the under-representation of other marginalized groups. The success of quotas may therefore add to the problem of reification.

For, given that gender quotas are designed to increase the number of female candidates and political representatives, they inevitably work with the category of 'women' as a single entity. Yet there are widely rehearsed theoretical and practical problems inherent in focusing on women as a group. Black feminists, particularly in the US and Britain, argued throughout the 1980s and 1990s that it is problematic to conceptualize women as a group: focusing attention on the inequalities and differences between men and women tended to marginalize the inequalities and differences among women (Collins 2000; Mohanty 1991; Spellman 1988). More recently, the poststructuralist critique of taking women as a category has become influential. Here it is argued that taking women as a category will close off intersectionality and fail to respond to the fluidity and mutability of social identities. Adopting women as a category of political analysis and activism works to inscribe and constitute the category rather than reflect and represent it (Brown 1995; Butler 1990). These arguments not only have had a significant impact on feminist theory during recent years, but also appear to resonate with popular sentiments, which tend to be individualist and hostile to group-based politics. A key concern, then, is whether gender quotas reify gendered identities or lead to policy-making that unsettles existing gendered practices.

This issue has been an explicit concern in South Asia, where debates on quotas have concentrated on the issue of differences among women, focusing in particular on 'the elite nature of representative politics in terms of both class and caste, and of women in political life in particular' (Rai *et al.* 2006:222). Writing in relation to India and Pakistan, Rai *et al.* note that:

> The age, education, socio-economic status and political background of the elected women seem to have a crucial effect on their access to

> both state and community resources needed for performing their roles as representatives in local government. (Rai *et al.* 2006:237)

In India the majority of elected women are from lower socio-economic strata in terms of both education and class and in Pakistan more than half of the women are illiterate and very few own land; while in Bangladesh elected women had a better socio-economic status than average rural women (Rai *et al.* 2006:238). Rai *et al.* suggest that 'more research needs to be done to explain the differences between India and Pakistan on one hand and Bangladesh on the other' (Rai *et al.* 2006:238).

Where descriptive representation is conceived purely in terms of the sex of the representative the socio-economic and cultural differences among women are obscured, and certain (though clearly not always the same) collectivities tend to get privileged while others are marginalized. For instance, intensive lobbying by women's groups led to the new Scottish Parliament being 37.2 per cent women, but including not a single ethnic minority representative. The 'unrepresentative' ethnic composition of the female representatives rarely features in quota debates, however, given that the issue of the representation of ethnic minorities is generally regarded as different in nature from the question of women's representation (Childs 2002). When the Sex Discrimination (Election Candidates) Act 2002 was introduced in Britain, making it permissible for political parties to adopt positive action measures in relation to female candidate selection, there was much discussion about the normative and pragmatic wisdom of promoting 'all-women shortlists, but not all-black ones or all-Asian ones' (Lester, 2003), with ethnic minority spokespeople arguing that this 'equality agenda shoves blacks and Asians to the back of the queue' (Woolley, *Guardian* 29 January 2003). The debate as to whether the act should apply to ethnic minorities in addition to women was one of the most difficult questions surrounding the bill (Russell 2001), indicating that one of the most significant limitations of quotas as a group representation strategy is that they inevitably operate with an undifferentiated category of women and fail to address the marginalization of groups other than women. It is unclear how they could be practically implemented in ways more sensitive to questions of multiple inequalities and intersectionality.

At a theoretical level, one influential response to this concern entails reframing the collectivity of women as a social rather than an identity or interest group. Sensitive to the concerns relating to essentialism and institutionalism, Young argues influentially that a retreat from conceptualizing women as a collective altogether would obscure oppression as a systematic, structured, institutional process and so fail to provide an alternative to liberal individualism (Young 1997:17). She therefore proposes that gender be theorized as multiple, and women constituted as a social group understood in relational, not essentialist, terms (Young 1997:21). However, while this proposal has theoretical appeal, it is difficult to discern its practical impact on quota strategies, which continue to work with biological notions of sex as the basis for defining the group to be given representational guarantees and rarely require the sort of inclusive deliberation in pursuit of social justice that Young proposes. Indeed advocates of gender quotas have generally been notably silent in relation to the justice claims of other social groups, rarely arguing for their extension to groups other than women. In this way advocates of quotas are not generally recommending 'microcosmic' representation as has often been suggested, in which the legislature forms a microcosm or representative sample of the electorate (Mansbridge 2003), but rather endorse a form of 'selective' representation, in which only certain groups are given greater descriptive representation (Mansbridge 2003).

Where Young offers a theoretical criterion for selecting which social groups merit greater descriptive representation based on a typology of five faces of oppression (Young 1990), practical decisions as to which groups require candidate quotas have rarely been so systematic. Some polities, in which consociational political systems institutionalize the representation of key religious or linguistic groups, have long operated with a system of guaranteeing representation of specific groups. For instance, Belgium has a tradition of segmented pluralism that makes it ideologically and institutionally receptive to the principle of quotas for multiple social groups (Meier 2004), whereas in France the state commitment to republicanism makes it profoundly hostile to the idea of selective representation (Krook 2005). This meant that whereas Belgian advocates of gender quotas argued for an extension of an existing quota logic to women, advocates of gender quotas (or parity) in France argued that 'women are not a group not a community nor a category nor a minority. They are simply one half of humanity' (Guigou 1998:4), thereby denying the legitimacy of other groups' demands for greater descriptive representation.

This indicates that the 'selection' of groups for guaranteed representation is in reality a socially determined process, influenced by a diverse array of factors over and above any normative determination of the oppression faced by that group. While gender quota strategies can therefore avoid the objections raised against microcosmic representation, in that they aspire not to 'pictorial adequacy' but to social justice (Phillips 1995:47), their advocates ought to address the issue, raised by their endorsement of selective representation, of the relative status of other social groups' claims to similar representational guarantees. While feminist theorists have generally defended selective representation for oppressed groups in general (Phillips 1995; Young 1990), the practical pursuit of quota strategies has tended to focus on women as a homogeneous and solitary group only. However, given the growing concerns about both intersectionality and multiple inequality strands, it may be time now for advocates of quota strategies to start thinking about whether, and how, these mechanisms might be reformulated to make them more sensitive to complex diversity, rather than simply sex difference.

Conclusion

Governments around the world are more and more adopting mechanisms for increasing levels of female representation, and gender quotas are one of the most important – and successful – mechanisms available for pursuing this goal (Dahlerup and Freidenvall 2005). Yet gender quotas remain highly controversial: the strength of both pragmatic and normative concerns about the use of quotas ensures that they remain deeply contentious in many quarters. Concerns relate to the way in which equality, representation, politics and gender are figured in quota strategies (Bacchi 2006), giving rise to anxieties about unfairness, essentialism and assimilation. While many of those who articulate concerns about gender quotas are not overly concerned about the under-representation of women generally, it is notable that among those who *are* concerned to secure equal political representation for women, anxieties about quotas as a mechanism by which to achieve this continue to abound.

First, the 'unfairness concern' is based on the fact that quotas are a form of positive action, which some perceive as discriminating against other candidates of equal or greater merit. Second, the 'essentialism concern' is based on the fact that gender quotas operate with the category of 'women' as a single entity at a time when there are widely rehearsed theoretical and practical problems inherent in assuming such homogeneity among women as a group, which is compounded by the assumed link between the descriptive and substantive representation of women. The concern here is not only the lack of empirical evidence that women consistently act for women, but also the normative concern about positing any predetermined notion of what acting for women might entail. Third, the 'assimilation concern' arises from an anxiety about the narrowing of the conception of democratic inclusion inherent in quota discourses to the existing institutions of representative liberal democracy. Of course, the 'democracy' argument for women's increased representation proposes that women should enter into positions of power because they will engage in political activity differently, revitalizing democracy and thereby improving the nature of the public sphere. Yet sceptics question whether the increased democratization of politics will ever really be secured through better access to existing structures of representative politics. Deliberative or radical democrats, for instance, could argue that the increasing global focus on gender quotas might work to divert attention from more radical reform, while offering a kind of pseudo-legitimacy for existing representative democracy.

How one goes about trying to establish and evaluate the consequences of quotas will inevitably be framed by one's perception of why the under-representation of women might matter, and therefore the nature of the problem that gender quotas might be expected to address.

First, if one's interest in quotas is framed by the justice argument, one would probably focus exclusively on the numbers of women present in parliaments and political bodies following their implementation. However, this may raise the 'assimilation concern' that this limits our attention to issues of numerical inclusion in existing political structures and renders broader issues of democratic transformation non-pertinent.

Second, if on the other hand one's concern with quotas is framed by the 'women's interests' argument, one would no doubt look for indicators that women's presence in political bodies leads to altered policy agendas and programmes. This approach may, in turn, raise the 'representation concern' that the attempt to correlate increased numbers of female representatives with more 'women-friendly' policy agendas may suggest a link between descriptive and substantive representation that underplays the complexity of the representative's multifaceted role (which may include party loyalty, constituency accountability, personal morality and so forth).

Third, if one's interest in the consequences of quotas is framed by the 'democratic argument' then one would look for shifts in the nature of political engagement. This, though, could raise the 'essentialist concern' that by looking for ways in which women 'do politics differently' one may be complicit in perpetuating ideas of gender differences and thereby constituting particular norms of femininity in the political sphere which may work to reinforce narrowly prescribed conceptions of gender roles.

It is common to find quotas justified with reference to both rights-based and utility-based arguments, and politicians have often argued that quotas are 'right in principle' and 'essential in practice', given that women's votes are key to electoral success (Harman and Mattinson 2000:3). While the utilitarian arguments invoked by politicians appeal to electoral considerations, those invoked by feminist scholars and activists have tended to appeal more widely on the basis of the social benefits that will accrue from recognizing the specificity of women's different voice. Where equal representation for women and men is conceived as a 'question of rights' (Mateo Diaz 2005:113), quotas are constructed as an affirmative action strategy required to address a structural inequality in the current opportunities available to women to become political representatives. Where it is conceived as a 'question of utility', quotas are constructed as a means of increasing the competence and performance of the political system by better representing the electorate, extending the political agenda and diversifying the styles of political engagement. Where the rights-based argument treats the under-representation of women in politics 'as akin to their under-representation in management or the professions' and therefore depicts politics as simply one profession among many, and women's claim to political equality as nothing more than an equal-opportunities claim to an interesting job (Phillips 1998:230–1), the utility-based arguments place very specific demands upon female parliamentarians, demanding that they 'make a difference' (Childs 2004; Russell 2003) as a result of their presence. It has frequently been suggested that the first argument is impoverished in that it fails to capture the distinctive role of political representatives as participants in a democratic process, whereas the other two more adequately recognize the needs of women as members of a group (Phillips 1998; Sapiro 1998:162). But it is this very appeal to women as a group that makes the second argument so problematic, relying as it does on the worryingly essentialist claim that women as a group have distinct interests as women and that the election of women will ensure their representation (Phillips 1998:234).

Even if one found these claims normatively compelling, there is an empirical difficulty in basing one's support for quotas on this argument, given that current electoral systems provide few mechanisms of accountability for social groups rather than constituents. This particular argument in favour of the increased representation of women, should one wish to make it, would therefore seem to be better served by the strategy of reserved seats rather than by quotas, given that reserved seats set aside a fixed percentage of legislative seats for members of selected groups, filled through election by voters registered on separate rolls

(Htun 2004:440, see also Jenkins 1999). Quotas are designed to address the problem of inequality of opportunity in relation to candidate selection, facilitating the greater integration of the marginalized group into the existing political system. They are not designed to introduce group-specific forms of representation that augment or challenge existing party systems. It therefore seems inappropriate to expect quotas to secure the improved representation of women as a group in this sense, even were this felt to be a desirable goal. Similarly, given that quotas are a mechanism for integrating women into existing party systems, it seems equally misplaced to expect them to result in a transformation of those very systems. As with the representation argument, the problem here is that quotas integrate women into existing party systems and processes, encouraging even those women who aspire to explore more deliberative or radical political practices to accept existing forms of democratic engagement. It could therefore be that the women's policy agencies and/or gender mainstreaming, in its participative-democratic form, in fact offer more appropriate resources for revitalizing democracy in that they explicitly foster deliberation with women in civil society and facilitate deliberative policy-making in a way that gender quotas simply do not.

While the representation and democracy arguments are problematic, the justice argument can and should be deployed to defend gender quotas, given that inequality of outcome suggests that opportunities for candidate selection are structurally unequal. Because it makes no appeal to consequentialist arguments about what women will do once they enter the legislature, this argument avoids the problems of essentialism that haunt the other two arguments. Nonetheless, it is worth noting that mainstreaming a gender equality perspective in relation to the reformulation of electoral systems may offer a better solution to the problem of structural discrimination in the long run than do gender quotas, which are a reactive positive action measure and fail to address the wider systemic problem at its origin. However, given that policy-making in relation to electoral systems can be an infrequent event, quotas may represent an effective temporary equality measure that has the beneficial result of focusing attention on the inadequacy of the existing system and the need for a more profound revision in due course. The consequentialist representation and democracy arguments are troubling because they inevitably require group characteristics to be prescribed and so pander to essentialism. If women really were a cohesive identity group with an explicit set of interests and policy concerns, reserved seats would appear to be a better solution to the problem of their under-representation because this mechanism would allow representatives to speak to a new agenda rather than integrating into existing political parties. Alternatively, where there are specific concerns that women's organizations mobilize around, women's policy agencies may be better placed to get these issues on to the policy agenda given that they – unlike female representatives – have a remit to advocate women's issues.

5

Feminist Advocacy? Policy Agencies

Introduction

This chapter considers the operation of women's policy agencies in relation to two challenges: the fragmentation of the women's movement and the restructuring of the state. Paradoxically, women's policy agencies have emerged to represent the voice of the women's movement within the state just as the women's movement was fragmenting into a series of diverse groups and loosely aligned networks, with no ideological core, and the state appeared to be being 'hollowed out', with its traditional responsibilities being dispersed vertically (to local and supranational institutions) and horizontally (to courts, executive agencies and civil society organizations).

In light of these challenges, the chapter asks whether women's policy agencies offer a form of group representation that manages to transform the gendered norms operating within state bureaucracies while also representing the diversity of perspectives among the women they claim to speak for. It focuses, in other words, on the ability of women's policy agencies to successfully negotiate the twin dangers of assimilation (into newly restructured state practices and forms of governance) and essentialism (with regard to the increasingly diverse constituency of women on whose behalf the agencies claim to speak).

Where the movement is fragmented and its demands are contested, the function of these agencies may well entail the active portrayal of 'women as a group' rather than the simple reflection of them, such that they serve as a surrogate for women's civil society voice, producing particular representations of women's political identities that may not capture the diversity among women, and privileging particular conceptions of gender equality that may structurally disadvantage some gendered identities while privileging others. Moreover, the difficulty of representing the diversity of women's civil society voices appears increasingly to be negotiated via an appeal to professionalized feminist NGOs which adopt an increasingly technocratic mode of operation.

It has been argued that in securing policy action women's policy agencies and women's movements together are more effective than large numbers of women in the legislature. Yet the fragmentation of the women's movement and restructuring of the state both have profound implications for the ability of women's policy agencies to represent women and women's issues within state bureaucracies. The representative function of women's policy agencies is challenged, given that both the constituency they aim to represent and the institution they hope to influence have been rendered more complex than early models of state feminism anticipated (Oustshoorn and Kantola 2007).

Women's policy agencies increasingly appear to represent women's interests in ways that actively constitute those gendered identities that are compatible with government rationalities, offering technical expertise on a new policy concern rather than providing a representative mechanism for women's civil society voices. Whether women's policy agencies still have a central democratic function in this context is open to question.

Women's Policy Agencies as Group Representation

Political representation is usually discussed within mainstream political science in terms of how accurately elected representatives reflect the interests of voters. However, there is a growing recognition that we need to focus attention on alternative sites of political representation, recognizing that 'constituents' and 'representatives' need not be members of electoral districts and elected parliamentarians respectively, and looking 'more closely at the democratic status of non-electoral representation' (Saward 2006:415). Although feminist political scientists have concentrated much of their attention on the representation of women in national legislatures, they have also explored alternative forms of representation, recognizing that while the use of gender quotas to increase the number of women representatives is more commonly depicted as group representation, the use of women's policy agencies to increase the profile of women's issues and interests might also be viewed as a group representation strategy.

Both gender quotas and women's policy agencies aim to secure the substantive representation of women, offering two distinct models of group representation. Quotas involve people 'marked by a particular group characteristic' representing the members of this group by securing a more equitable distribution of representative positions, so bringing a wider range of perspectives into play, without requiring these 'representatives' to follow group policies or concerns (Phillips 1999:40–1). Defending this form of group representation against its critics, Phillips distinguishes it from a second, corporatist form of group representation, in which accountable representatives refer back to and speak for their group. Phillips suggests that while the first form of group representation is 'looser, less predictable, and less accountable, it is also less likely to lock people into narrowly bounded political identities' (Phillips 1999:41). It does not treat people as if they are exclusively defined by group characteristics, nor does it expect them to view everything from a narrowly 'group' point of view.

The form of group representation pursued by women's policy agencies might be thought to map closely onto the corporatist form of group representation as defined by Phillips, to the extent that femocrats are expected to speak for the women's movement, to promote women's issues and to engage in policy-making from women's point of view. This would suggest that femocrats are more likely to be locked into narrowly bounded political identities than are female legislators, but are also more likely to be predictable and accountable. However, this model of corporatist group representation only partially describes the way in which women's policy agencies operate, for while femocrats do claim to speak for the women's movement in a way that female parliamentarians are not required to do, there are no formal mechanisms of accountability by which the women's movement might hold them to account (Franceschet and Macdonald 2004).

This is why Goetz argues that 'it is muddled thinking' to expect women's policy agencies to be accountable to women's movements, for they are directly accountable, like all other bureaucratic units, to the elected government (Goetz 2005:6). She suggests that to hold policy agencies directly accountable to the women's movement is to expect women's policy agencies to perform a 'representative function even though the staff and leadership of these agencies are not directly elected' (Goetz 2005:6). Nonetheless, while this lack of formal accountability to the women's movement creates problems (to be considered in the next section), women's policy agencies can be understood to perform a representative function, notwithstanding their lack of accountability, not least because they generally make a representative claim. Representation is 'a *process* in which the relationship between citizens and representatives continues over time' (Thompson 1988:136), and which entails the practice of making claims to be representative. The representative claim is constitutive in that it constructs a constituency in whose interests the representative claims to speak: 'representatives construct portrayals or depictions of the represented, in order to be able to represent them' (Saward 2006:414). When women's policy agencies claim to help the actors 'that speak for women and gender equality' to enter government policy-making arenas, and bring 'women's interests and gender equality issues into public policy discussion, formulation and implementation' (Mazur 2005:3), they are making just such a representative claim. The danger with the form of group representation offered by women's policy agencies resides in the possibility that they may represent 'women' and their interests in ways that fail to do justice to the diversity among women, and yet offer no mechanisms by which they might be held to account for their 'unrepresentativeness'. Given the fragmentation of the women's movement, and the diversity of perspectives held by women, any attempt at group representation should entail processes by which a diverse group might be represented without reifying the group in a manner that is too unitary to be sensitive to the contradictions and antagonisms within as well as between groups.

It is therefore significant that Weldon suggests that women's policy agencies are best placed to represent marginalized groups, without assuming a false homogeneity of interest or identity, in a manner that reflects group diversity (Weldon 2002:1155, Weldon 2004). Reflecting on the relative merits of the two models of group representation offered by gender quotas and women's policy agencies, Weldon claims that women's policy agencies and women's movements in combination 'provide more effective avenues of expression for women' than do women in the legislature (Weldon 2002:1153). She reads the case for gender quotas as invoking a form of group representation in which individual legislators stand for their group, having opinions or behaviour that is favourable to women because of their shared experiences: it is their personal experiences that are argued to be the basis of their claim to be representative (Weldon 2002:1154–5), and argues that this model of representation is limited because of the weakness of the presumed link between the personal experience of the individual representatives and their knowledge of the group perspective (Weldon 2002:1155).

The descriptive representation that is privileged in gender quota strategies is generally argued to lead to substantive representation because of the presumed links between identity (being a woman), experiences (gaining first-hand knowledge of the way in which gendered practices impact on women) and perspectives (developing a set of preferences and policy priorities on the basis of these experiences) (Mansbridge 1999). But if different women have different experiences (because of their differential positioning in relation to practices of ethnicity, sexuality and so on) they will no doubt have different perspectives. Weldon therefore suggests that individual women in the legislature are not particularly well placed to reflect the diversity within women-as-a-group given that they cannot share a set of experiences that are similar to those of all marginalized group members, and can draw only on their own personal experiences.

The logic of this argument suggests that an individual can represent a group only if their experiences map onto those of the group, which can occur only if there is no within-group diversity:

> [I]f she is a white, straight, middle class mother, she cannot speak for African American women, or poor women, or lesbian women on the basis of her own experience. Any more than men can speak for women merely on the basis of theirs. (Weldon 2002:1156)

Weldon suggests that this attempt to read group perspectives from individual identities is problematic: group perspectives can only really be grasped via group interaction, which will frequently involve conflict and contestation (Weldon 2002:1157). The interactive nature of group perspective is, she argues, more readily represented by women's policy agencies in consultation with women's movement organizations than by female legislators reflecting on their own personal experiences: notwithstanding their diversity, 'women's movements are likely to come closer to articulating women's perspective than a disparate, unorganized group of women in the legislature' (Weldon 2002:1161). The general upshot of her analysis is that women's policy agencies and women's movements together are more effective than large numbers of women in the legislature at securing policy action. This suggests that gender quotas are not the only – or indeed the most effective – means of securing group representation and democratic justice for women.

The issue then is whether women's policy agencies represent women's civil society 'voice' in a manner that acknowledges the fragmentation of the women's movement and represent the diversity among women. Weldon suggests that they are well placed to do this because they facilitate consultation with women's movement organizations. This focuses attention on how consultative women's policy agencies are in practice, which organizations in particular they consult with, and what form this consultation takes. In order to explore these issues, the next section will focus on who the policy agencies claim to represent, and the following one on how this representation occurs.

The Fragmentation of the Women's Movement

The substantive representation of women is variously conceived as entailing the introduction of feminist ideas, women's interests, or gender equality into policy-making processes and outcomes. Yet the multiplicity of understandings as to what gender equality entails, the frequent disjuncture between feminist and female ideas, the diversity among women and the corresponding differences among their interests, all serve to unsettle the representative claim made by women's policy agencies. Given that the femocrats found in women's policy agencies and the female legislatures found in national parliaments have become the privileged speakers for women's interests (Hobson 2003), and assuming that not all women share the same interests, it is important to ask which interests in particular they privilege.

Feminism has become increasingly sensitive to diversity among women and to intersections with other egalitarian movements. The women's movement is no longer, if ever it was, a cohesive entity with a single set of goals, and the pursuit of state feminism inevitably needs to reflect this. Research that evaluates the success of women's policy agencies has tended to focus on the extent to which the agencies are effective in assisting the 'women's movement in reaching its goals'. Yet it is not at all clear what the women's movement is, nor what its goals entail. Indeed, feminist scholars acknowledge that there is no concept 'women's movement' applicable to cross-national longitudinal comparative research (Beckwith 2000). What counts as the women's movement varies significantly in differing contexts, and can include national networks, organizations inside institutions, and grassroots groups. Broadly speaking, a women's movement is taken to refer to any political mobilization aimed at improving the condition of women (Molyneux 1998); 'a range of struggles by women against gender inequality' (Basu 1995:9); a subset of sociopolitical movements that are 'characterized by the primacy of women's gendered experiences, women's issues, and women's leadership and decision making' (Beckwith 2000:437). Although many feminists have claimed that women's movements are an important avenue of group representation (Dobrowolsky 1998), it is nonetheless recognized that they are 'an imperfect incarnation of "women's voice"', because 'subgroups of women are always dominated or excluded' (Weldon 2002:1161).

Democracy within the women's movement has been subject to contestation, with the assumption of movement unity being challenged by black and Third World feminists (Eschle 2001:117–44). The turn to social movement politics, rather than formal representative politics, had initially been inspired by a suspicion of representation given that in practice it had generally entailed men speaking on women's behalf, thereby marginalizing rather than institutionalizing women's voices. The embrace of social movement politics signalled a commitment to direct democracy, giving women the 'right to speak as women' in an unmediated fashion (Passerini 1994:237). In the prefigurative politics of the early second-wave women's movement, the commitment to non-hierarchical deliberation was intended to generate both consensus and raised consciousnesses (Phillips 1991). However, from the outset many women experienced the structurelessness of social movement politics as a tyranny (Freeman 1984), the demand on one's time as a burden (Phillips 1991) and the emphasis on consensus as stifling (Jones 1990). Although many feminists continued to take 'the movement' as a unified political actor, expressing a coherent feminist sisterhood (Melucci 1996; Morgan 1984), those marginalized by its claim to a consensual inclusive feminist sisterhood have been increasingly vocal in their critique of the way in which self-identified feminists obscure the lack of democratic inclusion within the movement itself (Mohanty 1998). Shorn of the formal mechanisms of accountability entailed in institutional politics, it has been difficult for the women's movement to maintain its representative claim.

The unity of the women's movement was therefore inevitably challenged by the assertion that it privileged a First World, heterosexual, white women's consensus, failing to acknowledge either the diversity of women or the importance of other social movements. During the 1980s and 1990s accounts of the ways in which feminist organizations had campaigned on issues that further disadvantaged black or immigrant women began to surface within many Western states (Amos and Parmer 1984; Caraway 1991), leading to charges that the women's movement was a white movement, failing to acknowledge the struggles of black women (Amos and Parmer 1984). For instance, many black feminists have criticized the women's movement's tendency to depict women's oppression as residing in their confinement to the private sphere, given that in the wake of slavery many black women have been forced to engage in work outside the home: far from viewing the domestic sphere as a site of confinement, to be politicized, many black feminists have viewed it as a refuge and source of resistance (Collins 2000; Carby 1999).

The fragmentation of the women's movement intensified with the emergence of the cultural politics of recognition, which increasingly privileged identities rather than interests as the basis for political engagement. The logic of feminist standpoint theory, which had challenged objectivist knowledge claims from the perspective of female experiences, was extended to an increasingly diverse array of identity groups. The movement's creation of a women's voice, based on a feminist standpoint, had entailed 'immersion in a world divided between male and female experiences in order to critique the power of the former and valorise the alternative residing in the latter' (Ferguson 1993:3). The logic of claims that women spoke 'in a different voice' (Gilligan 1982) because of their different experiences (Chodorow 1978; Ruddick 1997) was taken up and extended to black and Third World women (Collins 2000; Mohanty 1991), complicating the vision of a world divided by experiences of gender alone.

The emergence of identity politics and the acknowledgement that the women's movement was not cohesive led to a fulsome debate among Anglo-American feminists in particular about 'intersectionality', in which the complex relation between gender, race, sexuality and class (plus, more recently, age and disability) was theorized, producing sensitivity to the ways in which these structural inequalities intersected. As Calhoun notes:

> To combine gender with race, language, sexual orientation, concrete interpersonal relations, and a host of other dimensions of identity is no easy or uncomplicated thing. But it is from the recognition of this complexity and these contradictions that we must start. (Calhoun 1995)

In Britain the intersectionality debate began at the end of the 1970s when black and other minority feminisms appeared on the political arena (Anthias and Yuval-Davis 1983). Demanding that their specific identities be recognized, an increasing number of groups asserted that only they could speak of their own experiences and struggle for their own empowerment. This frequently led to a perception that those who shared multiple marginalized identities faced challenges that were qualitatively different from those who did not (see Collins 2000; Crenshaw 1991), creating a 'hierarchy of oppression' that eroded a wider sense of solidarity. Many black British feminists, for instance, argued that they suffered 'triple oppression' as blacks, as women and as members of the working class (Yuval-Davis 2005).

As a result of the challenges posed by identity politics, many studies have suggested that the women's movement has declined in visibility and influence (Bagguley 2002; Ryan 1992; Threlfall 1996). Others emphasize its changing form, from the early radicalism, autonomy and challenge to the state in the 1970s 'to a more moderate, state-involved, and accommodationalist stance by the 1990s' (Banaszak *et al.* 2003:2). Even in the 1970s there were different sections of the women's movement, with some advocating revolutionary change (Firestone 1970; Morgan 1970) and others campaigning for specific policy reforms, but the movement largely insisted on its autonomy and focused on cultural change rather than on influencing states. However, in the 1980s and 1990s women's issues 'permeated many social and political groups and institutions', which meant that the women's movement no longer had a monopoly on advocating women's issues. Many political parties and state bureaucracies offered women access to political office. As such, the women's movement comprised 'loosely coupled networks that extended into many non-movement areas, permitting the formation of broad alliances and the aggregation of heterogeneous resources' (Banaszak *et al.* 2003:21).

Moreover, where the women's movement of the 1970s was characterized by informal local organizational structures, the 1990s were characterized by the growing influence of 'transnational feminism', signifying the aspiration to negotiate the different positions and interests of women in an era of globalization, with the term 'transnational' pointing to the increasing tendency of national feminisms to 'politicise women's issues beyond the borders of the national state, for instance, in United Nations women's world conferences or on the Internet' (Mendoza 2002:296). For example, Mendoza suggests that the 1990s signalled a 'shift from local activism to transnational activism' in Latin American feminisms, in which the locus of feminist activism moved extensively into the transnational arena (Mendoza 2002:306–7). This signalled a shift away from 'building an alternative public sphere along with community-based women's groups' towards the lobbying practices of globetrotting feminists 'now acting primarily in international conferences and coalescing within international feminist movements' (Mendoza 2002:307). In this context, the women's movement appears to have been eclipsed by 'an expansive, polycentric, heterogeneous discursive field of action', which has generated 'more formalized modalities of articulation or networking amongst the multiple spaces and places of feminist politics' that emerged during the 1990s (Alvarez 1999:184). In place of a cohesive women's movement, feminist activism tends to take the form of pluralized, professionalized, transnational NGO activism.

The emergence of transnational feminism therefore signals a division between informal local feminist activism and professionalized transnational feminist activism: indeed Mendoza deems this to represent 'a division of political labour whereby the professional feminist – the gender expert – has arrogated the global terrain to themselves without a clear basis of legitimation from local constituencies' (Mendoza 2002:309). Feminist global interventions therefore frequently reflect the power imbalances of the nations of origin of the distinct national feminisms that operate in the global arena. The notion of 'transnational feminism' replaces the earlier idea of 'global sisterhood' (Morgan 1984), which was abandoned in the face of challenges that it universalized the perspectives of First World, white, middle-class feminists (Mohanty 1991). However, it is not altogether clear that the idea of transnational feminism is any better placed to confront the challenges of diversity than was the earlier notion of the women's movement, given that it often entails an affirmation of the 'desirability of a political solidarity of feminists across the globe that transcends class, race, sexuality and national boundaries' (Mendoza 2002:296). Transnationalism can be used to expose the differences between women, highlighting the particularities of feminist movements (Kaplan *et al.* 1999), or to obscure them, where diverse women's movements are assumed to share a global feminist solidarity. While the term 'transnational' is sometimes used to refer to the concrete experiences of the transnational organizing of women across the globe, it also tends to imply a potential solidarity of women in the North and South (Bunch 1995), or even – critics suggest – Western feminist dominance in worldwide feminist movements that are entangled in global networks (Mendoza 2002:296–7; Narayan 1997).

The fact that 1761 organizations attended the Beijing NGO forum (Tinker 1999:96) suggests that, while the women's movement may have fragmented, women's activism has not declined. However, the idea of a singular movement has been eclipsed by a series of provisional alliances of loosely coupled networks. Following the early debates about identity politics that undermined the apparent cohesion of the women's movement, there has been a clear enthusiasm for 'principled coalitions' (Collins 2000:36) that allow for strategic alliances between groups with differing identities and knowledge (Yuval-Davis 1997). But these coalitions are always provisional and may not be realized, leaving the women's movement so highly fragmented that it no longer exhibits 'an identifiable ideological and social core', jeopardizing its 'ability to act strategically' (Banaszak *et al.* 2003:21). Eschle suggests that this 'tendency toward organisational fragmentation should, to some extent, be recognised as a healthy and necessary dynamic' (Eschle 2001:128). However, both the organizational fragmentation and political contestation among diverse women's groups indicates that one must recognize that women do not have essentially the same interests or the same identity, so one needs to pay attention to the multiplicity of demands and perspectives to which they can give rise. This makes the continued appeal to the notion of the women's movement as a collective actor problematic, demanding that we reflect on how women's policy agencies might represent such a multiplicity of demands and perspectives: to whom should they be accountable?

Representing a Movement?

In practice, much of the literature on women's policy agencies accepts the obvious diversity among women, and the great diversity among the interest groups in which they organize, which suggests that there will be competing – and frequently contradictory – perceptions of what constitutes women's interests, but nonetheless continues to assume that the women's movement is cohesive and women's voices consensual by default, by failing to devote attention to the issue of internal democracy within the movement. For example, the RNGS team define state feminism as 'the advocacy of women's movement demands inside the state' (Lovenduski *et al.* 2005:4) and measures the success of women's policy agencies in terms of the successful representation of any perspective advocated by a women's organization. Most of the case-studies that comprise the project describe 'women's movement characteristics' in terms of the specific features of a limited number of women's organizations and note that the movement is fragmented (Kamenitsa and Geissel 2005:120), highlighting a diversity within the movement that is not systematically interrogated. The contributions to the RNGS study show that even within one country at one time in relation to one policy issue there were a range of national networks, organizations, insider institutions and grassroots groups, many of which advanced different or competing goals.

For instance, the evaluation of the 'women's movement impact' on prostitution debates in the UK, conducted as part of the RNGS project, was complicated by the wide range of views expressed on this issue by various women's organizations, including informal alliances of mothers, women activists within political parties and organizations representing prostitutes. Community activists, many of them women, argue that prostitution creates an atmosphere of fear among local women and children and represents a public nuisance. A female MP raised the issue in Parliament, stating:

> I have sought this debate on behalf of my constituents who live in what should be a pleasant residential area, but which for decades has been blighted and unjustifiably stigmatised as a result of the nuisance and disturbance associated with street prostitution. (*Hansard* 1994:292)

Jones went on to argue that 'from a resident's perspective prostitution creates a poor environmental image … An atmosphere of fear is created for female residents and children.' Speaking on behalf of her constituents, local community women and the Mother's Union, this female MP called for 'zones of tolerance' to be introduced so that prostitution could be controlled and managed in order to reduce medical problems and impose as little strain as possible on local people.

Meanwhile the English Collective of Prostitutes argued that these proposals aimed to defend the value of some people's property at the expense of the civil rights of others (Kantola and Squires 2004). While prostitutes' organizations have had very little influence in national debates in the UK, they could be taken to represent (certain) women's interests in relation to prostitution policies. The RNGS framework aims to determine whether the UK women's policy agencies were successful in bringing the substantive concerns of the women's movement into the policy-making process: but in this case it was simply not clear whether the community groups or the prostitutes' organizations were to be taken as representative of the movement.

The most obvious response is to acknowledge that neither group is representative of a 'women's movement', and to recognize that there was no movement voice for the policy agency to represent in this case. This signals the extent to which the use of the blanket term 'women's movement' is problematic when evaluating the success of women's policy agencies in relation to the presumed goals of any such movement, for these are far from uniform. It is simply not clear what women's interests should be deemed to comprise, given that women's organizations do not articulate a single shared set of goals or perspectives.

Indeed, it frequently appears to be the case that the creation of women's policy agencies and the fragmentation of the women's movement coincide. For example, Mtintso argues that in South Africa there was a convergence of aspirations that characterized the women's movement during the 1980s, for while there was never just one set of women's interests, the political context at that time did create conditions for a coherent and cohesive movement. As this political context has changed, and women have been able to enter into the parliamentary and bureaucratic spheres, she argues, diversity has superseded commonality, with party political concerns eroding previous feminist loyalties (Mtintso 2001). This suggests that both the emergence of state feminism and the fragmentation of the women's movement may be symptomatic of increased political empowerment. Although the femocrats that work in women's policy agencies may claim to represent and draw strength from the women's movement, the declining cohesiveness of this movement may actually coincide with the growing influence of state feminism, rendering their claims constitutive rather than descriptive.

Numerous case-studies of women's policy agencies express concern that the agencies benefit only a small female elite (Franceschet 2002), or focus on only those issues that are compatible with the dominant state interests (Matear 1997; Waylen 2000), with scholars noting, for instance, that the Turkish women's policy agency 'kept the Islamist women's movement at a distance' (Gunes-Ayata 2001:164). In Latin America, scholars note, female relatives of victims of human rights violations or women campaigning to improve living conditions gained less access to women's policy agencies than to those that were self-proclaimed feminist groups (Friedman 2000). On the other hand, Franceschet and Macdonald suggest that in Chile women in state agencies have been much less willing to advocate social welfare policies than have women's autonomous organizations – which argued for these on the basis of women's difference – given that the government is committed to market and private-sector solutions (Franceschet and Macdonald 2004). SERNAM, the Chilean women's policy agency, has focused on women's civil and political rights rather than their socio-economic rights, failing to reflect the social demands of the autonomous women's organizations. As a result, many of the autonomous women's organizations feel that the more institutionalized policy community is marginalizing their demands. These examples indicate that women's experiences are diverse and that women's policy agencies tend to represent particular voices from within the women's movement, while failing to represent others.

All of this suggests that state feminism may offer a conceptualization of gender equality that 'serves to valorize some women while marginalizing others' (Mohammad 2005:249). For certain feminist voices inevitably get privileged when feminists enter into the state: which voices prevail will vary by institutional context, with those feminist voices that are most compatible with the wider policy frame inevitably predominating in state feminist bodies. For instance, Mohammad suggests that the Instituto de la Mujer, the state department for women established in Spain in 1982, used its location within the state to disseminate (and universalize) its vision of what counts as women's equality and how this might be achieved (Mohammad 2005:248). She argues that Spanish state feminism offers a conceptualization of gender equality that aims to make women equal to men by developing their opportunities and creating a 'model of Spanish womanhood capable of taking up these opportunities' (Mohammad 2005:249). Those capable of the necessary transformation are brought to the fore, while those not are relegated to the periphery. In this way the ideal of gender equality prescribes a particular model of womanhood and valorizes it over others.

While the way gender equality is conceived in particular national discourses will vary, the tendency to privilege state feminists who most clearly articulate a conception of gender equality that resonates with dominant policy frames appears to be standard. Hobson notes that in Sweden the feminists to be given policy-making roles were those who did not decouple class equality from gender equality (Hobson 2003), given that women's emancipation was cast as part of the labour movement's struggle for a just society (Palme 1972:235–43). As a result, gender-equality polices are nearly always presented as gender-neutral, rather than as a means of recognizing gender-distinctive claims (Hobson 2003). Significantly, immigrant women's groups were rendered invisible by this Swedish institutionalized feminism, which 'produced hegemonic representations of women's political identities' (Hobson *et al.* 2007), obscuring the experiences of immigrant and minority women (Mulanari 2001, cited in Hobson *et al.* 2007). The Swedish equality discourse that has been celebrated around the world as a model for empowering women politically and economically is, it appears, implicated in creating another inequality by entrenching a hierarchy between 'Swedes' and 'immigrants' (Towns 2002).

This tendency may be common among the Nordic countries, which have been regarded as model states in relation to gender equality, but which actually privilege a form of gender equality that is not well placed to deal with the challenge of multiculturalism. As Siim argues, the Nordic 'discourse of gender equality has increasingly become a means to legitimise discrimination and stigmatisation of ethnic minorities' (Siim 2007). The Danish gender discourse, and the state feminists who articulate it, have depicted young Muslim men as violent and young Muslim women as oppressed and victims of their 'culture', 'representing' Muslim women in ways that frequently compete with their own self-understanding of the conflicting demands of their religious and national cultures. Given that these Muslim women are under-represented in political parties, women's policy agencies and voluntary organizations, neither the Danish women's movement nor the Danish women's policy agencies give these particular women a voice. As Siim states, the democratic challenge is to create conditions for the voices of ethnic minority women to be heard in minority organizations as well as in the Danish public arena (Siim 2007). Whether women's policy agencies will facilitate or hinder this process is open to question, for the process of representing women entails not only the reflection of pre-existing identities and interests, but also the constitution of a 'group' on behalf of which the agencies speak, portraying those represented in order to be able to represent them (Saward 2006:414). Perhaps inevitably, the particular portrayal of women offered by many women's policy agencies privileges a particular form of gender identity, which silences rather than gives voice to various 'minority' women.

Women's policy agencies therefore appear somewhat paradoxical, emerging to represent the voice of the women's movement within the state just as that movement is fragmenting into a series of loosely aligned networks that have no identifiable ideological or social core (Banaszak *et al.* 2003:21). Where the movement is fragmented and its demands are contested, the function of these agencies may well entail the active portrayal of 'women as a group' rather than the simple reflection of them, such that they serve as a surrogate for women's civil society voice, producing particular representations of women's political identities that may not capture the diversity among women, and privileging particular conceptions of gender equality that may structurally disadvantage some gendered identities while privileging others.

State Restructuring

If the attempt to represent a group that fragmented just as the representative process was being established appears somewhat paradoxical, a further complication lies in the fact that the turn to state feminism occurred at precisely the moment when the nation-state entered a deep crisis of legitimacy and sovereignty and many people argued that the state was being 'hollowed out' (Rhodes 1994). As Banaszak *et al.* note, 'Ironically, women's movements have solidified relationships with the nation state and feminists have moved into state institutions and elected bodies at the same time as the traditional responsibilities afforded these institutions are dissipating through state reconfiguration' (Banaszak *et al.* 2003:22). This could of course be viewed cynically, whereby as power moves elsewhere the granting of access to the state becomes an easier gesture that doesn't actually entail the disruption of patriarchal power; or it could be viewed more positively, whereby state reconfiguration actually provides new political opportunities to women's movements (Beckwith 2003:198).

Throughout the 1980s and 1990s the state has 'reshaped, relocated and rearticulated its formal powers and policy responsibilities' (Banaszak *et al.* 2003:4). Though the process of state reconfiguration has been highly differentiated, Banaszak *et al.* outline four key features, which they label as 'uploading', 'downloading', 'lateral loading' and 'offloading'. Uploading describes the process of state authority shifting up to supranational organizations such as the EU, whereby individual member states have transferred formal decision-making competences in specific policy areas to the regional body. Downloading, by contrast, describes the process of state authority shifting down to sub-state bodies such as the newly established Scottish Parliament. These two processes represent a 'vertical reconfiguration' of the state (Banaszak *et al.* 2003:4). Horizontal reconfiguration of the state also occurs in the form of lateral loading, whereby power shifts across state spheres, from elected bodies to the courts or executive agencies of government. Offloading describes the process by which traditional state responsibilities shift to civil society organizations, including the market, family and community. Traditional neo-corporatist arrangements, which gave privileged state access to some industries and trade unions, have been replaced by 'partnerships' that provide new political opportunities to a diverse range of groups.

These reconfiguration processes are crucial for women's movements in so far as they provide both negative and positive opportunities that differ fundamentally from the state context that women's movements faced in the 1960s and early 1970s. First, downloading state powers in the form of devolution has given some feminists opportunities for engaging in constitutional design, helping to shape new state structures in the making (Brown 1995; Dobrowolsky and Hart 2003), and augmenting the recent focus on the representative and administrative branches of the state with an increased interest in the constitutional (Waylen 2006). Second, uploading state powers to regional and international bodies has increased women's opportunities to use supra-state institutions to put pressure on the state to increase women's representation, encouraging the development of transnational NGO activism (Oustshoorn 1999:3). Third, offloading state powers to civil society organizations, which leads to the use of 'partnerships' in policy-making and implementation, gives feminist NGOs new responsibilities and powers (Larner 2005; Newman 2001).

Various forms of state offloading have empowered certain feminist NGOs, further fragmenting the women's movement by creating a growing disjuncture between those groups that work with the state and those that do not. But, perhaps more significantly still, some forms of offloading threaten to replace the problematic – but democratic – process of group representation with a more bureaucratic process in which the technical pursuit of 'gender equality' becomes disentangled from the political process of defining its nature. For example, states seeking gender advice and knowledge increasingly contract NGOs to provide research on indicators of gender inequality, or evaluate the effectiveness of policy outcomes. With the growth in new public management (introducing private-sector techniques of governance into the public sector) there has been a notable tendency to devalue in-house policy expertise in favour of contracting out (Sawer 2005:7). Feminist NGOs are therefore increasingly involved in gender policy assessments, project execution and social services delivery (Alvarez 1999:182). These NGOs are 'the perfect sites to channel international funds' for those seeking alternatives to the state, and feminist organizations thereby become 'entangled with the development apparatus and neoliberal policies, and even financially dependent on them for this subsistence' (Mendoza 2002:308). In this way NGOs have become professionalized technical experts, in a contractual relationship to the state, rather than autonomous organizations advocating political change.

Although much of the financial support for NGOs in the developing countries came from private donors and bilateral and multilateral agencies keen to promote a thriving civil society, the criteria for determining which NGOs will be consulted rarely entails considerations relating to their ability to mediate with civil society constituencies, usually focusing on more technical criteria, and privileging those NGOs deemed politically trustworthy (Alvarez 1999:193, 198). These processes have given the NGOs better access to state policy-making, but have also increased their distance from more movement-oriented activities. Given that their role as gender experts frequently entails advising on or carrying out government women's programmes, the boundary between the policy community and appointed officials is blurred and the space for contestatory politics is lost to more technical endeavours. While many of the actors in these NGOs initially negotiated both technical expertise and critical advocacy roles, their involvement in the former has increasingly been bought at the expense of the latter.

The democratic challenge of realizing group representation that is sensitive to the diversity among women has increasingly been circumvented as states have turned to feminist NGOs as gender experts 'rather than as citizens' groups advocating on behalf of women's rights' (Alvarez 1999:183). This process occurs in place of 'wider *political* debates with the civil society constituencies with the highest stakes in gender-focused programmes' (Alvarez 1999:192; emphasis in original). NGOs therefore become surrogates for civil society rather than an intermediary to it, circumventing the pressure on governments to establish other democratic mechanisms through which women might express their voices. In this way the growth of women's policy agencies and professional feminist NGOs might be viewed as an anti-political rather than a democratic tendency. Indeed, in the absence of political debate women's policy agencies may actively construct women's interests with little input from women themselves (Bacchi 1999), doing more to facilitate a governance agenda than a democratic one.

It is for this reason that Nussbaum places great emphasis on national, electoral politics, for 'these governments have one thing in their favour: they are elected', and they are 'accountable to the people … in a way that international agencies and even extremely fine NGOs simply are not' (Nussbaum 2000:105). This focuses attention back on women parliamentarians, who are structurally required to represent their constituents. But it also suggests that we should be thinking about alternative democratic innovations, to complement the work of the professionalized NGOs, and provide a political voice to informal issue networks and civil society actors located with subaltern counter-publics (Fraser 1989).

A concern about assimilation therefore augments the essentialist concern that women's policy agencies actively portray women as a group in a homogenizing way, for there is a danger that these agencies will become an institutionalized means of representing women's interests in a way that actually constitutes those new gendered identities that are compatible with the norms of state governance. In this context, the confidence that women's policy agencies are best viewed as a product of women's movement activism which further facilitates women's interests, clearly affirms a liberal democratic belief in the state as a neutral institution to be used by any group able to develop the political capital to promote its own vision of the world. This, as Mohammad points out, contrasts with the conviction of earlier Marxist and radical feminists that the state was a capitalist, patriarchal state and that engagement with this state would inevitably compromise feminists and their autonomy. Recent feminist activism and research appears to have generally opted to embrace the former liberal conception of the state rather than the more critical analysis that typified earlier feminist practices. However, one does not need to embrace the Nietzschean claim that the state 'is the coldest of all cold monsters … whatever its says, it lies – and whatever it has, it has stolen' (Nietzsche 1969:75), in order to recognize that the role of women's policy agencies might not just be to reflect the voices of the women's movement actors, but rather that part of the function of these agencies might equally be the '"making up" of citizens capable of bearing a kind of regulated freedom' (Rose and Miller 1992:172).

If government is understood as a 'problematizing activity', in which the state poses its obligations in terms of the problems it seeks to address (Rose and Miller 1992:182), then the creation of women's policy agencies within state machineries signals that gender inequality has become an obligation of the state, an ill that it seeks to cure. For many states, gender inequality comes to be posed as a problem that it seeks to address because it is held to symbolize the operation of traditional cultural practices that act as a constraint on modernization and liberalization. For example, for a Spanish nation whose identity vacillates around 'the inward-looking Spain of traditionalist Catholic values' and 'liberal Spain of progress and free thought', the state repudiation of the traditional values of domestic femininity and institutionalization of equality feminism plays a key part in transforming Spanish national identity: egalitarian attitudes are regarded as synonymous with modernization, with women's association with paid employment rather than motherhood symbolizing the modernization of Spanish society (Mohammad 2005:254). As the Instituto de la Mujer states, 'the high increase in rate of women's [economic] activity constitutes a relevant indicator of the process of modernization in Spanish society' (Instituto de la Mujer 1993:30). Here, as in the Nordic countries, the promotion of gender equality by women's policy agencies frequently entails the depiction of 'traditional femininities', whether Catholic or Muslim, as problematic, actively representing those feminist demands that best fit with dominant policy paradigms while marginalizing others.

Accordingly, 'the world of Spanish state feminism is one in which equality is translated as the production of labour markets where women are equally 'free' to sell their labour' (Mohammad 2005:258). The Spanish women's policy agencies produce extensive materials informing and guiding women, which serve to 'produce a collective memory of women's history which acts as a basis for the formulation of gender equality programmes and provides legitimation for equality feminism' (Mohammad 2005:251). In this way the Spanish agencies teach women the techniques by which they might become better workers, representing women's interests in a way that is simultaneously constitutive of new gendered identities. Thus, the sharp fall in Spain's birth rate, now the lowest in Europe, is a reflection of the increased availability of contraception and information, but 'also the lower social value placed on motherhood and mothering' (Mohammad 2005:256).

In these circumstances, the task of women's policy agencies is to depict gender inequality in a way that 'both grasps its truths' and 're-presents it in a form in which it can enter the sphere of conscious political calculation' (Rose and Miller 1992:183). Femocrats therefore enter into a double alliance: on the one hand allying themselves with political authorities, focusing on their problems and offering expertise about this new policy concern; and on the other hand, forming alliances with women's organizations, translating their concerns into the rationalities of government, and offering to teach them the techniques by which they might become more modern citizens.

Conclusion

This chapter has considered arguments in favour of women's policy agencies as an important form of group representation, which may be better able than individual female legislators to represent the diversity among women. It has suggested that there is potential for this to be the case, given that these agencies explicitly aim to advocate women's issues, but ideally do so by consulting with particular women's organizations directly, thereby having a greater claim to being authorized by and accountable to women's organizations. However, it has also suggested that women's policy agencies tend to manifest the problem of essentialism to the extent that they claim to represent the women's movement as a homogeneous actor, when it is in reality highly fragmented. Moreover, it has suggested that women's policy agencies also tend to manifest the problem of assimilation to the extent that they adopt professionalized technocratic modes of operation and to conceptualize gender equality in ways that valorize those forms of gendered identity that best resonate with dominant policy paradigms. This suggests that the danger inherent in women's policy agencies is that they operate as an institutionalized means of representing women's interests in a way that constitutes new gendered identities compatible with the norms of state governance.

The next chapter will consider whether the emergence of gender mainstreaming unsettles or reinforces this tendency. The shift from advocating women's policy agencies to advocating gender mainstreaming that occurred between the mid 1970s and mid 1990s was generally perceived to reflect a growing recognition that the group-based essentialist logic underpinning women's policy agencies, which generated a presumption that there are specific sets of interests and policies that are distinctly female, was unsatisfactory. The shift to 'gender' rather than 'women' and to a concern with all policy arenas, rather than those deemed to address women's issues alone, was widely presented as a means of moving beyond this essentialist logic. However, for many critics of mainstreaming, this shift appears to have been bought at the cost of embracing further assimilation, addressing the limitations of a strategy of reversal in the hope of developing a more transformative policy that might be congruent with a strategy of displacement, only to find that it looks suspiciously like a strategy of inclusion.

6
Engendering Governance? Mainstreaming

Introduction

Gender mainstreaming is defended, at a theoretical level, as a transformatory new approach to equality. The central claim made in favour of gender mainstreaming as a gender equality strategy is that it offers a way of introducing gendered perspectives into the construction of equality norms, rendering it potentially more transformatory than those approaches that demand equal treatment in relation to norms that are not themselves questioned, or positive action approaches, which respond to the inequalities that result from structural bias but do not themselves unsettle the norms that generate this bias. Where the existence of false impartiality claims demands either acceptance of partial and discriminatory norms, via an equal-treatment approach, or the assertion of alternative marginalized norms, via a positive-action approach, mainstreaming appears to offer a way of displacing this dichotomy by reworking the norms in a manner more sensitive to the diverse realities of gendered practices. This political equality measure therefore appears, in theory at least, to be more firmly located within a strategy of displacement than are either gender quotas or women's policy agencies.

For instance, Rees suggests that where equal treatment is a 'legal redress to treat men and women the same', and positive action recognizes that there are differences between men and women and that specific measures are required to address disadvantages experienced by women as a consequence of those differences, mainstreaming 'ideally should involve identifying how existing systems and structures cause indirect discrimination and altering or redesigning them as appropriate' (Rees 2002:46–8). The aim of the mainstreaming strategy is to counteract gender bias within existing systems and structures: it addresses 'those very institutionalized practices that cause both individual and group disadvantage in the first place' (Rees 2000:3). Because it takes a systems approach, its advocates have argued that it has more transformative potential than previous equality policies. It takes us beyond the classic opposition between equal treatment and positive action by focusing on the structural reproduction of gender inequality and aiming to transform the policy process so that gender bias is eliminated. From this perspective, mainstreaming is depicted as a strategy of displacement, rather than inclusion or reversal. However, the practice of mainstreaming rarely seems to realize its theoretical potential as a strategy of displacement, and most of the critical reflections on mainstreaming practices focus on its complicity with neoliberal forms of governance, rendering it closer to a strategy of inclusion in practice. Indeed, it appears that:

> ten years after the Beijing conference, many feminists have come to see gender mainstreaming, not just as failing to be as transformative as they were hoping, but often even as actually damaging for women, distracting energy and resources with little if any visible effects. (Yuval-Davis 2005)

There appears to be a gap between the rhetoric and the reality of mainstreaming, with the transformative potential being subsumed by the institutionalized demands of technocratic governance, leading to a clear sense of disappointment and frustration among many of its advocates. Critics of mainstreaming practices are beginning to argue that they inevitably articulate a conception of gender equality that resonates with dominant policy frames, which may well entail embracing not only neoliberal techniques of governance but also marketized economic goals that construe gender equality in an integrationist rather than transformatory manner. Meanwhile, those who defend its current manifestations argue that, while the radical potential of mainstreaming is clearly constrained by its institutional context, mainstreaming nonetheless offers new opportunities for bureaucratic interventions that privilege evidence-based policy-making and so empower those able to articulate their perspectives via the objective rationalities that this approach requires and enables them to speak to all policy issues rather than only those traditionally considered to be 'gendered'.

Those not convinced by this line of argument have tended to respond by distinguishing between two distinct models of mainstreaming: the 'expert-bureaucratic' and 'participative-democratic' (Nott 2000; Donaghy 2004a), arguing that while the expert-bureaucratic model may be problematic in various regards, the participative-democratic model holds out more positive potential. This form of mainstreaming aims to allow women's civil society organizations to 'set the agenda', avoiding becoming rhetorically entrapped by policy frames that are antithetical to their own ambitions. However, if the expert-bureaucratic form of mainstreaming seems to collapse back into a strategy of inclusion by embracing dominant policy paradigms, this participative-bureaucratic form has a tendency to revert into a strategy of reversal in its embrace of group consultation processes and tendency to privilege 'women's voices', which raise once again the spectre of essentialism. This suggests that, if the transformative potential of mainstreaming is to be realized, other forms of democratic participation, which avoid the reductive logic of group identity and the practical difficulties of extensive consultation, may need to be considered. This chapter considers whether the participative-democratic model holds out the potential for a more transformative manifestation of mainstreaming: one that avoids the twin pitfalls of both assimilation and essentialism by engaging with multiple equality strands and offering a valuable means of negotiating the demands of diversity.

Mainstreaming as a Governance Strategy

Many accounts of the global diffusion of women's policy agencies and gender mainstreaming tend to privilege the role of transnational feminist networks, proffering an uplifting narrative in which women's policy agencies and gender mainstreaming emerge as feminist transformatory strategies that are actively and effectively disseminated by feminist actors and adopted by benign policy-makers. Exponents of these accounts tend to conceptualize mainstreaming as an agenda-setting process. Yet there are other, rather more sceptical, accounts of the rapid embrace of mainstreaming, which find significance in the fact that mainstreaming emerges in a neo-liberal era and is actively advocated by the key institutions of neo-liberal development. Those who take this perspective tend to view mainstreaming as an integrationist strategy.

From the former perspective, neo-liberalism stands in principled tension with gender mainstreaming. For example, True emphasizes the theoretical and political tensions between the two, suggesting that there is a conflict between feminist concepts and values and the broader ideological framework of neo-liberal economics, which acts as a constraining factor on mainstreaming (True 2003:383). She suggests that one of the two factors that 'seriously compromises' the success of mainstreaming is 'the conflict between the feminist goal of gender equity achieved through state-led redistribution and the neoliberal goal of efficiency achieved through market-driven economic growth' (True 2003:371). Similarly Teghtsoonian argues that while neo-liberalism affirms the norm of value-neutrality and fiscal restraint, mainstreaming aims to 'dismantle claims to neutrality which often mark the deeply gendered assumptions underlying … neoliberal policies' (Teghtsoonian 2004:279). For instance, while neo-liberalism entails the erasure of 'women' as a social and political category and focuses on de-gendered workers, citizens and consumers, mainstreaming is intended to draw attention precisely to the gendered structuring of people's lives; while neo-liberal policies have frequently had a 'debilitating and gender-specific impact on the lives of diverse groups of women', mainstreaming aims to remedy gender-based disadvantage; and while neo-liberal policies aim to achieve greater market-driven economic efficiency, mainstreaming pursues state-led gender equality. Teghtsoonian therefore suggests that mainstreaming is at odds with many aspects of 'business as usual' because it is 'more amenable to being framed as politicized – and therefore problematic – than seemingly neutral practices that involve "governing by numbers"' (Teghtsoonian 2004:279).

This suggests that the pursuit of mainstreaming gets 'distorted' and limited by its neo-liberal context such that mainstreaming is rendered compatible with neo-liberal objectives. The socially transformative potential of mainstreaming thereby runs the risk of getting lost as ideas about gender become institutionalized as international norms and policies (True 2003:387), such that they come to embrace the business case for mainstreaming – strategically at first and perhaps on a more principled level with time, thereby further entrenching the 'normalization of neoliberalism' (Hay 2004). Here mainstreaming is depicted as a political project that potentially challenges the presumptions and processes of neo-liberal governance, but frequently fails to realize its radical potential.

Yet the intriguing thing, if there is indeed such a clear-cut conflict between the feminist values embedded in mainstreaming and the neo-liberal context in which it gets implemented, is that the former has been adopted and implemented so enthusiastically by the institutions advocating the latter. As Teghtsoonian herself notes, 'the proliferation of gender-sensitive approaches to government policy has occurred during a period when neoliberalism has become well-established as a pervasive script informing the agendas of governments world-wide'

(Teghtsoonian 2004:268). Given the apparent tensions between the two emphasized by those who hold an agenda-setting conception of mainstreaming, their simultaneous development appears contradictory, especially as it is the international institutions created to implement neo-liberal policies that have played such a key role in introducing and disseminating mainstreaming practices. Development scholars have stressed the importance of gender entrepreneurs within the institutions of global governance as key facilitators of mainstreaming processes (Kardam 2000; Moser 2002; Razavi and Miller 1995), and some have suggested that James Wolfensohn (the then president of the World Bank) acted as a key gender policy entrepreneur following his attendance at the 1996 UN women's conference (O'Brien *et al.* 2000:43–4). Given this, it seems rather odd to represent neo-liberalism as simply a constraint upon the pursuit of mainstreaming, for its institutions have actively promoted the adoption of mainstreaming, which suggests that they perceived it to be positively useful in some way, facilitating the pursuit of their strategic aims.

Clearly the pursuit of neo-liberal governance and the implementation of gender mainstreaming have appeared perfectly compatible to a large number of policy-makers across the globe. This suggests either that neo-liberalism is more open to feminist political aims and practices than many of its critics have suggested, or that mainstreaming can be implemented in ways that are more compatible with a neo-liberal logic than many of its advocates had hoped. For this reason, one might reasonably view the two as inherently congruent, sharing similar technologies and ambitions. On the first account, mainstreaming has the potential to challenge neo-liberal institutions from within, bringing women's voices into the policy-making process and changing the political agenda, but may not always achieve this potential. On the second account, mainstreaming simply offers useful specialist knowledge and policy-making techniques that augment neo-liberal technologies of governance and facilitates the realization of the neo-liberal goal of greater economic efficiency, while holding out no radical transformative potential. For the former camp mainstreaming is, at heart, a democratic 'agenda-setting' project; for the latter it is no more than a technocratic integrationist project.

From this latter perspective gender mainstreaming represents the appropriate approach to the pursuit of gender equality in the context of governance, just as women's policy agencies represented an appropriate approach in the context of the modernist bureaucratic state. Gender mainstreaming practices appear entirely consonant with those governing styles in which boundaries between and within public and private sectors have become blurred, and where contracting, franchising and new forms of regulation, including new public management, predominate (Rhodes 1996; Stoker 1998). Authoritative decisions are not produced by a single hierarchical structure, such as a democratically elected legislative assembly and government, but instead arise from the interaction of a plethora of public and private, collective and individual actors. Good governance therefore requires that the state 'operates in a network with private interests and groups as a partner' (Merrien 1998:58), steering rather than managing in a 'post-bureaucratic' manner (Barzelay 1992:199). Mainstreaming might then be understood as a governance strategy (Shaw 2005), sharing many features with other technologies favoured by neo-liberal institutions.

Neo-liberal policy frames, which initially reflected an 'ideological commitment to the sanctity, inviolability or infallibility of the market', have become the *normalized* and *necessitarian* rhetoric of later administrations, arising

> from a conviction that an ongoing agenda of neoliberal reform is a condition of sustained economic growth and competitiveness in an economically interdependent world in which market participants can be assumed to form their expectations in a rational manner. (Hay 2004:507)

Market mechanisms have become a kind of 'test', or regulatory ideal, of good or efficient government (Hindess 2004:26), with technologies, such as accountability, audit and budget discipline, being deployed to reshape the priorities and self-understandings of those who are targeted by them (Larner 2000:13; Miller 1994; Rose 1996, 1999; Teghtsoonian 2004:278). These technologies have required managers and staff

> to translate their activities into financial terms, to seek to maximize productivity for a given income, to cut out waste, to restructure activities that [are] not cost-affective, to choose between priorities in terms of their relative costs and benefits, to become more or less like the financial managers of their own professional activities. (Rose 1999:152)

This turns public servants into 'calculating selves', who accord priority to the calculative technologies of accounting, which seem to accord 'an objectivity, neutrality, and legitimacy to decisions that otherwise appear to be subjective' (Miller 1994:227–53). In this context, the pursuit of gender mainstreaming inevitably gets framed as yet another technology of governance.

For instance, under new public management (NPM) public servants are instructed to act as private-sector managers with devolved responsibility in which government focuses on policy-setting and management rather than the direct production and delivery of services. This management model, which is argued to produce a more flexible and less regulated workplace, entails high levels of self-management and self-surveillance (Blackmore and Sachs 2001). The NPM style of government involves using a wide range of 'tools' like grants, loans, contracts, vouchers, and direct government provision, many of which rely on networks of non-governmental organizations to deliver government services, such that 'NPM and entrepreneurial government share a concern with competition, markets, customers and outcomes' (Rhodes 1996). This shift towards governance and new public management, with its greater reliance on third parties in the design, implementation and evaluation of policy, creates new pressures to ensure that policies are designed and delivered in a consistent and effective manner (Jordan, Wurzel and Zito 2005). One response to this pressure has taken the form of a growing reliance on evidence-based policy-making. As knowledge and research have become key assets in the production of policy, evidence-based inputs are given greater weight. For instance, a recent UK report, *Better Policy-Making*, emphasized the importance of evidence-based policy and the use of experts in the policy process to make it as inclusive as possible (Bullock *et al.* 2001:25). Where external actors are able to supply policy-relevant knowledge they are afforded greater authority, encouraging non-governmental organizations to frame their intervention in objective rather than interest-based terms. The growing use of 'gender experts' and implementation of 'analytic tools' such as gender impact assessments fit in with the logic, providing 'evidence' about the likely gendered impacts of proposed policy initiatives in order to render the policy-making process more 'effective'.

Notions of good governance have always stressed the importance of basing policy-making on factual evidence rather than on mere opinion (Rose 1991), but evidence-based policy-making has become particularly important over the last decade and is now the dominant model for evaluating claims in the policy process (Marston and Watts 2003). Research and expertise are required to ensure that policy outcomes align with policy intentions. Evidence-based policy-making is argued to facilitate greater transparency than was afforded by older models of incrementalism (Laforest and Orsini 2005). Such evidence-based policy-making privileges specific social science methodologies, frequently relying on quantitative studies that generate 'objective' truth claims. As Bacchi and Eveline note, 'dominant forms of mainstreaming are clearly congruent with this self-managed model of governance …' (Bacchi and Eveline 2004:103–4). By equating gender mainstreaming with the tools of this new style of governance, including processes of self-management and self-surveillance, mainstreaming comes to be viewed as 'an issue of human resource management' (Bacchi and Eveline 2004:104–5) rather than a transformatory political strategy. From this perspective, mainstreaming loses its radical potential and becomes institutionalized by the dominant technologies of governance.

Mainstreaming as the Democratization of Expertise

It is, though, possible to view the consonance between mainstreaming and neo-liberal forms of governance in a rather more positive light, for it has offered up new political opportunities that feminist NGOs have been quick to exploit. For instance, given the dominance of evidence-based policy-making, NGOs are called upon to produce knowledge that will further the goals of their organizations and sway policy-makers. This results in activist organizations abandoning contentious modes of advocacy in favour of more 'legitimate', evidence-based claims of expertise (Laforest and Orsini 2005). In order to produce such expert knowledge and develop their research capacity, feminist organizations inevitably require increasing levels of organizational stability and funding. Some scholars have interpreted this turn to knowledge production within advocacy organizations as symptomatic of the depoliticizing and managerialist dynamics of neo-liberal governance, focusing on the growth of consultancy services, and the demand for new expertise in fundraising and organizational management (Chasin 2000), which makes activists increasingly accountable to funding bodies rather than political constituencies (Richardson 2005:528). As Laforest and Orsini argue, 'while this shift creates opportunities for organizations which engage in research activities, it also constrains their options by closing off political spaces to forms of representation that may be unconventional or deemed too politicized' (Laforest and Orsini 2005:483–4). NGOs increasingly adopt professional forms of organization, adhere to social scientific standards of knowledge production and speak the language of rational empiricism. The negative reading of this is that in order to participate in governance processes, activists become 'responsible' in form and voice and lose their political edge: the processes involved in securing consultancies and generating 'objective' social scientific knowledge thereby bring groups into alignment with state objectives. It is therefore particularly interesting that so many feminist organizations have been so ready to become responsible 'evidence-producing' organizations peopled by 'gender experts'.

The more positive reading of the feminist turn to 'expertise' is that the emergence of evidence-based policy-making offers social activists in NGOs new opportunities for making new knowledge claims and for having these claims accepted given that evidence-based policy-making unsettles the monopoly on policy knowledge previously claimed by the traditional public servant (Laforest and Orsini 2005). Feminist NGOs have been given new opportunities to filter their knowledge claims into the policy-making processes, but – no doubt anticipating problems of credibility conferral were they to speak from subjective marginalized locations – have usually drawn on traditional social science methods and knowledge structures to do so.

This is particularly interesting given that feminist critiques of objectivity have long been influential (Code 1995; Harding 1991; Lloyd 1984; Prokhovnik 1999), with feminist theorists routinely arguing that empiricist epistemologies marginalize those whose knowledge is not readily amenable to objectification, driving a wedge between those perceived to be making special-interest claims and those capable of transcending their own narrow concerns to make objective judgements. For this reason many feminists (and others) rejected claims to impartiality, arguing that the apparently just liberal presumption of impartiality actually worked to privilege dominant interests (Tully 1995; Young 1990). Indeed, many theorists have suggested that one product of historical oppression and marginalization is the tendency to work with concrete and particular modes of reasoning (Collins 2000; Tronto 1993), given that a 'sense of vulnerability' impedes people's ability to take the abstract stance required of objective judgement and a lack of power and consequent inability to do something in the world renders people uncertain about their right to make such statements. This focuses attention on the psychological limitations placed upon marginalized people's construction of knowledge claims by their experiences of marginalization. Similarly, Fricker suggests that the conferral of credibility upon knowledge claimants is a process that favours those groups who are already privileged, for the norms of credibility will reflect the structures of social power (Fricker 1998). In this way Fricker complements the claims of earlier standpoint theorists (Harding 1991; Hartsock 1983), analysing the processes that prevent the knowledge claims of marginalized groups being accepted as true. In particular, the sorts of knowledge claims made the new politics of gender equality

323.4 SQ58 2007

Squires, Judith

---

gender equality

Buvinic, Mayra

323.3 EQ25

2008

Equality 4 women: where do we stand on millenium Development goal 3?

by marginalized groups that are closely bound to the social location or identity of that group are likely to unsettle the dominant norms of society and therefore be harder to integrate into existing bodies of knowledge (McConkey 2004:203). Social movement activists therefore not only need to make new knowledge claims, but also need to ensure that these claims are credible.

Feminists are generally sensitive to the fact that those deemed to be pursuing 'special interests' have frequently been depicted as subjective and partial, operating with value-laden knowledge only (Code 1995:17). It appears that many feminist NGOs are now drawing on this perception, motivating their own assertions of objectivity. The affirmation of gender mainstreaming by international organizations and its formal endorsement by national governments now allows feminist activists to articulate historically excluded knowledge in their capacity as 'gender experts' and to have these claims listened to. It also privileges a certain form of knowledge, produced by social scientific enquiry, which does not simply describe the world but also enacts it (Law and Urry 2004:391). This suggests that gender experts contribute to the enactment of certain sorts of gendered worlds. The emergence of evidence-based policy-making and of gender mainstreaming has created new opportunities for feminist activists to make gendered knowledge claims and to make new gendered realities, with the production of sex-disaggregated statistics proving to be a central tool in this process. The demand for such knowledge has led to a professionalization of feminist NGOs and to the increased use of empirical research to ground the knowledge claims of gender experts.

This tendency to marginalize those who do not articulate their demands in the appropriate form has not been lost on many women within civil society. A pamphlet of The Revolutionary Women of the Philippines, for example, argues that mainstreaming is 'an imperialist scheme for co-opting the world's women, buying off once committed activists' (Baden and Goetz 1997:6), while panellists in a forum organized by the Applied Socio-economic Research organization of Pakistan argued that gender analysis had become overly technocratic because of the professionalization of the women's movement. Meanwhile, Baden and Goetz argue that gender analysis, including the use of gender disaggregated statistics which are frequently undertaken to generate a more robust analysis of the likely impact of policies and so prevent policy failure, has the function of reducing 'gender' to a product:

> [T]he gender-disaggregation approach … tends to a static and reductionist definition of gender (as woman/man) … Bureaucratic requirements

> for information tend to strip away the political content of information on women's interests and reduce it to a set of needs or gaps, amenable to administrative decisions about the allocation of resources. (Baden and Goetz 1997:7)

So while this technocratic and depoliticized process of policy-making is empowering, in that it offers feminist NGOs and gender experts new sources of authority and avenues of influence, it should not be forgotten that the nature of the knowledge claims made by 'gender experts' remains contested, and that the world these claims enact is still 'provisional' and open to democratic challenge. For instance, the emphasis of quantitative measurements and empirical indicators has encouraged 'gender experts' to produce sex-disaggregated data, which focuses attention on sex differences rather than gendered processes. The large body of data on the number of women in national parliaments is one example of the emphasis on empirical indicators. The number of women in parliaments is measurable in a way that the effect of gendered practices on policy outcomes is not. As social-scientific knowledge production becomes a political strategy, those feminist NGOs with the resources to conduct and present empirical research will find it easier to impact on the policy-making process than those without them. While the empowerment this confers on some feminist organizations is to be welcomed, the processes of marginalization it inscribes on others should not be overlooked.

Mainstreaming as Rhetorical Entrapment

The production of sex-disaggregated data and the claims to gender expertise enact certain worlds, and the worlds they enact are most likely to be consonant with dominant policy priorities. The framing of gendered knowledge in terms of concerns about economic productivity, for example, will inflect the particular sort of claims made. Yet framing gendered knowledge in this way is precisely what mainstreaming seems to require. It must, as Verloo points out, convince these actors that policy-makers are a part of 'the problem' without alienating them from the mainstreaming project. In order to do so, it needs to 'resonate' with the existing frames within which regular actors operate: it needs to 'seduce' them (Verloo 2001:9).

Frame extension and bridging is needed to bring the goal of gender equality into alignment with the existing frames and norms of politicians and civil servants. In the context of contemporary governance, this usually means that gender equality is argued to be better for both women and men, to improve productivity, and to facilitate better, more modern government (Stratigaki 2004). Here mainstreaming becomes a way of thinking about users as distinct groups with differing needs, characteristics and behaviour, which matters if one is concerned about delivering customer and user satisfaction. The main concern here is that of assimilation. For instance, the 'business case' for mainstreaming is frequently the only case offered for 'why gender equality matters': as the UK Women and Equality Unit states on its website:

> [U]nfair discrimination is plainly wrong. It stops people realising their potential, and prevents businesses from using skills and talents to good effect … discrimination in employment has a huge price, beyond the tragic cost to individuals experiencing discrimination. It affects our productivity and profitability. The best [businesses and service providers] already know that good employment practices, based on equality and diversity, give them the competitive edge. (WEU 2003)

The necessity of engaging in this process of 'frame bridging' means that there is always a danger of 'rhetorical entrapment' (Verloo 2001:10).

As the pursuit of gender equality becomes rationalized as a means of gaining a competitive edge, gender experts increasingly embrace this rationality in their articulation of women's interests. For instance, a recent piece of research commissioned by the UK Women and Equality Unit stated that:

> Two women each week are killed by a partner or former partner, a total of over 100 deaths each year. The cost of the domestic homicide of adult women is an estimated £112 million each year … Domestic violence is a complex social problem with devastating consequences. It drains the resources of public and voluntary services and of employers and causes pain and distress to women and their families. The purpose of providing a figure for the 'cost' of domestic violence is to more clearly show its importance, by finding a way of translating these hardships into a common unit of account. (WEU 2004)

By putting the issue of domestic violence on the political agenda, arguing that the state should take responsibility for this ill in order to reduce the economic cost it entails, gender experts both represent the concerns of women and (knowingly) translate these concerns into the rationalities of government. As Shaw notes, this 'can lead to co-optation into political discourse of concepts such as "gender equality" but only once their meaning has been "transformed" and "corrupted" in the service of other policy priorities such as economic policies' (Shaw 2005:17).

The pursuit of gender equality comes to be articulated and defended in terms of consequentialist arguments of utility, most commonly focused on economic efficiency considerations, rather than rights-based arguments of justice. The potential strength of arguing from 'efficiency considerations' is that they enable one to raise gender equality considerations in relation to any policy, irrespective of its goals in a manner that 'should appeal to all policy makers' (Himmelweit 2002:50–1). The potential weakness of this approach is that it may privilege those concerns that fit most readily with dominant policy-making rationalities, thereby obfuscating the normative and contested nature of gender equality and privileging the 'objective' knowledge of gender experts.

The presentation of gender equality as a technology of government tends to locate it in relation to questions of utility rather than social justice, echoing – in form – the consequentialist arguments frequently deployed in favour of gender quotas. Arguments for gender equality are therefore focused on the socio-political benefits that it will bring, with the legitimacy of gender equality programmes being evaluated in terms of their good for society in general (Mateo-Diaz 2005:116, 234) and economic productivity in particular.

The dominance of neo-liberal economic governance means that mainstreaming is often framed by the pursuit of economic efficiency rather than gender justice (Hancock 1999:6–7), such that when successful, mainstreaming is depicted as a means of realizing economic competitiveness rather than as a constraint upon it (see Veitch 2005). As True notes, feminists working with institutions that embrace an ostensibly gender-neutral, neo-liberal, rational economic framework have to 'provisionally accept aspects of the neoliberal frame' (True 2003:385), which means that the case for gender mainstreaming is frequently a 'business case', which focuses on the efficiency gains to be made from investing in human capital (see OECD 2000). For example, True notes that an OECD ministerial-level workshop on gender mainstreaming 'showed governments how mainstreaming can promote strong economies, competitiveness and growth' (OECD 2000; True 2003:37). Similarly, gender policy-makers within the World Bank are under pressure to frame gender policy using appeals to productivity and quantifiable efficiency (Bedford 2006). Meanwhile, in a policy document produced by the World Bank for Beijing, the case for gender mainstreaming was made 'almost entirely on efficiency grounds, constructing a convergence between the interests of women and the promotion of economic liberalization' (Baden and Goetz 1997:9).

This approach is echoed in the way in which mainstreaming is framed by national governments around the globe. As Teghtsoonian notes, 'In the political context where neoliberalism prevails, it is unsurprising to find government ministries and departments – including women's policy agencies – emphasizing the relevance and utility of their activities for the private sector' (Teghtsoonian 2004:273). For instance, in Australia the Ministry of Women's Affairs encourages private-sector employers to take up gender analysis because it 'enables the private sector to tap into women's markets', which makes 'good business sense' (MWA 2001, cited in Bacchi and Eveline 2004:105). Similarly, Sharp and Broomhill argue that the women's budget process in Australia is limited by the government's commitment to fiscal restraint and economic restructuring, and note that mainstreaming may reinforce the normalization of neo-liberalism, with gender-based analysis adding a veneer of legitimacy to these measures – officials claiming that 'women would benefit in the long run with increased economic growth and jobs' (Sharp and Broomhill 2002:42). Meanwhile, most Latin American governments tend to view women's integration into the market as crucial to neo-liberal development (Alvarez 1999:191). Here gender equality considerations are a key dimension of state attempts to privatize social welfare provision and contain social discontent (Craske 1998:104). Gender becomes part of a policy lexicon as states focus on incorporating women into neo-liberal development programmes.

Similarly, within the EU, scholars note that market interests are increasingly privileged over social interests (Fredman 1992) and that social policy is being 'subsumed by the competitiveness agenda' (Kenner 2000:125). This inevitably informs the way in which mainstreaming is conceptualized and practised. Jill Rubery, for instance, suggests that the main objective of mainstreaming is 'that of moving the economy and society towards a position where women's employment is more likely to contribute towards both a stronger fiscal base and fighting social exclusion' (Rubery 2002:517). In this way she emphasizes the complementarities between EU economic objectives and the objectives of mainstreaming gender equality. Mosesdottir and Erlingsdottir provide some support for this account, analysing the implementation of mainstreaming at the EU level as part of the European Employment Strategy (EES), 1997–2002. They suggest that the 'EES treats gender problems first and foremost as a technical problem preventing the member states from achieving economic growth comparable with that of the US' (Mosesdottir and Erlingsdottir 2005:528).

Gender equality therefore gets measured as the difference between men and women in employment, unemployment and pay, as well as gender segregation. By requiring member states to adopt mainstreaming procedures to address these policy problems using these measures, the EU induces member states to identify common gender problems and then provides them with methodological tools to tackle them. For example, the female employment rate in the EU is to reach 60 per cent by the year 2010 (as agreed by the Lisbon Council 2000), and member states should provide childcare for at least 90 per cent of children between 3 years old and mandatory school age and for at least 33 per cent of children under 3 years of age by 2010 (as agreed by the Barcelona Council 2002). Unsurprisingly, the policy solutions of EU member states to gender problems 'harmonise with the objectives of the EES and have, therefore, a strong labour market orientation' (Mosesdottir and Erlingsdottir 2005:523). echo an increasingly widespread perception among feminist scholars, suggesting that gender equality is perceived 'more as a derived objective of economic growth rather than a question of social justice' (Mosesdottir and Erlingsdottir 2005:528).

As long as gender equality is framed by dominant considerations of utility with respect to other existing policy priorities, mainstreaming will remain an integrationist rather than a transformative practice, manifesting a strategy of inclusion rather than displacement. As Verloo rightly suggests, 'the strategy as conceptualised strengthens technocratic tendencies and consequently fails to contribute to empowering mechanisms' (Verloo 2005:361). Only when marginalized voices are included in the framing of policy priorities can mainstreaming be seen as a strategy of displacement. For, as Bacchi and Eveline argue, 'the best intentions of feminist reformers will be thwarted so long as gender analysis is positioned as an ex post commentary on proposed or existing policies' (Bacchi and Eveline 2004:99). In their view, to 'reconstitute mainstreaming as able to put neoliberal agendas into question requires a form of ex ante gender analysis which includes scrutiny of broad policy objectives' (Bacchi and Eveline 2004:99). For, while mainstreaming remains subservient to wider policy objectives, the possibility of contesting neo-liberal economic agendas is seriously compromised. What is needed, if mainstreaming is to be more than a strategy of inclusion, is 'deep evaluation', which entails putting into question the grounding premises of proposed or existing policies, which will be a creative rather than a reactive process (Bacchi and Eveline 2004:112). For this reason, advocates of mainstreaming as a transformative strategy turn, at this point, to those forms of mainstreaming that privilege democratic participation rather than bureaucratic expertise.

Mainstreaming as Democratic Participation

One of the key strengths of the expert-bureaucratic model of mainstreaming is its effectiveness in allowing gender experts an important role in the policy formation process (Woodward 2003). This in turn ensures that policy-making is based on 'gendered' knowledge, rather than on ideology or stereotypes (Beveridge and Nott 2002:301). However, there is clearly a danger that, once accepted as a norm that resonates with the dominant policy frame, mainstreaming will be adopted as a technocratic tool in policy-making, reducing the scope for wider consultation with 'non-experts' and so the likelihood that the policy agenda will reflect the particular experiences and concerns of women that do not resonate with the pre-existing policy framework, and ultimately depoliticizing the issue of gender inequality itself. For this reason the expert-bureaucratic approach to mainstreaming inevitably becomes an integrationist approach, introducing a gender perspective into existing policy paradigms without questioning them.

The strength of this approach lies in its ability to realize effective integration, but it is unlikely to realize the transformative potential claimed for mainstreaming as a frame of analysis given that it is framed as an effective means to the ends pursued by policy-makers, rather than as a challenge to them (Pollack and Hafner-Burton 2000). If the transformative potential of mainstreaming is to be realized in practice then we need both to explore the possibilities for transformation implicit within the expert-bureaucratic model, and to explore the possibility of persuading policy-makers to embrace a more participative-democratic model of mainstreaming.

Here it is important to recall that the Council of Europe detailed three types of mainstreaming tools: analytic (including statistics, research, checklists and gender impact assessments), educational (training, awareness-raising, manuals or experts), and consultation and participation (think tanks, hearings, expert meetings, databases, and the participation of both sexes in decision-making) (Verloo 2005:351). This last set of tools suggests that democratic debate about gender equality might reasonably be viewed as part of the mainstreaming process. However, this insight has generally been lost in the repeated appeal to the definition of mainstreaming provided by the report of the Group of Specialists to the

Council: 'the (re)organisation, improvement, development and evaluation of policy processes, so that a gender equality perspective is incorporated in all policies at all levels and at all stages, by the actors normally involved in policymaking' (Council of Europe 1998:15). This definition fails to make 'reference to the need to give voice to the feminist movement or to those suffering from gender inequality' (Verloo 2005:351). Indeed there is no discussion as to how a gender perspective might be derived. There is no reference to the possibility of opposing political ideas on gender equality, and the expertise mentioned seems unrelated to normative beliefs, which suggests that mainstreaming is 'beyond politics' (Verloo 2005:321). In this context it is telling that the European Women's Lobby has gained a legitimate role within EU policy-making by presenting itself as the (one and only) 'expert' voice of the feminist community.

Interestingly, the Council of Europe's definition of mainstreaming did involve a discussion of what a gender equality perspective entailed, and did acknowledge that this perspective would have to be struggled for in a political debate, yet when the definition travelled in policy circles this element of the account tended to get lost in translation (Verloo 2005:355). Because only the empty one-sentence definition travelled, the global diffusion of mainstreaming occurred shorn of the original Council of Europe emphasis on democracy. While the goal of gender equality has been embraced and pursued in numerous mainstreaming practices, debate as to what gender equality comprises, and how it is to be understood, has been rather marginal. The Council of Europe's call for a 'process approach to the goal' has not been included in the wider diffusion of its definition of gender mainstreaming: and the 'split between process and goal has made perversion of the strategy easier' (Verloo 2005:356). The emphasis on consultation and participation tools has been sidelined and the notion of gender equality as a product of political struggle is lost, while other commitments, such as increasing organizational effectiveness and economic productivity, have emerged as central to mainstreaming practices. Mainstreaming has, it becomes clear, been 'strategically framed' as a way of pursuing existing ends, rather than of challenging them (Hafner-Burton and Pollack 2000): it has become assimilatory rather than transformative, technocratic rather than democratic. For example, a study of gender mainstreaming in national employment practices in 12 European countries found that it usually entailed the continuation of previous policies, with women depicted as the subject of change rather than participants in the mainstreaming process (Pascual and Behning 2001).

By contrast, participative-democratic mainstreaming emphasizes the importance of creating mechanisms for women's groups within civil society to articulate their group perspectives. The key strength of this model lies in its aspiration to recognize the perspectives and concerns of women outside of the policy-making elite, countering the top-down approach to agenda-setting and problem-solving. Rather than relying on bureaucratic policy instruments, this approach focuses on the importance of consultation with non-governmental organizations and social movements, promising to open up policy development 'to groups previously under-represented in this process' (Kelly and Donaghy 2001).

While this approach to mainstreaming looks more likely to realize the transformative potential that theories of mainstreaming promise, there are weaknesses in this model, which echo those discussed in relation to women's policy agencies (see Chapter 5). Consultation with non-governmental organizations and social movements is not synonymous with the democratic participation of citizens. By focusing on particular organizations as representative of the women's movement, this approach has a tendency to privilege certain gendered identities over others, entrenching political opportunities structures that require one to speak 'as a woman', and a certain type of woman, first and foremost. The concern is that this may formalize and freeze identities that are actually subject to constant change and thereby undermine solidarity across groups. While the strength of this model lies in its concern to recognize group perspectives from outside the existing policy-making elite and to highlight the differential experiences of women and men, its weakness may reside in a tendency to reify group identities, obscuring both intra-group divisions and inter-group commonalities.

In order to see whether this is the case, one might look at Northern Ireland, given that while the expert-bureaucratic approach has been common elsewhere, the participative-democratic model has more closely characterized the development of mainstreaming in the devolved administrations in the United Kingdom, which have relied on the participation of community groups through a consultation process (Donaghy 2003:3). The Northern Ireland Act 1998 s. 75(1) gives public authorities a statutory duty to promote equality of opportunity. Here mainstreaming has been cast as involving not only assessing but also consulting on the likely impact of policies adopted or proposed by the authority on equality of opportunity. Donaghy suggests that this emphasis on consultation 'emerges as central to the spirit and framework of Northern Ireland's mainstreaming approach … placing it firmly within the participative-democratic model' (Donaghy 2003:8). Interestingly, civic actors and groups are treated as the equality 'experts' to be consulted on policy developments.

Comparative evaluations of mainstreaming find that: 'In Northern Ireland, impact assessment seems to have assumed a level of sophistication not currently seen elsewhere in the United Kingdom, and seems to be firmly established in the participatory-democratic mould' (Beveridge *et al.* 2000:401). However, this approach has not been without its problems. There have been difficulties in finding the groups and organizations with which to consult in all policy areas (for instance, how rural development policies would impact on transgendered people), and where they do exist community groups often lack the resources, including time, labour and funds, to respond to all the equality schemes put out for consultation. Groups who participate receive no remuneration for their expertise and there is some evidence that the burden placed on the civic groups by the consultations is unsustainable (Donaghy 2004; Tallion 2001).

In these circumstances the pressure to rely on funded, professionalized NGOs and to embrace the integrationist model of mainstreaming will inevitably grow. Here it is worth recalling Young's proposal that effective group participation requires the provision of public resources to support the self-organization of group members and to enable the group to analyse and generate policy proposals in institutionalized contexts (Young 1990:184). This suggests that a participative-democratic model of mainstreaming would require a more extensive injection of state funding into civil society than has currently been envisaged. Unlikely to find support among state advocates of current mainstreaming practices, this proposal also presents challenges to radical democrats, demanding as it does that consideration be given as to which groups should receive funding and recognition, and which not. For, while radical social and political theorists have tended in recent years to challenge liberal egalitarianism by celebrating diversity and affirming demands for group recognition, the existence of 'reactionary or disagreeable' forms of difference (Cooper 2004) demands that advocates of participative-democratic mainstreaming offer some criteria for determining which groups are to gain recognition in this consultation process. This challenge is particularly acute in the context of the growing concern to mainstream not only gender equality perspectives, but also wider 'diversity' considerations.

Conclusion

The gap between the theoretical potential and the practical limitations of mainstreaming is causing many gender equality advocates to question the desirability of mainstreaming practices. There is a growing sense that its transformative potential is being subsumed by the institutionalized demands of technocratic governance. The conception of gender equality that is generally being mainstreamed is one that resonates with dominant policy frames such that the mainstreaming process increasingly comes to be viewed as one more technique of neo-liberal governance. Although mainstreaming does offer new opportunities for bureaucratic interventions in evidence-based policy-making, empowering professionalized NGOs who are deemed to offer objective expert knowledge about gender equality, it also privileges a particularly technocratic rendering of what a gender perspective might entail.

So, whereas gender mainstreaming has been depicted as a radical transformatory equality strategy in theory, recent feminist evaluations of its implementation suggest that it is not always welcomed in practice. Its transformatory potential is all too frequently undermined by assimilatory pressures in practice. What promised to be a radical strategy of displacement looks like a particularly effective strategy of inclusion. Given the limitations of mainstreaming as currently implemented, there is clearly a need for the recuperation of its transformatory potential. Specifically, in order to capture the politically contested nature of equality perspectives, the technocratic consultation with gender experts needs to be complemented by more deliberative consultations with civil society actors.

7 Future Challenges: Negotiating Diversity

Introduction

The two most striking challenges now facing gender equality strategies are the reconfiguration of state practices to embrace technocratic modes of governance, and the widespread embrace of 'diversity' as a governmental priority. These two developments resonate in different ways with the twin concerns that have haunted the three political equality measures under consideration, namely: whether the mechanisms designed to facilitate women's increased political equality lead to the assimilation of women into existing political systems, rather than the transformation of those systems; and whether the mechanisms rely on essentializing notions of women and the women's movement, which fail to recognize a more complex social diversity. While the emergence of a technocratic mode of governance appears to accentuate and entrench concerns about assimilation, the emergence of 'diversity' as a central policy problem appears, by contrast, to confront and unsettle concerns about essentialism.

Where the last two chapters explored the ways in which the emergence of a technocratic mode of governance accentuates concerns about assimilation with respect to women's policy agencies and gender mainstreaming, this chapter interrogates the extent to which the growing concern with diversity might address concerns about essentialism. It argues that advocates of feminist political equality measures might usefully engage with the demands of diversity, reflecting on how these mechanisms might better deal with both the internal differentiation among women, and the interrelation between gender and other equality agendas. It considers mainstreaming practices in terms of diversity, aiming to determine whether and in what ways these might be reconfigured such that they engage with diversity, making this political equality mechanism both more inclusive and more democratic than it has generally been to date.

The chapter suggests that it no longer makes sense to conceive, or pursue, mainstreaming in relation to gender alone. If mainstreaming processes are to adequately address the full range of gender equality concerns they will inevitably need to engage with multiple equalities and their intersections. While there is evidence that mainstreaming is indeed being implemented in relation to other equality strands, there is less evidence of mainstreaming practices systematically addressing the intersections between these. The chapter articulates a conception of diversity mainstreaming that draws on the insights of both gender mainstreaming and intersectionality debates and concludes that mainstreaming theorists have much to gain from exploring the possible synergies between deliberative innovations and their own equality strategies.

From Gender to Diversity

Mainstreaming is most frequently understood as a policy 'to promote equality between men and women' (EU COM (96) 67 final). However, it is increasingly being adopted in relation to other forms of inequality, notably race and disability. This extension of mainstreaming practices to other forms of inequality needs to be understood in the context of the move within the European Union to extend its earlier focus on gender equality to multiple inequalities (Verloo and Lombardo 2006:1). The European Union now recognizes, in art. 13 EC, six key characteristics as requiring measures to combat discrimination: sex, racial and ethnic origin, disability, age, religion and sexual orientation. Given that gender equality advocates have long argued for the need to supplement anti-discrimination policies with mainstreaming practices, mainstreaming is increasingly being considered as a policy process that might realistically be extended beyond gender to address a whole range of other inequality concerns. This raises the prospect of gender mainstreaming becoming eclipsed by 'diversity mainstreaming'.

The promotion of diversity has emerged as a central political priority within Europe over the last few years. While the concept of equality has been central to the European Union's legal order, with the Charter of Fundamental Rights enshrining a range of equality principles (Shaw 2004), the concept of diversity has recently also been recognized explicitly in the EC Treaty: art. 149 EC protects the 'cultural and linguistic diversity' of the educational systems of the member states, while art. 151

EC calls upon the Union to respect the 'national and regional diversity' of member-states (Shaw 2004). Additionally, in 2003 the European Commission launched a five-year, EU-wide information campaign, 'For Diversity – Against Discrimination', aiming to 'promote the positive benefits of diversity for business and for society as a whole' (EC Green Paper 2004:13). These developments have led commentators to suggest that EU equality policies now comprise three strands: ensuring formal anti-discrimination, working towards substantive equality, and managing diversity (Bell 2003).

This European turn to diversity echoes the now ubiquitous appeal to diversity across the Atlantic. Diversity emerged as a significant concept in US affirmative action debates in 1996, with a Court of Appeals ruling that the race-conscious affirmative action program at the University of Texas (Austin) Law School could not be justified on the grounds of the desire to promote 'diversity', only to be overturned by a Supreme Court decision in 2003 in two cases (*Gratz v. Bollinger* and *Grutter v. Bollinger*), which established that promoting diversity could indeed provide the central justification for affirmative action policies. This ruling established diversity as a central concern in US college admissions debates, with the Association of American Universities and Colleges proclaiming diversity as 'a comprehensive institutional commitment and educational priority'. At the same time 'diversity management' emerged as a key human resource management strategy within the corporate sector and is now a central element of good business practice in North America, with 84 per cent of human resource professionals at Fortune 500 companies saying their top-level executives think diversity management is important. As the Society for Human Resource Management tell us: 'appropriate management of a diverse workforce is critical for organizations that seek to improve and maintain their competitive advantage' (13 September 2004). Accordingly, commentators predict that Europe will follow North America in embracing diversity management (Wrench 2005:74).

Within the corporate world diversity policies are depicted as an important complement to equal opportunity policies (Price 2003), and are widely argued to improve the quality of organizations' workforces and act as a catalyst for a better return on companies' investment in human capital. They are also argued to help businesses to capitalize on new markets, attract the best and the brightest employees, increase creativity, and keep the organization flexible (Cartwright 2001). The injunction to manage diversity rests on a 'business case', which maintains that companies need to reflect their customers (because where employees mirror the customers they can understand them, identify their needs and suggest potential new markets) and that diverse teams produce better results (because employees from diverse cultural and educational backgrounds will generate a 'dynamic synergy' of increased creativity). In this private-sector diversity perspective the quest for equality is translated into a theory of management, which retains a general hostility to regulation, but which is 'voluntarily assuming positive obligations to promote equality' (Barmes and Ashtiany 2003:289).

This approach focuses on organizational measures to achieve a positive working environment for a diverse workforce, which might entail differential treatment on grounds of race, sex or other barriers to participation, within the limits of formal equality laws and so long as the aim is to promote diversity. Among organizations that do not have customers *per se*, such as the International Monetary Fund, diversity is perceived as a matter of corporate legitimacy and accountability, enabling them to claim good governance in terms of being 'modern', representative and expertly staffed. For such organizations diversity management is less about managing a diverse workforce, or understanding a diverse customer base, than about legitimizing or transforming elite and unrepresentative workforces. The fact that such institutions also have diversity strategies and diversity managers, largely as a process of corporate legitimization, is testimony to the strength of the corporate diversity frame.

This corporate discourse advocates not just 'valuing diversity' but 'managing diversity', locating diversity in relation to corporate human resource management and conceiving it primarily as a means of producing economic productivity rather than social justice (Wrench 2002). As the Society for Human Resource Management states:

> Under this scenario, capitalizing on diversity is seen as a strategic approach to business that contributes to organizational goals such as profits and productivity. It also does not involve any legal requirements and is not implemented just to avoid lawsuits. Managing diversity moves beyond valuing diversity in that it is a way in which to do business and should be aligned with other organizational strategic plans. (Society for Human Resource Management 2004)

In this context, some theorists adopt a highly sceptical view of 'diversity', locating the emergence of diversity management within the logic of Taylorized capitalism (Hennessey 2000) and deploring the replacement of a moral issue by a business strategy (Wrench 2002:10).

Feminists have also been rather sceptical about this shift from an exclusive focus on gender to a more wide-ranging concern with diversity and multiple inequalities (Woodward 2005). There are fears that the recognition of multiple inequalities will generate a 'hierarchy of oppression' in which different equality groups fight over scarce resources and institutional access. Moreover, one of the consequences of the growing European concern to devise institutions and laws that address multiple inequalities is the establishment of equality commissions and policy agencies that frequently replace dedicated women's policy agencies, thereby apparently eroding many of the institutional gains made by feminists during the past decade.

In addition, there is a profound concern among many feminists that other equality strands may have demands that run counter to those of women's equality groups. For instance, many feminists have expressed concern that the recognition of ethnic minority and religious group rights may limit and erode the pursuit of gender equality (Okin 1999; Shachar 2001; Skjeie 2007), leading to anxieties that a multiple equalities agenda may undermine rather than facilitate gender justice. Okin argued that while most cultures entail practices that disadvantage women, some minority cultures affirm particularly oppressive practices, such as polygamy, and that to affirm these cultures via multicultural exemptions would be to erode hard-won gender equality norms (Okin 1999). Critics of this argument, on the other hand, view it as assuming a hierarchy of cultures and defending one particular vision of gender equality that is simply insensitive to cultural diversity. The apparent difficulties entailed in accommodating minority cultures and respecting women's rights (Reitman 2005) have at times encouraged critics of multiculturalist policies to use gender equality 'as part of the demonisation of minority cultural groups' (Phillips 2006:3). While some of the concerns about multicultural exemptions clearly appeal to women's rights considerations in a rather strategic way, to justify otherwise apparently illiberal social attitudes, there are deeply felt concerns among gender equality advocates that the pursuit of a cultural or religious equality agenda may conflict with their own (Skjeie 2007). The extension of mainstreaming processes to fields other than gender has therefore been perceived by some feminists as a worrying development, signalling a diminution of concern with gender and a marginalization of feminist concerns in the policy agenda. However, it is hard to discern normatively persuasive grounds for refusing to extend equality considerations to other oppressed social groups, or for considering the differences among individuals within these groups. One of the virtues of a diversity agenda lies in the possibilities it opens up for considering the similarities in the nature of equality claims being made by peoples across groups, as well as the differences within them.

Intersectionality: Additive and Transversal

Rather than viewing the diversity agenda as a straightforward threat to gender equality, it is important to recognize that it may empower some women, where their particular concerns have not been prioritized in dominant gender equality discourses. Tellingly, while there is a clear anxiety among many feminists about the diversity agenda, there is evidence that the way in which feminists respond to the diversity agenda will depend both on the status of the women's policy agencies relative to other equality strands and the dominant normative framing of gender equality in relation to questions of intersectionality. Where women's policy agencies have the greatest relative status and where gender equality has been conceived in a way that fails to consider issues of intersectionality, the diversity agenda is likely to be perceived primarily as a threat (Squires 2006). For these reasons, Nordic state feminist responses to the challenges of diversity are likely to be particularly anxious given that gender equality has such a privileged status in these countries and has not generally been attentive to differences among women (Hobson *et al.* 2007; Siim 2007), frequently obscuring the experiences of immigrant and ethnic minority women (Mulanari 2001; Towns 2002). Where, as in the UK, other equality strands have achieved legal or institutional gains from which women may benefit, and where feminists have accepted the importance of intersectionality considerations, the diversity agenda is likely to be perceived primarily as an opportunity for advancement.

Diversity is not an external agenda, imposed upon gender equality debates: it has been subject to an 'extensive theoretical investigation' by feminist theorists (Shaw 2004:3), who have long recognized the importance of understanding intersectionalities and multiple identities (hooks 1981, 1989). For instance, intersectionality was central to debates in Britain at the end of the 1970s concerning the 'triple oppression' of black, working-class women (Anthias and Yuval-Davis 1983). More recently, a concern with 'intersectionality' was central to feminist preparations for the 2001 UN World Conference Against Racism (Yuval-Davis 2005). As Collins suggests, 'viewing gender within a logic of intersectionality redefines it as a constellation of ideas and social practices that are historically situated within and that mutually construct multiple systems of oppression' (Collins 2000:263). This suggests that there are good feminist reasons for being concerned with intersectionality, and for considering the ways in which gender mainstreaming practices might take multiple inequalities and the intersections between them into account more systematically than has been the case to date.

One of the central dynamics in feminist debates about intersectionality has been whether to interpret intersectionality as an additive or a constitutive process, framed by identity or transversal politics (Yuval-Davis 1994, 1997). An identity politics generates an additive model of intersectionality, in which each axis of discrimination is distinct. One of the dangers of this approach to multiple discriminations, popularized by American scholars (Crenshaw 1991), is the tendency for each axis of discrimination to become isolated from all the others (Shaw 2004:21). One of the strengths of the additive approach, however, is that it remains attentive to the distinctive nature of each inequality strand, avoiding an over-simplistic assumption that all inequalities are of the same order and therefore amenable to the same sort of policy response. It allows one to differentiate between different kinds of differences (Yuval-Davis 2006:199). As the European Women's Lobby suggests, 'different equality agendas have their specific dynamics of inclusion, exclusion and marginalization and consequently need specific analysis and actions in order to find the best strategies' (European Women's Lobby 2004:2).

By contrast, an alternative epistemological approach, which unsettles standpoint arguments by introducing a more dialogical approach to the diversity (Benhabib 1992), advocates the creation of strategic alliances based on a transversal politics (Cockburn 1998; Eschle 2001; Yuval-Davis 1994, 1997). Transversal politics was developed in contradistinction to both universalistic and identity politics. Challenging both the false neutrality of the integrationist approach of universalistic politics and the essentializing reification of identity politics that adopted a strategy of reversal, this approach emphasizes the importance of communication – both horizontally and vertically – needed to construct a radical political collective (Guattari 1974). Where the addititive model of identity politics leads to fragmentation, the dynamic model of transversal politics allows for a more integrated approach. From the transversal perspective, any attempt to essentialize 'blackness', 'womanhood' or 'working-class' as a specific form of concrete oppression 'conflates identity politics narratives with descriptions of positionality' (Yuval-Davis 2005).

Transversal politics entails three key features (Yuval-Davis 2004:16): first, a dialogical standpoint epistemology, which recognizes that as the world is seen differently from different standpoints any one standpoint will be 'unfinished' and dialogue between those with different standpoints will produce a fuller knowledge (Collins 2000:236); second, the principle of encompassment, in which differences are recognized as important but encompassed by a broader commitment to equality (Yuval-Davis and Werbner 1999); third, a distinction between positioning, identity and values, whereby people who identify themselves with a social category can be positioned differently in relation to a range of social locations and can also have very different social and political values (Yuval-Davis 1997, 2004). Together these three principles make an interactive universalism possible (Benhabib 1992:227), as participants engage in dialogue to negotiate a common political position, mutually reconstructing themselves and others in the process. What follows from this transversal approach has profound implications for the conceptualization of diversity mainstreaming. Rather than attempting to develop gender, race, disability, sexuality and age mainstreaming as discreet processes, it offers the potential for developing a more cohesive diversity approach.

Diversity Mainstreaming

If mainstreaming processes are to adequately address the full range of equality concerns confronting us today, they will inevitably need to engage with multiple equality strands, and the ways in which they intersect. There ought therefore to be potential to take the lessons learnt from attempts to develop gender mainstreaming practices and to apply them to a newer agenda of diversity mainstreaming.

To date, the diversity agenda has largely taken the form of an anti-discrimination approach and has not yet really echoed the developments in gender equality, which moved from anti-discrimination alone to embrace issues of equality of outcome and mainstreaming processes (Rees 1998). Given the current normative concerns and legal requirements to consider equality in relation to various strands, including age, disability, race, religion, sexuality and gender, mainstreaming is increasingly required to speak to diversity. This means that, while mainstreaming emerged in relation to gender equality debates, it is now frequently implemented in relation to a wide range of inequality strands. The EU, for example, which claims to be in favour of an integrated approach to combat 'multiple discrimination' (European Commission 2004:3), depicts itself as a learning institution capable of transferring knowledge achieved in the area of gender to the treatment of other inequalities (Verloo 2005).

Within the EU, mainstreaming is now being used to address race inequality (Shaw 2005) and disability (European Commission 2005) and many development agencies promote the concept of disability mainstreaming (Disability KaR 2006). The British Equal Opportunities Commission defines mainstreaming as a way of mainstreaming equal opportunities generally, not gender equality in particular, stating that:

> Mainstreaming equality is essentially concerned with the integration of equal opportunities principles, strategies and practices into the everyday work of Government and other public bodies from the outset, involving 'every day' policy actors in addition to equality specialists. In other words, it entails rethinking mainstream provision to accommodate gender, race, disability and other dimensions of discrimination and disadvantage, including class, sexuality and religion. (EOC http://www.eoc.org.uk)

Similarly, though dropping the mention of 'class' as is all too common in debates about equality and diversity (Coole 1996), the devolved administrations in Scotland, Wales and Northern Ireland are currently pursuing 'equalities mainstreaming' (Chaney 2003; Donaghy 2004: Mackay and Bilton 2000). Here mainstreaming works with a multiple equality approach, requiring due regard for the need to promote equality of opportunity: (a) between persons of different religious belief, political opinion, racial group, age, marital status or sexual orientation; (b) between men and women generally; (c) between persons with a disability and persons without; and (d) between persons with dependents and persons without (Donaghy 2004; McCrudden 2001).

However, while the trend to extend mainstreaming to multiple equality strands is clear, Shaw suggests that 'there has been limited progress with mainstreaming techniques away from the field of gender' (Shaw 2005:6) and 'no comprehensive programme of equality mainstreaming cutting across various equality grounds' (Shaw 2005:6) at the EU level. Similarly, other commentators note that where diversity is considered it is frequently listed as a factor 'in addition to gender' (CIDA 1999:6), and while attention is sometimes drawn to multiply marginalized women the focus of mainstreaming remains on 'gender-in-general' (Teghtsoonian 1999:5). The process of extending mainstreaming from gender to other equality strands, and of creating 'diversity mainstreaming' practices, demands that the nature of mainstreaming be rethought. As Verloo rightly notes, 'the fact that inequalities are dissimilar means that such 'equality mainstreaming cannot be a simple adaptation of current tools of gender mainstreaming' (Verloo 2006:222). There is still some way to go in terms of developing mainstreaming processes that address multiple inequalities (Hankivsky 2005).

There is, inevitably, a division of opinion among feminists as to whether this extension of mainstreaming to embrace 'diversity' rather than just gender is a positive development. Sceptical of the move, Woodward asks whether 'gender will fall out of mainstreaming' (Woodward 2005:2), noting that 'to mainstream' is a policy verb now frequently used without the prefix 'gender' as a technique for inserting a policy theme horizontally. A recent Belgian evaluation of mainstreaming concluded that:

> there is a real fear that GM will be used as a strategy to stop support for specific target actions for women. There is also a fear that gender mainstreaming will disappear in a larger whole of diversity policy, wherein the specificity of gender will not be accounted for. It needs to be made clear that GM is not just a synonym for diversity policy, and that GM should not hinder positive actions being taken for (specific groups of) women. (Van Roemberg and Spee 2004:65 cited in Woodward 2005)

More generally, critics of mainstreaming view it as encouraging a shift away from a focus on 'women's issues and a reduction in specific programmes targeted at women' (True 2003:369). This tendency to view the emergence of the diversity frame as a threat is informed by an additive model of intersectionality, in which the various equality strands are viewed as discrete and competing. The argument that the consideration of other inequalities will dilute efforts spent on gender mainstreaming and result in the loss of understanding of the specific structural causes of gender inequality (Woodward 2003) relies on the idea that blacks and migrants are competing with women for resources, which in turn implies that there are no women among the blacks or migrants, and no blacks or migrants among the women.

On the other hand, Rees argues that limiting mainstreaming to gender equality is conceptually flawed given the diversity among women and men, and suggests that one of the real virtues of this approach is that mainstreaming allows for the recognition of cross-cutting diversity in a manner that neither the equal treatment nor positive discrimination models is able to do (Rees 2002:54). Similarly Beveridge and Nott argue that there is a logical tension within gender mainstreaming, for it is impossible to focus on 'the real lives of people' and to see only gender (Beveridge and Nott 2002:311). They therefore conclude that the mainstreaming concept calls into question the privileged position of gender, as opposed to other equality strands such as race, disability, age, sexuality and religious belief (Beveridge and Nott 2002:311). Following up this insight some theorists have expressly advocated a more committed embrace of diversity mainstreaming, arguing that gender mainstreaming is inherently limited and flawed 'because it always prioritizes gender as *the* axis of discrimination', and should be replaced by an alternative and broader strategy of diversity mainstreaming (Hankivsky 2005:978). What is needed, Hankivsky suggests, is 'a broader approach to mainstreaming, one that is able to consistently and systematically reflect a deeper understanding of intersectionalities'. Similarly, Shaw suggests that mainstreaming is the appropriate policy mechanism for implementing a diversity perspective (Shaw 2005:23). But, if it is difficult to determine what a 'gender perspective' is, how much more difficult will it be to determine what a diversity perspective might be?

Given the ways in which mainstreaming has tended to be implemented, the attempt to apply it to other equality strands in addition to gender has generally been conceived as an additive technical process rather than a more genuinely integrated approach to intersectionality. The theoretical challenge is to articulate a conception of diversity mainstreaming that draws on the best insights of gender mainstreaming and intersectionality debates, drawing on the participative-democratic approach to the former and the transversal approach to the latter. Central to the articulation of both these elements is a form of deliberative democratic exchange, which encourages interaction between advocates of distinct equality strands and fosters the development of cross-cutting rather than competing goals. For, given the plurality of equality agendas held by diverse groups and the difficulty of ascertaining the nature of these by bureaucratic mechanisms alone, the role of inclusive deliberation should be stressed when attempting to develop mainstreaming practices in relation to diversity rather than just gender. This would transform mainstreaming from a technocratic tool to an institutional manifestation of deliberative democracy.

Attempts to develop mainstreaming processes based on an identity politics that generates an additive model of intersectionality will inevitably result not in a coherent practice of diversity mainstreaming – but in a series of distinct, and frequently competing, mainstreaming processes taking each inequality as a separate consideration. The expert-bureaucratic model of diversity mainstreaming therefore appears to require the embedding of a series of parallel technical mainstreaming practices. These practices would however inevitably tend to treat each equality strand separately: seeking statistics disaggregated by a series of classifications (age, gender, religion and so on), and carrying out serial impact assessments with respect of these categories. Yet such an approach to mainstreaming does not engage directly with the issue of 'diversity': rather it approaches its constituent elements in a piecemeal fashion.

One might therefore look to the alternative participative-democratic model of gender mainstreaming as the basis for developing a more genuinely diversity-focused model of mainstreaming. Yet the embrace of a participative-democratic mainstreaming model does not in and of itself ensure that diversity would be addressed in a more integrated manner than this. For here mainstreaming would require a broadening out of the range of actors involved in the policy-making process, via a visible increase in social dialogue through the institutionalization of consultation practices, the creation or consolidation of advisory bodies representing a series of distinct social groups or an increase in government investment with a view to equipping their respective representatives with the necessary skills to participate in policy-making (Beveridge *et al.* 2000; Daly 2005:442–3; Donaghy and Kelly 2001; Mackay and Bilton 2000; Mazey 2002; Squires and Wickham-Jones 2001). The difficulty with these attempts to extend mainstreaming to equality considerations other than gender is that they too remain additive and fail to engage with the issue of intersectionality as long as they concentrate on separate consultations with existing social groups. Fragmentation inevitably arises from this additive approach given the emphasis placed on identity politics, whereby political judgements were held to develop from one's own standpoint. These standpoints are generally held to attach to groups rather than individuals, meaning that any member of that group could speak for all other members of that category. However, marginalized voices within identity groups have challenged repeatedly the representativeness of the representative voice, thereby leading to the multiplication of representative voices (Yuval-Davis 2004:7), which ultimately renders this approach unworkable.

Although, at a theoretical level, diversity mainstreaming requires a 'truly integrated analysis, one that systematically captures the interstices of all factors of oppression' (Hankivsky 2005:993), there have been limited attempts to pursue this challenge to date, with various forms of mainstreaming generally being undertaken in isolation. However, intersectional analysis has been introduced into gender mainstreaming analyses as a means of considering the 'full diversity of women's experiences' (Center for Women's Global Leadership 2001:1), using disaggregated data collection, contextual analysis, an intersectional review of policy initiatives, and the implementations of intersectional policy initiatives (see Center for Women's Global Leadership 2001). There is clearly the potential here to implement a transversal approach to intersectionality, analysing 'the differential ways in which different social divisions are concretely enmeshed and constructed by each other and how they relate to political and subjective construction of identities' (Yuval-Davis 2005). But there is also the danger that this form of mainstreaming will simply become another facet of a rather more bland form of diversity management.

Interestingly, Rees is attuned to the potential consonance between mainstreaming and diversity management. She argues that there are three key principles in mainstreaming: treating the individual as a whole person; democracy; and justice, fairness and equity (Rees 2005:564). Treating the individual as a whole person entails challenging stereotypical assumptions and embracing difference while at the same time avoiding the pitfalls of biological essentialism. One of the tools she pinpoints as pursuing this principle is the modernization of human resource management (Rees 2005:565). However, she suggests that the motivation for mainstreaming is linked more to justice, fairness and equity than it is to the business case that underpins diversity management. Yet her own account of the mainstreaming tools that aspire to treat the individual as a whole person sound very similar to the practices articulated by human resources managers implementing diversity management. Rees therefore acknowledges that 'many of the tools invoked to mainstream equality and to manage diversity are the same or similar' (Rees 2005:568), while maintaining that the former is motivated by social justice and the latter by a business case. But what difference, in practice, will motivation make if the tools are the same? Can we to be confident that different sorts of outcome will result? Perhaps we need to take a closer look at the tools.

The role of 'democracy' as one of the key principles of mainstreaming becomes particularly central here, as this is where we might be able to distinguish most clearly between diversity mainstreaming and diversity management, between the pursuit of social justice and greater economic productivity. Although Rees states that democracy is an integral part of the mainstreaming process, she does not detail the manner in which this manifests itself. When it comes to outlining the tools that deliver on this principle Rees lists the following: transparency in government; legislation on gender balance; consultative procedures; and national machineries for women. She notes that quota policies are often used to secure gender-balanced decision-making, but suggests that quotas are better viewed as positive action policies rather than a mainstreaming tool (Rees 2005:566). Interestingly, she doesn't elaborate on consultation and national machineries for women, despite having listed them. This suggests an awareness of the importance of locating mainstreaming in relation to democratic innovations, but a lack of clarity as to what this framing might entail.

In fact, the democratic tools appropriate to diversity mainstreaming will vary depending on the approaches to intersectionality adopted. The additive model of intersectionality suggests that series of discrete impact assessments are needed (assuming a technocratic mainstreaming model), possibly supplemented with consultation with a range of spokespeople for the various inequality strands (allowing for a more participative-democratic rendering of mainstreaming). However, neither of these processes promises to address issues of transversal intersectionality, for which a more deliberative approach to mainstreaming is required. This approach suggests that mainstreaming processes should be concerned with equalizing participation within decision-making institutions and processes in order to allow people an equal capacity to shape the social and physical world in which they live. The shift from identity to transversal politics therefore demands that we direct our attention away from the idea that people represent groups by virtue of a shared identity, and towards the idea that advocates can broaden their horizons by engaging in dialogue with others. The claim to speak for others cannot be based on identity alone; it must be a product of a dialogic process.

Of course, while transversal feminist politics depend on as comprehensive a dialogic approach as possible (Yuval-Davis 2004:35), opportunities for dialogue are inevitably constrained by existing structural inequalities and social norms. In practice, as we saw in the last chapter, the dialogues that have taken place between femocrats and women in civil society have generally been conversations with feminist NGOs, which are directly accountable only to their funders. The professionalization of feminist politics, whereby a business network of trained gender experts has largely replaced social movement activism, means that the nature of the dialogue has become increasingly bound by the conventions of rationalist epistemologies and the predetermined strategic goals. The values that emerge from this dialogue, the feminist values advocated by femocrats and gender experts, are delimited by the horizons of the participants. A wider dialogue, encompassing a greater diversity of participants, would no doubt produce different – and more democratic because more inclusive – values. This suggests that the elitism of professional feminist NGOs and the expertise of those engaged in evidence-based policy-making may need to be countered by other, more deliberative, devices.

Significantly, Yuval-Davis's commitment to a transversal rather than additive conception of intersectionality leads her to emphasize democratic dialogue rather than group consultation or diversity management as central to mainstreaming processes. The fact that transversal intersectionality requires contextual analysis makes deliberation particularly central, for as Yuval-Davis suggests: 'The differential positionings of the participants in such a dialogue from which they gaze at the situation should be acknowledged while they should not be considered representatives of any fixed social groupings' (Yuval-Davis 2005). The transversal approach to intersectionality therefore lends weight to the importance of using deliberative rather than statistical mechanisms, for here the complexity of intersectional analysis can be accommodated more readily. Where the mainstreaming tool appropriate to the additive model is the collection and analysis of disaggregated data by experts, the tool appropriate to the transversal model is closer to the dialogue facilitated by citizen's juries and deliberative forums currently being explored in various forms of democratic innovation, not widely associated with mainstreaming practices.

This in turn suggests that if mainstreaming is to become diversity mainstreaming rather than 'simply' gender mainstreaming or diversity management, its advocates should explore these forms of democratic innovation rather more closely than they have done to date. Mainstreaming needs to be located in relation to democratic theory in order to facilitate its engagement with diversity, which requires a participative-democratic approach to mainstreaming in addition to an expert-bureaucratic one precisely because it uses both disaggregated data and democratic dialogue as its centrals tools of analysis: disaggregated data in order to establish where inequality of outcome indicates that existing norms result in structural discrimination, and democratic dialogue in order to negotiate new equality norms that are more inclusive and therefore genuinely impartial.

Deliberation and Diversity

Distinguishing between incumbent and critical democracy, Blaug suggests that the former describes 'liberal, realist, representative, institutional and protective' democratic practices and the latter describes 'deliberative, direct, developmental and personal' democratic practices (Blaug 2002:105–6).

The incumbent model conceives democracy as an institutionalized, rule-governed procedure, where participation becomes primarily instrumental and ethical considerations are subsumed to the adjudication of interests and aggregation of preferences. Its strength lies in its effectiveness, its power to centrally command resources and the stability it offers. Its weakness lies in its tendency to degenerate into competitive elitism (Blaug 2002:105). The critical model, by contrast, conceives democracy as a response to suffering, which entails face-to-face debate within local and peripheral sites and involves resistance to elite governance. Its strength lies in its rapid transformation of citizen capacities, interrelationships and self-descriptions. Its negative side lies in its lack of attention to concrete institutions and procedures and disengagement with power politics.

Contemporary democratic theorists aiming to revitalize existing democratic practices in the face of obvious political disaffection within democratic regimes frequently aspire to bring critical practices into the institutions of incumbent democracy. These include electoral innovations such as electronic voting, compulsory voting and reducing the voting age; consultation innovations such as public opinion surveys, community visioning, participatory theatre, citizens' panels and focus groups; deliberative innovations such as citizens' juries, deliberative opinion polling and consensus conferences; and direct democracy innovations including referenda (Smith 2005). These innovations are motivated by a desire to increase and deepen citizen participation in the political decision-making process.

Of these practical innovations, it is the deliberative democratic practices that have most obviously captured the imagination of democratic theorists. Deliberative approaches are argued to have significant advantages over consultative approaches. Standard techniques of consultation tend to attract citizens who already have a strong political interest, moreover the relationship between consultation and decision-making is not always clear and feedback rarely provided; as a result there is widespread scepticism that consultation is used to legitimate decisions that have already been made. This raises concerns about the model of 'participative-democratic' mainstreaming advocated by many feminists as an alternative to the expert-bureaucratic model, for those practices that have been labelled as participative-democratic to date tend to rely on consultation rather than deliberation. By contrast, deliberative approaches bring together a cross-section of the population so that all citizens have an equal opportunity to participate, and the outcomes of deliberation reflect citizen's considered judgements rather than given preferences. Attempts to increase and deepen the participation of citizens in mainstreaming processes might therefore usefully entail deliberative innovations.

It makes particular sense for mainstreaming theorists to engage with theories of deliberative democracy, which have attempted to explore 'discursive mechanisms for the transmission of public opinion to the state' (Dryzek 2000:162). Significantly, advocates of deliberative democracy – in a move akin to that made by advocates of mainstreaming – suggest that the idea of democracy revolves around the transformation of preferences, rather than simply their aggregation. The basic impulse behind deliberative democracy is the notion that people will modify their perceptions of what society should do in the course of discussing this with others. The point of democratic participation is to manufacture, rather than to discover and aggregate, the common good. The ideal is one of democratic decision-making arising from deliberative procedures that are inclusive and rational (Miller 2002:202). A deliberative decision will have taken all relevant evidence, perspectives and persons into account, and will not favour some over others on morally arbitrary grounds (Williams 2000). Legitimacy here requires not only a lack of bias, but also inclusivity. The deliberative project is 'to conceive of how we might reflect critically, and impartially, on principles of justice without abstracting from concrete needs and interests that are particular to some social group or other' (O'Neill 1997:55). This will be possible only if we can ground these principles in a 'reasonable yet open and unrestricted dialogue in the public domain' (O'Neill 1997:56). In other words, we find in the deliberative democracy literature very similar concerns to those within the mainstreaming literature, though the language is different: both aspire to bring diverse perspectives to bear on the formulation of norms and policies in order that contingent distortions and systematic limitations might be exposed and replaced by more impartial norms or policies. It is for this reason that it makes sense to think about mainstreaming in relation to deliberative democracy.

This recommendation needs to be tempered, though, by the significant feminist critiques of deliberative theories, especially in their Habermassian formulation (Meehan 1995), including in particular the gender-blindness of Habermas's work (Benhabib 1992); the marginalization of the aesthetic-expressive (Coole 1996a; Sitton 2003; Squires 1998); and the restrictive formulation of the public sphere (Everingham 1994; Fraser 1996). Accepting the gravity of these critiques, an appeal to deliberative democracy would ideally be grounded in a non-Habermassian dialogical ethics, in which consensus presupposes communication, not vice versa. Nonetheless, what deliberative democrats offer theorists of mainstreaming is a concern with the quality and form of engagement between citizens and participatory forums, stressing in particular the importance of political equality and inclusivity, and of unconstrained dialogue (Smith 2005:39). Deliberative democrats, like gender mainstreaming theorists, suggest that if the decision-making process is inclusive and dialogue unconstrained, a greater understanding between different perspectives is more likely to be realized, and outcomes more widely accepted by participants likely to be achieved. The emphasis that deliberative democrats place on inclusion and dialogue offer rich resources to counter the technocratic tendency in the integrationist model of mainstreaming. Where the integrationist model emphasizes the importance of 'gender expertise' and creates an elite body of professional gender experts, a deliberative rendering of diversity mainstreaming would emphasize the importance of dialogue with diverse social groups. This is particularly significant given that the move to consider diversity rather than simply gender equality renders the process of mainstreaming infinitely more complex.

Moreover, if theories of deliberation have much to offer theories of mainstreaming, the reverse might also be true. For although deliberative democrats have placed great emphasis on inclusion and deliberative decision-making they have had relatively little to say about the practical institutional arrangements that might facilitate such inclusive deliberation: the deliberative democracy literature remains highly abstract and 'fails to engage with the "messy" and more detailed task of institutional design' (Smith 2003:79). Indeed, when one does look at the institutional arrangements proposed by deliberative democrats they appear to embody not simply the dialogical conception of impartiality, but rather a two-track model in which the monological and the dialogical have distinct roles, located within clearly demarcated political practices (Squires 2002:133–56).

For example, Habermas suggests that legitimacy is based on 'rationally motivated agreement' that is produced in 'un-deformed public spheres' through actual processes of deliberation. The general public sphere is not a mere 'back room' of democratic politics, but rather an 'impulse-generating periphery that surrounds the political centre: in cultivating normative reasons, it affects all parts of the political system without intending to conquer it.' In other words he draws a clear distinction between 'un-deformed', informal or weak public spheres where public opinion may be formed, and the strong, 'arranged', formal sites of institutionalized dialogue, which must be open to influence from the weak public spheres (Habermas 1996:147). This implies that political decisions in complex and pluralistic societies can be rational and hence legitimate in a deliberative-democratic sense – that is, rationally authored by the citizens to whom they are addressed – if institutionalized decision-making procedures follow two tracks. Political decisions must be both open to inputs from an informal, vibrant public sphere (contexts of discovery) and appropriately structured to support the rationality of the relevant types of discourse and to ensure implementation (contexts of justification). This two-track model of deliberative democracy distinguishes between communication oriented toward mutual understanding on the one hand and instrumental action and politics on the other.

However, while the deliberative-democratic literature has focused on the importance of active civil society and the reinvigoration of the public sphere, there is surprisingly little attention as to how the deliberations from within civil society are to be transmitted to the more formal arena of political decision-making. In one of the rare exceptions, Smith maps out three models for the transmission of public opinion into decision-making: mediation, citizens' forums, and citizen initiatives and referendums (Smith 2003:80). Mediation brings together different parties who are in dispute and aims to achieve resolution of conflict such that all parties involved are satisfied and in agreement as to the way forward (Smith 2003:81). Citizen forums include deliberative opinion polls (in which a cross-section of the population is asked to discuss an issue of public concern and the individual views are recorded), and citizens' juries (in which a selection of citizens are asked to come to a collective decision on a specified issue after a period of deliberation) (Smith 2003:86–7). Citizen initiatives and referendums allow citizens to vote directly on policy issues (Smith 2003:93). Smith suggests that there is no single 'best' design and that the models need not be thought of in isolation but could be combined.

Deliberative innovations such as citizens' juries, consensus conferences, deliberative opinion polls and deliberative mapping are growing in number and significance (see Smith 2005:39–55). Evidence suggests that these mechanisms do indeed facilitate the capacity to produce recommendations on complex public policy issues that are informed by a wide variety of experiences and viewpoints (Smith 2005:55). One practical example of this type of development can be found in the UK Women's Unit establishment of women's juries, providing 'an opportunity for women whose voices are not normally heard to contribute more directly to the policy-making process' (Ruddock 1998:col. 409). In addition to strengthening their links with women's organizations and reviewing the Women's National Commission, the Unit aimed to

> reach out to women who do not join organisations to hear the views of those who do not normally take part in consultative exercises. They

> are the people who most often feel cut off and alienated from the world of politics and government. (Ruddock 1998: col. 614)

They did this by establishing two pilot women's juries, building on the model of citizens' juries, in which a small group of citizens is asked to take part in an informed and extended discussion on a policy question. This was conceived as a 'a deliberative process. It is not like a focus group, which researches public opinion. The jury model is intended to improve and enrich our democratic practice', complementing the normal channels of consultation and decision-making, 'adding a distinctive voice that is not usually heard, especially in the House' (Ruddock 1998: col. 614). The two juries made over sixty recommendations, covering a range of issues including the regulation of childcare, parental leave, and part-time working. While these were women's juries, there is no reason why this model could not be extended to encompass citizens' juries in light of the growing commitment to diversity mainstreaming.

This suggests that the participatory-democratic model of mainstreaming may usefully explore the resources of deliberative democracy in general, and citizens' juries in particular, especially in the context of an attempt to negotiate diversity in a transversal rather than an additive manner. These mechanisms should be considered in relation to mainstreaming policies, and the potential of integrating these deliberative transmission mechanisms into a transformative model of mainstreaming should be explored. This would generate a model of mainstreaming that is deliberative, rather than bureaucratic or consultative, and that aims primarily to denaturalize and thereby politicize policy norms, rather than to pursue neutral policy-making or to recognize marginalized voices. The strengths of this potential model are that it would be sensitive to diverse citizen perspectives without reifying group identities, thereby avoiding the charge of essentialism, and would allow deliberations for within civil society to be transmitted to the formal arena of political decision-making without becoming rhetorically entrapped, thereby avoiding the charge of assimilation.

Conclusion

There has been a twofold focus in recent feminist campaigns and scholarship: one focusing on women's political representation and promoting strategies to increase their descriptive presence in the electoral sphere in the form of gender quotas, and the other focusing on women's political interests and promoting strategies to increase their substantive realization in the bureaucratic sphere in the form of women's policy agencies and gender mainstreaming. While these two strategies have been linked in policy debates, with practitioners endorsing a twin-track strategy entailing both campaigns to increase women's representation in decision-making bodies and the establishment of gender machineries, they have not been as closely linked in theoretical debates as one would expect. Significantly, there is no body of literature that considers the interactions between gender quotas and gender machineries. This matters, I think, because quotas offer a mechanism for securing increased participation in one particular electoral moment. Yet democratic participation could usefully be conceived more broadly than this. The emergence of governance brings with it changes in the nature of both politics and policy-making, creating new sites of democratic engagement. Governance emerges as a response to the new reality of network society, whereby new networks erode the power of previously powerful institutions, redefining state authority in ways that are characterized by greater flexibility and experimentation. These policy networks unsettle traditional top-down bureaucratic structures, changing the way in which policy-making is conducted. These developments allow for the possibility of both technocratic governance and 'expansive democracy' and will only entail the latter if actors are attuned to the need to facilitate new forms of democratic inclusion.

There is an emerging rhetorical claim that neo-liberal forms of governance have given way to a new form of joined-up, inclusive governance, 'characterised by relationships of collaboration, trust and, above all, partnership' (Larner and Craig 2005:402). Some have argued that these new forms of governance are simply a 'compensatory mechanism for the inadequacies of the market mechanism' (Jessop 2002:455). Others argue that these partnerships represent a new form of governance based on trust and collaboration (Newman 2001, 2006; Rhodes 1994, 1996, 2000). This could be viewed as a 'roll-out' form of neo-liberalism (Peck and Tickell 2002), promoted by those intent on distancing themselves from the 'roll-back' form of neo-liberalism in order to create improved social integration and better facilitate the regulation of capital (Larner and Craig 2005:403). Whereas earlier forms of governance required managers with bureaucratic skills, this newer form of partnership governance requires 'strategic brokers', who have the ability to network with community activists and promote change, creating a newly professionalized cohort of 'social entrepreneurs' (Larner and Craig 2005:405). Interestingly, women are disproportionately represented in these brokering roles (Larner and Craig 2005:420), suggesting that this new mode of governance has both facilitated, and been facilitated by, feminist demands for greater political inclusion and critiques of hierarchical modes of government.

Significantly, state feminists have acted as key strategic brokers, working with feminist activists and women's organizations to create partnerships with a professionalized network of 'gender experts'. Together, the strategic brokers within women's policy agencies and social entrepreneurs within women's NGOs have created powerful new forms of governance designed to improve the social integration of women. This has clearly empowered many women politically, but it has also 'governmentalized' their professional functions and political ambitions.

Governance focuses on the ability of decision-makers to secure compliance with policy decisions both inside and outside bureaucracies. As Goetz notes, 'when it comes to gender-equality policy measures, considerable state capacity is required to compel compliance with what both state employees, policy or service clients, and the general public may view as profoundly counter-cultural policy goals' (Goetz 2005:5). Given the nature of the demands placed on the state by a gender-equality policy agenda, there have inevitably been 'serious gender-specific capacity failures in all of the public institutions targeted in the governance agenda' (Goetz 2005:5). The rapid and extensive introduction and implementation of gender quotas, women's policy agencies and gender mainstreaming have worked to address this issue, with varying degrees of success globally. Yet, however successful they have been in this regard, it is important to note that this pursuit of effective governance does not necessarily include notions of democratic justice.

Although many feminist advocates of women's policy agencies consider these institutions to have a representative function, the staff in these agencies are in fact directly accountable to the elected government rather than to the women's movement, or particular organizations within it. Similarly, while many advocates of gender mainstreaming have stressed its participatory function, allowing women's perspectives to be taken into account in the policy-making process, mainstreaming practices actually rely on technocratic data collection and impact assessments carried out by professionalized gender experts. These are primarily mechanisms of governance rather than democratic voice. The recent feminist preoccupation with these mechanisms reveals a shift of focus away from democratic participation and the pursuit of political equality, and towards governance and the implementation of gender-equality policy measures. While the latter is clearly important, it is crucial to maintain a commitment to the former, for without inclusive deliberation as to what gender equality entails – and therefore what form gender-equality policies should take – the pursuit of gender equality can itself become an exclusionary process, undertaken for considerations of utility rather than justice. To mainstream gender is not necessarily to democratize the state (Rai 2003). Future feminist political practices need to be attentive not only to fostering modes of governance that take the pursuit of gender equality as a policy goal, but also to ways of facilitating a more inclusive democratic debate as to what gender equality comprises.

Bibliography

Ackerly, B. and S. Moller Okin (1999) 'Feminist social criticism and the international movement for women's rights as human rights', in I. Shapiro and C. Hacker-Cordón (eds) *Democracy's Edge*. Cambridge University Press, 134–62.

Agacinski, S. (2001) *Parity of the Sexes*, trans. L. Walsh. New York: Columbia University Press.

Alvarez, S. (1999) 'Advocating feminism: the Latin American NGO boom', *International Feminist Journal of Politics* 1(2):181–209.

Amos, V. and P. Parmer (1984) 'Challenging imperial feminism', *Feminist Review* 17:3–20.

Anderson, E. (1999) 'What is the point of equality?', *Ethics* 109:287–337.

Anderson, M. (1993) 'The concept of mainstreaming: experience and change', in *Focusing on Women: UNIFEM's Experience of Mainstreaming*. New York: United Nations Development Fund for Women, 1–32.

Anthias, F. and N. Yuval-Davis (1983) 'Contextualizing feminism: gender, ethnic and class divisions', *Feminist Review* 15 Winter:62–75.

Araujo, C. and A. Garcia (2006) 'The experience and impact of quotas in Latin America', in D. Dahlerup (ed.) *Women, Quotas and Politics*. London and New York: Routledge: 83–11.

Armstrong, C. (2003) 'Opportunity, responsibility and the market: interrogating liberal equality', *Economy and Society* 32(3):410–27.

Armstrong, C. (2006) *Rethinking Equality*. Manchester University Press.

Arranz, F., B. Quintanilla and C. Velázquez (2000) 'Making Women Count in Spain' in F. Beveridge *et al.* (eds) *Making Women Count: Integrating Gender into Law and Policy-making*, Aldershot: Ashgate, 107–129.

Bacchi, C. (1999) *Women, Policy and Politics: The Construction of Policy Problems.* London*:* Sage.

Bacchi, C. (2004) 'Beijing's Legacy: Mainstreaming and Electoral Quotas for Women', paper presented at the University of Adelaide, August, 2004.

Bacchi, C. (2006) 'Arguing for and against quotas', in D. Dahlerup (ed.) *Women, Quotas and Politics*. London and New York: Routledge 32–51.

Bacchi, C. and J. Eveline (2004) 'Mainstreaming and neoliberalism: a contested relationship', *Policy and Society: Journal of Public, Foreign and Global Policy* 22(2):98–18.

Baden, S. and A.-M. Goetz (1997) 'Who needs [sex] when you can have [gender]? Conflicting discourses on gender at Beijing', *Feminist Review* 56 Summer:3–25.

Bagguley, P. (2002) 'Contemporary British feminism: a social movement in abeyance?', *Social Movements Studies* 1(2):169–85.

Baldez, L. (2001) 'Coalition politics and the limits of state feminism in Chile', *Women and Politics* 22(4):1–28.

Baldez, L. (2002) *Why Women Protest: Women's Movements in Chile*. Cambridge University Press.

Baldez, L. (2004) 'Elected bodies: gender quota law for legislative candidates in Mexico', *Legislative Studies Quarterly* 29(2):231–58.

Ballington, J. and D. Dahlerup (2006) 'Gender-quotas in post-conflict states: East Timor, Afghanistan and Iraq', in D. Dahlerup (ed.) *Women, Quotas and Politics*. London and New York: Routledge: 249–58.

Ballington, J. and A. Karam (2005) *Women in Parliament: Beyond Numbers*. Stockholm: International Institute for Democracy and Electoral Assistance.

Banaszak, L., K. Beckwith and D. Rucht (eds) (2003) *Women's Movements Facing the Reconfigured State,* Cambridge University Press.

Barmes, L. and S. Ashtiany (2003) 'The diversity approach to achieving equality: potential and pitfalls', *Industrial Law Journal* 32:274–96.

Barry, B. (2001) *Culture and Equality*. Cambridge: Polity Press.

Barzelay, M. (1992) *Breaking Through Bureaucracy: A New Vision for Managing Government*, Berkeley: University of California Press.

Basu, A. (ed.) (1995) *The Challenge of Local Feminisms: Women's Movements in Global Perspective*. Oxford: Westview.

Beauchamp, T. (1998) 'In Defense of affirmative action', *Journal of Ethics* 2:143–58.

Beckwith, K. (2000) 'Beyond compare? Women's movements in comparative perspective', *European Journal of Political Research* 37:431–68.

Beckwith, K. (2003) 'The gendering ways of states: women's representation and state reconfiguration in France, Great Britain, and the United States', in L. Banaszak, K. Beckwith and D. Rucht (eds) *Women's Movements Facing the Reconfigured State*. Cambridge University Press.

Bedford, K. (2006) 'Problematic partnerships how heteronormativity influences the practices of world bank gender staff', paper presented at Political Studies Association Woman and Politics Conference, 11 February, Edinburgh.

Bell, M. (2003) 'The right to equality and non-discrimination', in T. Hervey and J. Kenner (eds) *Economic and Social Rights under the EU .Chatter of Fundamental Rights: A Legal Perspective*. Oxford: Hart, 91–110.

Benhabib, S. (1992) *Situating the Self*. Cambridge: Polity.

Benhabib, S. (1996) (ed.) *Democracy and Difference: Contesting the Boundaries of the Political*. Princeton University Press.

Benhabib, S. (2002) *The Claims of Culture: Equality and Diversity in the Global Era*. Princeton University Press.

Beveridge, F. and J. Shaw (2002) 'Introduction: mainstreaming gender in European public policy', *Feminist Legal Studies* 10(3–4):209–12.

Beveridge, F. and S. Nott (2002) 'Mainstreaming: a case for optimism and cynicism', *Feminist Legal Studies* 10(3–4):299–311.

Beveridge, F., S. Nott and K. Stephen (2000) 'Mainstreaming and the engendering of policy-making: a means to an end?', *Journal of European Public Policy* 7(3):385–405.

Blackmore J. and J. Sachs (2001) 'Women leaders in the restructured university', in A. Brooks and A. Mackinnon (eds) *Gender and the Restructured University*. Buckingham: Open University Press, 45–66.

Blaug, R. (2002) 'Engineering democracy', *Political Studies* 50(1):102–16.
Bohman, J. and W. Rehg (eds) (1997) *Deliberative Democracy*. Cambridge, MA: MIT Press.
Booth, C. and C. Bennett (2002) 'Gender mainstreaming in the European Union: towards a new conception and practice of equal opportunities?', *European Journal of Women's Studies* 9(4):430–46.
Boserup, E. (1970) *Women's Role in Economic Development*. London: Allen & Unwin.
Boylan, M. (2002) 'Affirmative action: strategies for the future', *Journal of Social Philosophy* 33(1):117–30.
Breitenbach, E. (2004) 'The Scottish Executive and Equality', published in *Etudes Ecossaises*, no.9 and presented at ESRC Seminar Series, 'Public Policy, Equality and Diversity in the Context of Devolution'.
Breitenbach, E., A. Brown, F. Mackay and J. Webb (eds) (2002) *The Changing Politics of Gender Equality in Britain*. Basingstoke, Palgrave.
Bretherton, C. (2001) 'Gender Mainstreaming and EU enlargement: swimming against the tide?', *Journal of European Public Policy* 8(1):60–81.
Brown, A., T. Donaghy, F. Mackay and E. Meehan (2002) 'Women and constitutional change in Scotland and Northern Ireland', in K. Ross (ed.) *Women, Politics, and Change*. Oxford: Oxford University Press, 71–84.
Brown, W. (1988) *Manhood and Politics: A Feminist Reading in Political Theory*. Totowa, N.J: Rowman & Littlefield.
Brown, W. (1995) *States of Injury: Power and Freedom in Late Modernity*. Princeton University Press.
Bullock, H., J. Mountford and R. Stanley (2001) *Better Policy-Making*. Centre for Management and Policy Studies, available at: http://www.policyhub.gov.uk/docs/betterpolicymaking.pdf
Bunch, C. (1995) 'On globalizing gender justice: women of the world unite', *Nation* 11 September: 230–36.
Butler, J. (1990) *Gender Trouble*. New York: Routledge.
Calhoun, C. (1995) *Critical Social Theory: Culture, History and the Challenge of Difference*. Cambridge, MA: Blackwell.
Caraway, N. (1991) *Segregated Sisterhood: Racism and the Politics of American Feminism*. Knoxville: University of Tennessee Press.
Carby, H. (1999) *Cultures in Babylon: Black Britain and African America*. London: Verso.
Carney, G. (2003) 'Communicating or just talking? Gender mainstreaming and the communication of global feminism', *Women and Language* 26(1):52–61.
Carney, G. (2004) 'Researching gender mainstreaming: a challenge for feminist IR', paper presented at the International Studies Association Annual Conference, Montreal.
Carroll S. J. (2001) 'Representing women: women state legislators as agents of policy related change', in S. J. Carroll (ed.) *The Impact of Women in Public Office*. Bloomington, Indiana: Indiana University Press, 3–21.
Cartwright, R. (2001) *Managing Diversity*. Oxford: Capstone Express Exec.
Casqueira Cardoso, J. (2000), 'Making women count in Portugal', in F. Beveridge *et al.* (eds) *Making Women Count: Integrating Gender into Law and Policy-making*, Ashgate. Aldershot, 77–106.

Catt, H. (2003) 'How can women MPs make a difference? Reconsidering group representation and the responsible party model', Occasional Paper, Centre for the Advancement of Women and Politics, Queens University, Belfast. Available at: http://www.qub.ac.uk/cawp/research/Catt.pdf

Caul, M. (1999) 'Women's representation in parliament: the role of political parties', *Party Politics* 5(1):79–98.

Caul, M. (2001) 'Political parties and the adoption of candidate gender quotas: a cross-national analysis', *Journal of Politics* 63(4):1214–29.

Celis, K. (2004) 'Substantive and descriptive representation: investigating the impact of the voting right and of descriptive representation on the substantive representation of women in the Belgian Lower House (1900–1979)', paper presented at the Annual Meeting of the American Political Science Association, 2–5 September, Chicago.

Celis, K. (2005) 'Reconciling theory and empirical research: methodological reflections on women MP's representing women ('s Interests)', paper presented at the ECPR General Conference, Budapest.

Center for Women's Global Leadership (2001) 'Holding on to the promise: women's human rights and the Beijing +5 Review', available at: www.cwgl.rutgers.edu/globalcenter/gcpubs.html

Chaney, P. (2002) 'Women and the post-devolution equality agenda in Wales', paper presented to the Gender Research Forum, Women and Equality Unit, 11th February.

Chaney, P. (2003) 'Increased rights and representation: women and the post-devolution equality agenda in Wales', in A. Dobrowolsky and V. Hart (eds) *Women Making Constitutions: New Politics and Comparative Perspectives*. Basingstoke: Palgrave, 173–85.

Chaney, P. and R. Fevre (2002) 'Is there a demand for descriptive representation? Evidence from the UK's devolution programme', *Political Studies* 50(5):897–915.

Chappell, L. (2000) 'Interacting with the state: feminist strategies and political opportunities', *International Feminist Journal of Politics* 2(2):244–75.

Chappell, L. (2002) 'The femocrat strategy: expanding the repertoire of feminist activists', *Parliamentary Affairs* 55(1):85–98.

Chappell, L. (2002a) *Gendering Government: Feminist Engagement with the State in Australia and Canada*. Vancouver: UBC Press.

Chasin, A. (2000) *Selling Out: The Gay and Lesbian Movement Goes to Market*. New York: St. Martin's Press.

Childs, S. (2002) 'Concepts of representation and the passage of the Sex Discrimination (Election Candidates) Bill', *Journal of Legislative Studies* 8(3):90–108.

Childs, S. (2002a) 'Hitting the target: are Labour women MPs "acting for" women?', in K. Ross (ed.) *Women, Politics and Change*. Oxford: Oxford University Press, 143–53.

Childs, S. (2004) 'A feminised style of politics? Women MPs in the House of Commons', *British Journal of Politics and International Relations* 6(1):3–19.

Childs, S. (2004a) *New Labour's Women MPs: Women Representing Women*. London: Routledge.

Childs, S. and M. Krook (2005) 'The substantive representation of women: rethinking the critical mass debate', paper presented at the American

Political Science Association Annual Meeting, Washington, DC, 1–4 September.

Childs, S. and J. Withey (2006) 'The substantive representation of women: the case of the reduction of VAT on sanitary products', *Parliamentary Affairs* 59(1):10–23.

Chodorow, N. (1978) *The Reproduction of Mothering*. Berkeley: University of California Press.

CIDA (1999) *Policy on Gender Equality*. Available at: www.un.org/womenwatch/daw/beijing/platform/instituto.htm

Cockburn, C. (1998) *The Space Between Us: Negotiating Gender and National Identities in Conflict*. London: Zed Books.

Code, L. (1995) 'How do we know? questions of method in feminist practice', in S. Burt and L. Code (eds) *Changing Methods: Feminist Transforming Practice*. Peterborough: Broadview, 13–43.

Collins, P. H. (2000) *Black Feminist Thought: Knowledge, Consciousness and the Politics of Empowerment*. New York: Routledge. 1st edition 1990.

Commission of the European Communities (1996) *Communication from the Commission: Incorporating Equal Opportunities for Women and Men into All Community Policies and Activities*. COM(96)67 final of 21 February.

Commission on the Status of Women (CSW) 49 2005. Available at: http://www.thewnc. org.uk/wnc_work/csw_2005.html

Coole, D. (1996) 'Is class a difference that makes a difference?', *Radical Philosophy* 77, 17–25.

Coole, D. (1996a) 'Habermas and the question of alterity', in M. P. d'Entreves and S. Benhabib (eds) *Habermas and the Unfinished Project of Modernity*. Cambridge: Polity.

Cooper, D. (2004) *Challenging Diversity: Rethinking Equality and the Value of Difference*. Cambridge University Press.

Council of Europe (1996) 96/p9444/EC http:/eur-lex.europa.ev

Council of Europe (1998) *Gender Mainstreaming: Conceptual Framework, Methodology and Presentation of Good Practice*. Final Report of Activities of the Group of Specialists on Mainstreaming. EG-S-MS (8) 2, Strasbourg.

Council of Europe (2003) 5th European Ministerial Conference on Equality between Men and Women, http://www.humanrights.coe.int/equality/Eng/WordDocs/e%20MEG-5%203%20declaration%20and%20plan%20of%20action.doc

Cowley, P. and S. Childs (2003) 'Too spineless to rebel? New Labour's women MPs', *British Journal of Political Science* 33(3):345–65.

Craske, N. (1998) 'Remasculinisation and the neoliberal state in Latin America', in V. Randall and G. Waylen (eds) *Gender, Politics and the State*. London: Routledge, 100–119.

Crenshaw, K. (1991) 'Mapping the margins: intersectionality, identity politics, and violence against women of color', *Stanford Law Review* 43(6):1241–99.

Dahlerup, D. (1998) 'Using quotas to increase women's political representation', in A. Karam (ed.) *Women in Parliament Beyond Numbers*. Stockholm: IDEA.

Dahlerup, D. (2005) 'About quotas', available at: http://www.quotaproject.org/aboutQuotas.cfm

Dahlerup, D. (ed.) (2006) *Women, Quotas and Politics*. London and New York: Routledge.

Dahlerup, D. and L. Freidenvall (2005) 'Quotas as a "fast track" to equal representation for women. Why Scandinavia is no longer the model', *International Feminist Journal of Politics*. 7(1):26–48.
Daly, M. (2005) 'Gender mainstreaming in theory and practice', *Social Politics* 12(3):433–50.
Department for International Development (2002) *Gender Manual: A Practical Guide for Development Policy-Makers and Practitioners*. London: DFID.
Diamond I. and N. Hartsock (1998) Beyond interests in politics: a comment on Virginia Sapiro's 'When are women's interests interesting?', in A. Phillips (ed.) *Feminism and Politics*. Oxford University Press, 193–203.
Directory of National Machineries for the Advancement of Women, available at: http://www.unescap.org/esid/gad/Issues/Machineries/DAWNational_Machineries_26May2006.pdf
Disability KaR (2006) 'Mainstreaming disability in development', available at: http://www.disabilitykar.net/learningpublication/disabilitydevelopment.hmtl
Division for the Advancement of Women (2005) 'The role of national machineries in promoting gender equality and the empowerment of women: achievements, gaps and challenges for the future', EGM/National Machinery/2004/BP.1.
Dobrowolsky, A. (1998) 'Of special interest: interest, identity and feminist constitutionalism activism', *Canadian Journal of Political Science* 31(6):707–42.
Dobrowolsky, A. (2000) 'Intersecting identities and inclusive institutions: women and a future transformative politics', *Journal of Canadian Studies* 35(4):240–61.
Dobrowolsky, A. (2002) 'Crossing boundaries: exploring and mapping women's constitutional interventions in England, Scotland, and Northern Ireland', *Social Politics* 9(2):293–340.
Dobrowolsky, A. and V. Hart (eds) (2003) *Women Making Constitutions: New Politics and Comparative Perspectives,* Basingstoke: Palgrave.
Dolowitz, D. and D. Marsh (1996) 'Who learns what from whom: a review of the policy transfer literature', *Political Studies*, XLIV, 343–57.
Donaghy, T. B. (2003) 'Mainstreaming equality in public policy making', paper presented at the 19th IPSA World Congress, Durban.
Donaghy, T. B. (2004) 'Applications of mainstreaming in Australia and Northern Ireland', *International Political Science Review* 25(4):393–410.
Donaghy, T. B. (2004a) 'Mainstreaming: Northern Ireland's participative-democratic approach', *Policy and Politics* 32:49–62.
Dryzek, J. (2000) *Deliberative Democracy and Beyond*. Oxford University Press.
E/CN.6/1988/3 listed in the Directory of National Machineries for the Advancement of Women DAW.
Edwards, J. and C. Chapman (2003) 'Women's political representation in the National Assembly for Wales', *Contemporary Politics* 9(4):397–414.
Edwards, J. and L. McAllister (2002) 'One step forward, two steps back? Women in the two main political parties in Wales', in K. Ross (ed.) *Women, Politics, and Change*. Oxford: Oxford University Press, 154–66.
Eisenstein, H. (1996) *Inside Agitators: Australian Femocrats and the State*. Philadelphia, PA: Temple University Press.
Elgood, J., L. Vinter and R. Williams (2001) *Man Enough for the Job? A Study of Parliamentary Candidates*. London: Equal Opportunities Commission.

Elgstrom, O. (2000) 'Norm negotiations the construction of new norms regarding gender and development in EU foreign aid policy', *Journal of European Public Policy* 7(3), 457–476.

Elman, A. (2003) 'Engendering state theory: feminists engage the state', *Review of Policy Research* 20(3):549–56.

Elson, D. (2000) 'Gender Budget Initiatives as an Aid to Gender Mainstreaming', paper presented at Ministerial Conference of Gender Mainstreaming, Competitiveness and Growth, OECD, Paris, 23–24 November.

Elster, J. (ed.) (1998) *Deliberative Democracy*. Cambridge University Press.

Eschle, C. (2001) *Global Democracy, Social Movements and Feminism.* Boulder, CO: Westview.

European Commission (1996) *Communication on mainstreaming: Incorporating equal opportunities for women and men into all Community Policies and activities* (COM(96)67).

European Commission (2004) 'Equality and non-discrimination Annual Report 2004', available at: www.ec.europa.eu/employment_social/

European Commission (2005) 'Disability mainstreaming in the European employment strategy', paper available at: http://www.euroblind.org/fichiersGB/2005mainst.htm

European Women's Lobby (2004) 'Response to the Commission's Fundamental Rights Agency Public Consultation Document.'

Eveline, J. and C. Bacchi (2005) 'What are we mainstreaming when we mainstream gender?', *International Feminist Journal of Politics* 7(4):496–512.

Everingham, C. (1994) *Motherhood and Modernity*. Milton Keynes: Open University Press.

Facon, P., A. Hondeghem and S. Welen (2004) *Gelijkekansenbeleid onderweq*. Brugge: Die Keure.

Ferguson, K. (1993) *The Man Question: Visions of Subjectivity in Feminist Theory*. Berkeley: University of California Press.

Firestone, S. (1970) *The Dialectic of Sex*. New York: Bantam.

Fishkin, J. (1991) *Democracy and Deliberation: New Directions for Democratic Reform*. New Haven, CT: Yale University Press.

Fishkin, J. (2000) 'The quest for deliberative democracy', in M. Saward (ed.) *Democratic Innovation*. London: Routledge.

Flammang, J. (1985) 'Female officials in the feminist capital', *Western Political Quarterly* 38: 94–118.

Franceschet, S. (2002) 'State feminism and social movements: the impact of Chile's Servicio Nacional de la Mujer on Women's Activism', *Latin American Research Review*, 38(1): 9–40.

Franceschet, S. and L. Macdonald (2004) 'Hard times for citizenship: women's movements in Chile and Mexico', *Citizenship Studies* 8(1):3–23.

Franzway, S., D. Court and R. Connell (1989) *Staking a Claim: Feminism, Bureaucracy and the State*. Cambridge: Polity.

Fraser, N. (1989) *Unruly Practices: Power, Discourse and Gender in Contemporary Social Theory*. Cambridge: Polity Press.

Fraser, N. (1995) 'Recognition or redistribution? A critical reading of Iris Young's "Justice and the Politics of Difference"', *Journal of Political Philosophy* 3(2):166–80.

Fraser, N. (1996) *Justice Interruptus: Critical Reflections on the Postsocialist Condition*. New York: Routledge.
Fraser, N. (2007), 'Mapping the feminist imagination: from redistribution to recognition to representation' in J. Browne (ed.) *The Future of Gender*. Cambridge: Cambridge University Press.
Fredman, S. (1992) 'European Community discrimination law: a critique' *Industrial Law Journal* 21(2): 119–134.
Fredman, S. (1997) *Women and the Law*. Oxford University Press.
Fredman, S. (2001) 'Equality: a new generation?', *Industrial Law Review* 30:145–68.
Fredman, S. (2002) *The Future of Equality in Britain*. Manchester: Equal Opportunities Commission. http://www.eoc.org.uk/PDF/a_future_of_equality_in_britain.pdf
Freeman, J. (ed.) (1984) *Women: A Feminist Perspective*. Palo Alto, CA: Mayfield.
Fricker, M. (1998) 'Rational authority and social power: towards a truly social epistemology', *Proceedings of the Aristotelian Society*, 98(2): 159–177.
Friedman, E. (2000) *Unfinished Transitions: Women and the Gendered Development of Democracy in Venezuela, 1936–1996*. University Park: Pennsylvania State University Press.
Gamson, W. (1975) *The Strategy of Social Protest*. Homewood: Dorsey Press.
Gaspard, F., C. Servan-Schreiber, and A. Le Gall (1992) *Au Pouvoir, citoyennes!: liberté, égalité, parité*. Paris: Seuil.
Gilligan, C. (1982) *In a Different Voice*. Cambridge, MA: Harvard University Press.
Goetz A.-M and S. Hassim (2003) *No Short-Cuts: African Women in Policy and Policy-Making*. London: Zed.
Goetz, A.-M. (1998) 'Mainstreaming gender equality to national development planning', in C. Miller and S. Razavi (eds) *Missionaries and Mandarins: Feminist Engagement with Development Institutions*. London: Intermediate Tech Public with UNRISD.
Goetz, A.-M. (2003) 'National women's machinery: state-based institutions to advocate for gender equality', in S. Rai (ed.) *Mainstreaming Gender, Democratizing the State: Institutional Mechanisms for the Advancement of Women*. Manchester: Manchester University Press, 69–95.
Goetz, A.M. (2004) 'Gender and Accountability', in A. Dobrowolsky and V. Hart (eds) *Women Making Constitutions: New Politics and Comparative Perspectives*. Basingstoke: Palgrave Macmillan, 52–67.
Goetz, A.-M. (2005) 'Advocacy administration in the context of economic and political liberalisation', paper presented to the UN Division for the Advancement of Women meeting on National Machinery, 29 November– 2 December, Rome. Available at: http://www.ub.org/womenwatch/daw/egm/ nationalm2004/
Gopal Baidya, B. (2005) 'The role of national mechanisms in promoting gender equality and the empowerment of women: lessons from Nepal' EGM/National Machinery/ 2004/EP.3.
Grey, S. (2002) 'Does size matter? Critical mass and New Zealand's women MPs', *Parliamentary Affairs* 55(1):19–29.
Guattari, F. (1974) *Psychoanalyse et Transversalité*. Paris: Maspéro.
Guerrina, R. (2003) 'Gender, mainstreaming and the EU Charter of Fundamental Rights', *Policy, Organisation and Society*, 22(1):97–115.

Guigou, E. (1998) 'Projet de loi constitutionelle relatif à l'égalité entre les femmes et les hommes', speech to the French National Assembly, December 15, http://www.justice. gouv.fr/discours/d151298.htm

Gunes-Ayata, A. (2001) 'The politics of women's rights in Turkey', in J. H. Bayes and N. Tohidi (eds) *Globalization, Gender, and Religion: The Politics of Women's Rights in Catholic and Muslim Contexts*. Basingstoke and New York: Palgrave Macmillan.

Habermas, J. (1996) *Between Facts and Norms*. Cambridge: Polity.

Hafner-Burton, E. and M. Pollack (2000) 'Mainstreaming gender in the European Union', *Journal of European Public Policy* 7(3):432–56.

Hafner-Burton, E. and M. Pollack (2002) 'Mainstreaming gender in global governance', *European Journal of International Relations*, 8(3), 389–373.

Hajer, M. and H. Wagenaar (2003) *Deliberative Policy Analysis: Understanding Governance in a Network Society*. Cambridge University Press.

Hancock, L. (ed.) (1999) *Women, Public Policy and the State*. South Yarra, Australia: Macmillan.

Hankivsky, O. (2005) 'Gender mainstreaming vs. diversity mainstreaming: a preliminary examination of the role and transformative potential of feminist theory', *Canadian Journal of Political Science* 38(4) 997–1001.

Harding, S. (1991) *Whose Science? Whose Knowledge?: Thinking from Women's Lives*. Ithaca, NY: Cornell University Press.

Harman, H. and D. Mattinson (2000) *Winning for Women*. London: Fabian Society.

Hartsock, N. (1983) 'The feminist standpoint', in S. Harding, and M. Hintikka (eds) *Discovering Reality*. London: Riedell.

Hausmann, M. and B. Sauer (eds) (2007) *Gendering the State in the Age of Globalisation. Women's Movements and State Feminism in Post Industrial Democracies*. New York: Rowman and Littlefield.

Hay, C. (2004) 'The normalizing role of rationalist assumptions in the institutional embedding of neoliberalism', *Economy and Society* 33(4):500–27.

Hennessey, R. (2000) *Profit and Pleasure: Sexual Identities in Late Capitalism*. London: Routledge.

Himmelweit, S. (2002) 'Making visible the hidden economy: the case for gender-impact analysis of economic policy', *Feminist Economics* 8(1):49–70.

Hindess, B. (2004) 'Liberalism: what's in a name?', in W. Larner and W. Walters (eds) *Global Governmentality. Governing International Spaces*. London, Routledge, 23–39.

Hobson, B. (2003) *Recognition Struggles and Social Movements*. Cambridge University Press.

Hobson, B., M. Carson and R. Lawrence (2007) 'Recognition struggles and transnational arenas: negotiating identities and framing citizenship', forthcoming in *Critical Review of Social and Political Philosophy*, 10(4).

Holzer, H. and D. Neumark (2000) 'Assessing affirmative action', *Journal of Economic Literature* 38:483–568.

Honculada J. and R. Ofreneo (2003) 'The national commission on the role of Filipino women, the women's movement and gender mainstreaming in the Philippines', in S. Rai (ed.) *Mainstreaming Gender Democratizing the State?* Manchester: Manchester University Press, 131–45.

hooks, b. (1981) *Ain't I a Woman: Black Women and Feminism*. Boston: South End.

hooks, b. (1989) *Talking Back: Thinking Feminist, Thinking Black*. Boston: South End.

Hoskyns, C. (1992) 'The European Community's policy on women in the context of 1992', *Women's Studies International Forum*, 15(1): 21–8.
Hoskyns, C. (1996) *Integrating Gender: Women, Law and Politics in the European Union*. London: Verso.
Htun, M. (2002) 'Puzzles of women's rights in Brazil', *Social Research* 69(3):733–51.
Htun, M. (2004) 'Is gender like ethnicity? The political representation of identity groups', *Perspectives on Politics* 2(3):439–58.
Htun, M. N. and M. P. Jones (2002) 'Engendering the right to participate in decision-making: electoral quotas and women's leadership in Latin America', in N. Craske and M. Molyneux (eds) *Gender and the Politics of Rights and Democracy in Latin America*. New York, Palgrave.
Inglehart, R. and P. Norris (2003) *Rising Tide: Gender Equality and Cultural Change Around the World*. Cambridge University Press.
Instituto de la Mujer (1993) *Equal Opportunities for Women: Second Plan of Action 1993–1995*. Madrid: Instituto de la Mujer.
Jacquot, S. (2003) 'Sequences of policy change: European gender equality policies and the emergence of the gender mainstreaming principle, 1989–1996', paper presented at the ECPR General Conference, Marburg. Available at: http://www.essex.ac.uk/ ecpr/events/generalconference/papers/
Jahan, R. (1995) *The Elusive Agenda: Mainstreaming Women in Development*. Atlantic Highlands, NJ: Zed.
Jenkins, L. D. (1999) 'Competing inequalities: the struggle over reserved seats for women in India', *International Review of Social History* 44:53–75.
Jessop, B. (2002) *The Future of the Capitalist State*. Cambridge: Polity.
John, P. (1999) 'Ideas and interests; agendas and implementation: evolutionary explanations of policy change in British local government finance', *British Journal of Politics and International Relations* 1(1):39–62.
Jones, K. (1990) 'Citizenship in a woman-friendly polity', *Signs*, 15(4): 781–812.
Jones, L. (1994), speech in the House of Parliament, reported in *Hansard* 19 July: 292.
Jones, M. (1996) 'Increasing women's representation via gender quotas: the Argentine Ley de Cupos', *Women and Politics* 16(4):75–98.
Jones, M. (1998) 'Gender quotas, electoral laws and the election of women: lessons from the Argentine Provinces', *Comparative Political Studies* 31(1):3–21.
Jones, M. (2004) 'Quota legislation and the election of women: learning from the Costa Rican experience', *Journal of Politics* 66, 1203–23.
Jordan, A., R. Wurzel and A. Zito (2005) 'The rise of "new" policy instruments in comparative perspective: has governance eclipsed government?', *Political Studies* 53(3):477–96.
Kabeer, N. (2003) *Gender Mainstreaming in Poverty Eradication and the Millennium Development Goals: A handbook for Policy-makers and Other Stakeholders*. Prepared for Commonwealth Secretariat/ICRC/CIDA. http://web.idrc.ca/ev.php?=42969_201& ID2-DO_TOPIC (July 23, 2004).
Kamenitsa, L. and B. Geissel (2005) 'WPAs and political representation in Germany', in J. Lovenduski (ed.) *State Feminism and Political Representation*. Cambridge: Cambridge University Press, 106–29.
Kantola, J. (2006) *Feminists Theorize the State*. Basingstoke: Palgrave.
Kantola, J. and J. Squires (2004) 'Discourses surrounding prostitution policies in the UK', *European Journal of Women's Studies* 11(1):77–101.

Kaplan, C., N. Alarcon and M. Moallem (eds) (1999) *Between Woman and Nation: Nationalisms, Transnational Feminisms, and the State*. Durham, NC: Duke University Press.

Karam, A. (ed.) (1998) *Women in Parliament: Beyond Numbers*. Stockholm: International Institute for Democracy and Electoral Assistance.

Kardam, N. (2000) 'Global gender norms, donor funding and local realities: The Turkish case', paper presented at workshop on Human Rights and Globalization, University of California, Santa Crus, December.

Kardam, N. (2005) 'The role of national mechanisms in promoting gender equality and the empowerment of women: Turkey experience', EGM/ National Machinery/ 2004/EP.2.

Kardam, N. and S. Acuner (2003) 'National women's machineries: structures and spaces', in S. Rai (ed.) *Mainstreaming Gender, Democratizing the State: Institutional Mechanisms for the Advancement of Women*. Manchester University Press.

Keck, M. and K. Sikkink (1998) *Activists Beyond Borders: Advocacy Networks in International Politics*. Ithaca, NY: Cornell University Press.

Kelly, R. and T. Donaghy (2001) 'Doing their duty: implementing statutory duty under section 75 of the Northern Ireland Act 1998', paper presented at the Political Studies Association of Ireland Annual Conference, Galway, November.

Kenner, J. (2000) 'The paradoxes of the social dimension', in P. Lynch, N. Neuwahl and W. Rees (eds) *Reforming the European Union: From Maastricht to Amsterdam*. London: Longman, 108–29.

Klausen, J. and C. Maier (eds) (2001) *Has Liberalism Failed Women? Assuring Equal Representation in Europe and the United States*. Basingstoke: Palgrave.

Krook, M. (2004) 'Gender quotas as a global phenomenon: actors and strategies in quota adoption', *European Political Science* 3(3):59–65.

Krook, M. (2005) 'Contested equalities: national and international laws and norms in gender quota debates', Political Studies Association Annual Conference, Leeds, 5–7 April.

Krook, M. (2005a) 'Politicizing representation: campaigns for candidate gender quotas worldwide', PhD dissertation, Department of Political Science, Columbia University.

Krook, M. (2006) 'Reforming representation: the diffusion of candidate gender quotas worldwide', *Politics and Gender* 2(3):303–26.

Krook, M. (2007) 'Candidate gender quotas: a framework for analysis', *European Journal of Political Research*, 46: 367–94.

Krook, M., J. Lovenduski and J. Squires (2006) 'Western Europe, North America, Australia and New Zealand: mapping the debates, adoption and implementation of gender quotas in the context of citizenship models', in D. Dahlerup (ed.) *Women, Quotas, Politics*. London and New York: Routledge, 194–221.

Kwesiga, J. (2003) 'The national machinery for gender equality in Uganda: Institutionalised gesture politics?', in S. Rai (ed.) *Mainstreaming Gender, Democratizing the State: Institutional Mechanisms for the Advancement of Women*. Manchester: Manchester University Press, 203–22.

Lacey, N. (2004) 'Feminist legal theory and the rights of women', in K. Knop (ed.) *Gender and Human Rights*. Oxford University Press.

Laforest, R. and M. Orsini (2005) 'Evidence-based engagement in the voluntary sector: lessons from Canada', *Social Policy and Administration* 39(5):481–97.

Larner, W. (2000) 'Neoliberalism: policy, ideology, governmentality', *Studies in Political Economy* 63:5–26.
Larner, W. (2003) 'Neoliberalism?', editorial, *Environment and Planning D: Society and Space* 21(5):509–12.
Larner, W. (2005) 'Neoliberalism in (regional) theory and practice: the stronger communities action Fund in New Zealand', *Geographical Research* 43(1):9–18.
Larner, W. and D. Craig (2005) 'After neoliberalism? Community activism and local partnerships in Aotearoa New Zealand', *Antipode* 37(3):402–24.
Law, J. and J. Urry (2004) 'Enacting the social', *Economy and Society* 33(3):390–410.
Lester, Lord (2003), cited in Anne Perkins, 'Lib Dem Seeks Better Defined Equality Law', *The Guardian,* Thursday 16 January, available at: http://www.guardian.co.uk/ guardianpolitics/story/0,,875495,00.html
Liebert, U. (2003) 'Between diversity and equality', in U. Liebert (ed.) *Gendering Europeanisation*. Brussels, Peter Lang.
Lister, R. (1997) *Citizenship: Feminist Perspectives*. Basingstoke: Macmillan.
Lloyd, G. (1984) *The Man of Reason: 'Male' and 'Female' in Western Philosophy*. Minneapolis: University of Minnesota Press.
Lombardo, E. (2003) 'EU gender policy: trapped in the Wollstonecraft dilemma', *European Journal of Women's Studies* 10(2):159–80.
Lombardo, E. (2005) 'Integrating or setting the agenda? Gender mainstreaming in the European constitution-making process', *Social Politics* 12(3):412–32.
Lovecy, J. (2002) 'Gender mainstreaming and the framing of women's rights in Europe: The contribution of the Council of Europe', *Feminist Legal Studies* 10 (3–4):271–83.
Lovenduski, J. (1981) 'Toward the emasculation of political science: the impact of feminism' in D. Spender (ed.), *Men's Studies Modified*. Oxford: Pergamon Press, 83–97.
Lovenduski, J. (1996) 'Sex, gender and British politics', in J. Lovenduski and P. Norris (eds) *Women in Politics*. Oxford: Oxford University Press, 3–18.
Lovenduski, J. (1997) 'Gender politics: a breakthrough for women?', *Parliamentary Affairs* 50(4):708–19.
Lovenduski, J. (2005) *Feminizing Politics*. Cambridge: Polity.
Lovenduski, J., C. Baudino, M. Guadaqnini, P. Meier and D. Sainsbury (2005) (eds) *State Feminism and Political Representation*. Cambridge University Press.
Mackay, F. (2001) *Love and Politics: Women Politicians and the Ethic of Care*. New York: Continuum.
Mackay, F. (2004) 'Gender and political representation in the UK: the state of the "discipline"', *British Journal of Politics & International Relations* 6(1):99–120.
Mackay, F. and K. Bilton (2000). *Learning from Experience: Mainstreaming Equal Opportunities*. Governance of Scotland Forum, University of Edinburgh.
Mackay, F., F. Myers and A. Brown (2003) 'Towards a new politics? Women and the constitutional change in Scotland', in A. Dobrowolsky and V. Hart (eds) *Women Making Constitutions: New Politics and Comparative Perspectives*. New York: Palgrave, 84–98.
Mansbridge, J. (1999) 'Should blacks represent blacks and women represent women? A contingent "yes"', *Journal of Politics* 61(3):628–57.
Mansbridge, J. (2001) 'The descriptive political representation of gender: an anti-essentialist argument', in J. Klausen and C. Maier (eds) *Has Liberalism*

Failed Women? Assuring Equal Representation in Europe and the United States. Basingstoke: Palgrave, 19–38.

Mansbridge, J. (2003) 'Rethinking representation', *American Political Science Review* 97(4):515–28.

Mansbridge, J. (2005) 'Quota problems: combating the dangers of essentialism', *Politics and Gender* 1(4): 622–38.

Marques-Pereira, B. (2000) 'Quotas and parity in Belgium within a European framework', paper presented at the International Political Science Association World Congress, Quebec, August.

Marques-Pereira, B. (2001) *La répresentation politique des femmes en Amérique Latine*. Bruxelles: L'Harmattan.

Marston G. and R. Watts (2003) 'Tampering with the evidence: a critical appraisal of evidence-based policy', *The Drawing Board: An Australian Review of Public Affairs* 3(3): 143–163.

Matear (1997) 'The institutionalisation of the women's movement in Chile', in E. Dore (ed.) *Gender Politics in Latin America: Debates in Theory and Practice*. New York: Monthly Review Press, 84–100.

Mateo Diaz, M. (2002) 'Do quotas matter? Positive actions in the Belgian parliament', *Res Publica* 44(1):49–72.

Mateo Diaz, M. (2005) *Representing Women? Female Legislators in West European Parliaments*. Oxford: ECPR.

Matland, R. (1998) 'Women's Representation in National Legislatures: Developed and Developing Countries', *Legislative Studies Quarterly* 23(1): 109–25.

Matland, R. (2005) 'Explaining Women's Representation: The Role of Legislative Recruitment and Electoral Systems', paper presented to the UN Division for the Advancement of Women meeting on National Machinery, 29 November–2 December, Rome. Available at: http://www.ub.org/womenwatch/daw/egm/nationalm2004/

Matland, R. and D. Studlar (1996) 'The contagion effect of women candidates in single-member district and proportional representation electoral systems: Canada and Norway', *Journal of Politics* 58(3):707–33.

Mazey, S. (2000) 'Introduction: integrating gender – intellectual and "real world" mainstreaming', *Journal of European Public Policy* 7(3):333–45.

Mazey, S. (2002) 'Gender mainstreaming strategies in the EU: delivering on an agenda?', *Feminist Legal Studies*, 10(3): 227–240.

Mazur, A. (2002) *Theorising Feminist Policy*. Oxford University Press.

Mazur, A. (2005) 'The impact of women's participation of leadership on policy outcomes: a focus on women's policy machineries', paper presented and the United Nations Expert Group Meeting on Equal Participation of Women and Men in Decision-Making Processes, 24–27 October.

Mazur, A. (ed.) (2001) *State Feminism, Women's Movements and Job Training: Making Democracies Work*. London/New York: Routledge.

McBride, D. and A. Mazur (2006) 'Women's movements, women's policy agencies and democratization', paper presented at the Conference of Europeanists, Council for European Studies, March 30–April 2, Chicago.

McBride, D. (2003) 'Reconceptualising the Women's Movement: discourses, actors and states', paper presented at the International Studies Association Annual Convention.

McBride, D. (2005) 'Femocrats in a cold climate: US women's policy machinery in the era of Republican dominance', paper presented at ECPR Joint Workshops, Universidad de Granada, 14–19 April.
McConkey, J. (2004) 'Knowledge and acknowledgement: epistemic justice as a problem of recognition', *Politics* 24(3):198–205.
McCrudden, C. (2001) 'Equality', in C. J. Harvey (ed.), *Human Rights, Equality and Democratic Renewal in Northern Ireland.* Oxford: Hart.
McDowell, L. (1991) 'Life without father and Ford', *Transactions of the Institute of British Geographers* 16(4):400–19.
McKay, J. (2004) 'Women in German politics: still jobs for the boys?', *German Politics* 13(1):56–80.
Meadowcroft, J. (2000) 'Sustainable development: a new(ish) idea for a new century?', *Political Studies* 48(2):370–87.
Meehan J. (ed.) (1995) *Feminists Read Habermas*, London: Routledge.
Meier, P. (2000) 'The evidence of being present: guarantees of representation and the Belgian example', *Acta Politica* 35(1): 64–85.
Meier, P. (2000) 'From theory to practice and back again: gender quota and the politics of presence in Belgium', in M. Saward (ed.) *Democratic Innovation.* London: Routledge, 106–16.
Meier, P. (2004) 'The Belgian perspective', *Party Politics* 10(5):583–600.
Melucci, A. (1996) *Challenging Codes: Collective Action in the Information Age*. New York: Cambridge University Press.
Mendoza, B. (2002) 'Transnational feminisms in question', *Feminist Theory* 3(3):295–314.
Merrien, F. (1998) 'Governance and modern welfare states', *International Social Science Journal* 155:57–65.
Mies, M. and V. Shiva (1993) *Ecofeminism*. London: Zed Books.
Miller, D. (2002) 'Is deliberative democracy unfair to disadvantaged groups?', in M.P. d'Entreves (ed.) *Democracy as Public Deliberation: New Perspectives*. Manchester University Press 201–25.
Miller, P. (1994) 'Accounting and objectivity: the invention of calculating selves and calculable spaces', in A. Megill (ed.) *Rethinking Objectivity*. Durham, NC: Duke University Press, 239–64.
Millett, K. (1970) *Sexual Politics*. New York: Ballantine Books.
Ministry of Women's Affairs, New Zealand (2002) *Briefing to the Incoming Minister*. Wellington.
Mohammad, R. (2005) 'The Cinderella complex – narrating Spanish women's history, the home and visions of equality: developing new margins', *Transactions of the Institute of British Geographers* 30(2):248–61.
Mohanty, C. (1998) 'Critical feminist genealogies: on the geography and politics of home and nation', in E. Shohat (ed.) *The Age of Globalization*. Amherst: University of Massachusetts Press.
Mohanty, C. T. (1991) 'Under Western eyes: feminist scholarship and colonial discourses', in C. T. Mohanty, A. Russo, and L. Torres (eds) *Third World Women and the Politics of Feminism*. Indianapolis: Indiana University Press, 51–80.
Molyneux, M. (1998) 'Analysing women's movements', *Development and Change* 29(2):219–45.
Morgan, R. (1970) *Sisterhood is Powerful*. Random House.
Morgan, R. (1984) *Sisterhood Is Global*. Doubleday Books.

Moser, C. (2002) 'Mainstreaming gender in international organizations', Public Hearing on Globalization and Gender, available at: http://e-education.uni-muenster.de/ enquete/papers/CarolineMoser/ weltto114_ stell003.pdf
Moser, C. (2005) 'Has gender mainstreaming failed?', *International Feminist Journal of Politics* 7(4):576–90.
Mosesdottir, L. and R. Erlingsdottir (2005), 'Spreading the word across Europe: gender mainstreaming as a political and policy project', *International Feminist Journal of Politics*, 7(4): 513–31.
Mtintso, T. (2001) 'Towards a movement for transformation of gender relations and the achievement of gender equality', *Umrabulo*, no.11 http://www.anc.org.za/ancdocs/pubs/umrabulo/umrabulo11e.html
Mulanari D. (2001) 'Race/ethnicity in a Nordic context: a reflection from the Swedish borderlands', in A. Johansson (ed.) *Svensk Genusforskning i Världen*. Götebörg: Nationella sekretariet för genusförskning.
Murphy, C. (ed.) (2003) *Egalitarian Politics in the Age of Globalization*. Basingstoke: Palgrave.
Murray, R. (2004) 'Why didn't parity work? A closer examination of the 2002 election results', *French Politics* 2:347–62.
Narayan, U. (1997) *Dislocating Cultures: Identities, Traditions, and Third-World Feminism*. London: Routledge.
Newman, J. (2001) *Modernising Governance*. London: Sage.
Newman, J. (2006) 'Destabilising "governance", and unsettling "diversity": thinking governance through feminist and queer perspectives', paper presented at the 'Rethinking Governance from Feminist and Queer Perspectives' Workshop, University of Kent, Canterbury, 29 June.
Nickel, J. W. (1995) 'Discrimination and morally relevant characteristics', in S. Cahn (ed.) *The Affirmative Action Debate*. London: Routledge, 3–4.
Nietzsche, F. (1969) *Thus Spake Zarathustra*. Harmondsworth: Penguin.
Norris, P. (1997) 'Equality strategies and political representation', in F. Gardiner (ed.) *Sex Equality Policy in Western Europe*. New York: Routledge, 46–59.
Norris, P. (2000) 'Women's representation and electoral systems', in R. Rose (ed.) *The International Encyclopedia of Elections*. Washington, DC: CQ Press, 348–51.
Norris, P. (2004) *Electoral Engineering: Voting Rules and Political Behaviour*. New York: Cambridge University Press.
Norris, P. and J. Lovenduski (1995) *Political Recruitment: Gender, Race and Class in the British Parliament*. Cambridge University Press.
Nott, S. (2000) 'Accentuating the positive: alternative strategies for promoting gender equality', in F. Beveridge, S. Nott, and K. Stephen (eds) *Making Women Count: Integrating Gender Into Law And Policy-Making*. Aldershot: Ashgate.
Nussbaum, M. (2000) *Women and Human Development: The Capabilities Approach*. Cambridge University Press.
O'Brien, R., A.-M. Goetz, J. Scholte and M. Williams (2000) *Contesting Global Governance: Multilateral Economic Institutions and Global Social Movements*. Cambridge University Press.
O'Neill, S. (1997) *Impartiality in Context*. New York: State University of New York Press.
OECD (2000) 'Gender mainstreaming: competitiveness and growth conference proceedings', Paris, 23–24 November. Available at: http://www.oecd.org/subject/gender_mainstreaming

Okin, S. M. (1989) *Gender, Justice and the Family*. New York: Basic Books.
Okin, S. M. (1999) 'Is multiculturalism bad for women?' in J. Cohen and M. Howard (eds) *Is Multiculturalism Bad for Women?* Princeton University Press, 7–26.
Okin, S. (2003) 'Poverty, well-being and gender: what counts, who's heard', *Philosophy and Public Affairs* 31(3):280–316.
Organisation for Economic Co-operation and Development (2004) 'Gender mainstreaming', http://www1.oecd.org/subject/gender_mainstreaming/about/ August 29.
Oustshoorn, J. (ed.) (2004) *The Politics of Prostitution. Women's Movements, Democratic States and the Globalisation of Sex Commerce*. Cambridge University Press.
Oustshoorn J. and J. Kantola (eds) (2007) *Changing State Feminism*. Basingstoke: Palgrave.
Palme, O. (1972) 'The emancipation of man', *Journal of Social Issues* 28(2):237–46.
Pascual, A. and U. Behning (eds) (2001) *Gender Mainstreaming in the European Union Employment Strategy*. Brussels: European Trade Union Insitute.
Passerini, L. (1994) 'The interpretation of democracy in the Italian women's movement of the 1970s and 1980s', *Women's Studies International Forum* 17(2–3):235–39.
Pateman, C. (1970) *Participation and Democratic Theory*. Cambridge: Cambridge University Press.
Pateman, C. (1988) *The Sexual Contract*. Cambridge: Polity Press.
Pateman, C. (1989) *The Disorder of Women*. Cambridge: Cambridge University Press.
Peck, J. and A. Tickell (2002) 'Neoliberalizing space', *Antipode* 34(3):380–404.
Peschard, J. (2003), *The Quota System in Latin America: General Overview*, paper presented at the Regional Workshop on 'The Implementation of Quotas: Latin American Experience', IDEA, Lima, Peru, February, 23–24.
Peschard, J. (2005) 'The quota system in Latin America: general overview', in International IDEA Quota Workshop Report, Stockholm: IDEA, 173–86.
Pettman, J. J. (2005) 'Review', *International Feminist Journal of Politics* 7(4):621–3.
Phillips, A. (1991) *Engendering Democracy*. Oxford: Polity Press.
Phillips, A. (1995) *The Politics of Presence*. Oxford: Clarendon.
Phillips, A. (1997) 'What has socialism to do with sexual equality?', in J. Franklin (ed.) *Equality*. London: Institute for Public Policy Research, 102–21.
Phillips, A. (1999) *Which Equalities Matter?* Cambridge: Polity.
Phillips, A. (2004) 'Defending equality of outcome', *Journal of Political Philosophy* 12(1):1–19.
Phillips, A. (2006) 'Multiculturalism Without Culture', paper presented at the 'Beyond feminism vs. multiculturalism' Conference, London School of Economics, 17 November, available at: http://www.kcl.ac.uk/depsta/law/events/06_07/femworkshop/Anne% 20Phillips%20Beyond%20Feminism%20v%20Multiculturalism.pdf
Phillips, A. (ed.) (1998) *Feminism and Politics*. Oxford University Press.
Pitkin, H. (1967) *The Concept of Representation*. Los Angeles: University of California Press.
Polanyi, K. (1975) *The Great Transformation: The Political and Economic Origins of Our Time*. Boston, MA: Beacon.

Pollack, M. and E. Hafner-Burton (2000) 'Mainstreaming gender in the European Union', *Journal of European Public Policy* 7(3):432–56.

Price, A. (2003) *Human Resource Management in a Business Context*. International Thomson Business.

Prokhovnik, R. (1999) *Rational Woman*. London: Routledge.

Puwar, N. (2004) 'Thinking about making a difference', *British Journal of Politics and International Relations* 6(1):65–80.

Quota Project (2006) Available at: http://www.quotaproject.org/

Rai, S. (ed.) (2003) *Mainstreaming Gender, Democratizing the State: Institutional Mechanisms for the Advancement of Women*. Manchester: Manchester University Press.

Rai, S., F. Bari, N. Mahtab and B. Mohanty (2006) 'Gender quotas in the politics of empowerment – a comparative study', in D. Dahlerup (ed.) *Women, Quotas and Politics*. London and New York: Routledge, 222–45.

Randall, V. (1982) *Women and Politics: An International Perspective*. University of Chicago Press.

Ravens-Roberts, A. (2005) 'Gender mainstreaming in United Nations peacekeeping operations: talking with talk, tripping over the walk', in D. Mazurana, A. Ravens-Roberts and J. Parpart (eds) *Gender, Conflict and Peacekeeping*. Lanham, MD: Rowman & Little.

Razavi, S. and C. Miller (1995) 'From WID to GAD: conceptual shifts in the women in development discourse', UNRISD Occasional Paper for the Fourth Conference on Women, Beijing 1995, OP 1, Geneva: UNRISP/ UNDP.

Rees, T. (1998) *Mainstreaming Equality in the European Union: Education, Training, and Labour Market Policies*. London: Routledge.

Rees, T. (2000) 'Mainstreaming equality', in Sophie Watson and Lesley Doyal (eds) *Engendering Social Policy*. Buckingham: Open University Press.

Rees, T. (2002) 'The politics of "mainstreaming" gender equality', in E. Breitenbach, A. Brown, F. Mackay and J. Webb (eds) *The Changing Politics of Gender Equality in Britain*. Basingstoke: Palgrave, 45–6.

Rees, T. (2005) 'Reflections on the uneven development of gender mainstreaming in Europe', *International Feminist Journal of Politics* 7(4):555–74.

Regents of the University of California v. Bakke, 438 U.S. 265 (1978), available at: http://caselaw.lp.findlaw.com/scripts/getcase.pl?court=US&vol=438&invol=265

Reitman, O. (2005) 'Multiculturalism and feminism: incompatibility, compatibility or synonymity?', *Ethnicities* 5(2):216–47.

Rhodes, R. (1994) 'The hollowing out of the state: the changing nature of the state in Britain', *Political Quarterly* 65(2):138–51.

Rhodes, R. (1996) 'The new governance: governing without government', *Political Studies* 44(4), 652–67.

Rhodes, R. (2000) 'The governance narrative: key findings and lessons from the ESRC's Whitehall programme', *Public Administration* 78(2):345–63.

Richardson, D. (2005) 'Desiring sameness? The rise of a neoliberal politics of normalization', *Antipode* 37(3):515–35.

Richardson, J. (2000) 'Government, interest groups and policy change', *Political Studies*, 48, 1006–25.

Riley, J. (2004) 'Some reflections on gender mainstreaming and intersectionality', *Development Bulletin* 64:82–6.

Robeyns, I. (2003) 'Sen's capability approach and gender inequality: selecting relevant capabilities', *Feminist Economics* 9(2/3):61–92.

Robeyns, I. (2007) 'Sen's Capability Approach and feminist Concerns', in S. Alkire, F. Comim and M. Quizilbash (eds) *The Capability Approach: Concepts, Measures and Applications.* Cambridge: Cambridge University Press.

Roemburg, B. van and S. Spee (2004). *Gender Mainstreaming: kritische analyse van gender mainstreaming als theoretisch concept en als beleidsinstrument.* Steunpunt Gelijkekansenbeleid, Universiteit Antwerpen.

Rose, N. (1991) 'Governing by numbers: figuring our democracy', *Accounting Organisations and Society* 16(7):673–92.

Rose, N. (1996) 'Governing "advanced" liberal democracies', in A. Barry, T. Osborne and N. Rose (eds) *Foucault and Political Reason: Liberalism, Neo-Liberalism and Rationalities of Government.* Chicago: University of Chicago Press, 37–64.

Rose, N. (1999) *Powers of Freedom: Reframing Political Thought.* Cambridge University Press.

Rose, N. and P. Miller (1992) 'Political power beyond the state: problematics of government', *British Journal of Sociology* 43(2): 173–205.

Roseau, S. (2005) 'The role of national mechanisms in promoting gender equality and the empowerment of women: the Antigua and Barbuda experience', EGM/National Machinery/2004/RP.10.

Ross, K. (2002) 'Women's place in "male" space: gender and effect in parliamentary contexts', *Parliamentary Affairs* 55(1):189–201.

Rubery, J. (2002) 'Gender mainstreaming and gender equality in the EU: the impact of the EU employment strategy', *Industrial Relations Journal* 33(5):500–22.

Ruddick, S. (1997) 'Maternal thinking', in D. Meyers (ed.) *Feminist Social Thought: A Reader.* New York: Routledge.

Ruddock, J. (1998) 'House of Commons Hansard Debates', available at: www.publications.parliament.uk/pa/cm/cmhansard.htm

Russell, M. (2000) *Women's Representation in UK Politics: What Can Be Done with the Law?* London: The Constitution Unit.

Russell, M. (2001) *The Women's Representation Bill: Making it Happen.* London: The Constitution Unit.

Russell, M. (2003) 'Women in elected office in the UK, 1992–2002: struggles, achievements and possible sea change', in A. Dobrowolsky and V. Hart (eds) *Women Making Constitutions: New Politics and Comparative Perspectives.* New York: Palgrave, 68–83.

Ryan, B. (1992) *Feminism and the Women's Movement: Dynamics of Change in Movement Ideology and Activism.* London: Taylor & Francis.

Sacchet, T. (2003) 'The political potential of gender quotas in Latin America: beyond numbers', paper presented at the 2nd ECPR Conference, Marburg, September.

Sapiro, V. (1998) 'When are interests interesting? The problem of political representation', in A. Phillips (ed.) *Feminism and Politics.* Oxford University Press, 169–92.

Sauer, B. (2005) 'What happened to the model student? Austrian state feminism in the 1990s', paper presented at the ECPR Joint Sessions, Granada, 14–19 April.

Saward, M. (1998) *Terms of Democracy.* Cambridge: Polity.

Saward, M. (2006) 'Democracy and citizenship: expanding domains', in J. Dryzek, B. Honig and A. Phillips (eds) *Oxford Handbook of Political Theory*. Oxford University Press, 400–19.

Saward, M. (ed.) (2000) *Democratic Innovation: Deliberation, Representation and Association*. London: Routledge.

Sawer, M. (1990) *Sisters in Suits: Women and Public Policy in Australia*. Sydney: Allen & Unwin.

Sawer, M. (1995) 'Feminism in glass towers? The office of the status of women in Australia', in D. Stetson and A. Mazur (eds) *Comparative State Feminism*. London: Sage, 22–39.

Sawer, M. (1996) 'Femocrats and eurocrats: women's policy machinery in Australia, Canada and New Zealand', part of the UN Research Institute for Social Development Occasional Paper Series. New York: United Nations.

Sawer, M. (2002) 'The representation of women in Australia: meaning and make-believe', *Parliamentary Affairs* 55: 5–18.

Sawer, M. (2005) 'Gender equality in the age of governing for the mainstream', paper presented at the United Nations for the Advancement of Women, 29 November–2 December 2004, Rome.

Schmidt, G. and K. Saunders (2004) 'Effective quotas, relative party magnitude and the success of female candidates', *Comparative Political Studies* 37(6):704–34.

Schwindt-Bayer, L. (2004) 'Women's representation in Latin American legislatures: policy attitudes and bill initiation behavior', paper presented at the Annual Meeting of the Midwest Political Science Association, Chicago, IL, April 15–18.

Sen, A. (1992) *Inequality Re-examined*. Oxford: Clarendon.

Sen, A. (2004) 'Dialogue capabilities, lists and public reason', *Feminist Economics* 10(3):77–80.

Sevenhuijsen, S. (1998) *Citizenship and the Ethics of Care*. London: Routledge.

Shachar, A. (2001) *Multicultural Jurisdictions Cultural Differences and Women's Rights*. Cambridge: Cambridge University Press.

Sharp, R. and R. Broomhill (2002) 'Budgeting for equality: the Australian experience', *Feminist Economics* 8(1):25–47.

Shaw, J. (2002) 'The European Union and gender mainstreaming: constitutionally embedded or comprehensively marginalised?', *Feminist Legal Studies* 10(3–4), 213–26.

Shaw, J. (2004) 'Mainstreaming equality in European Union law and policy-making', report published by the European Network Against Racism (ENAR).

Shaw, J. (2005) 'Mainstreaming equality and diversity in the European Union', *Current Legal Problems* 58:255–312.

Shaw, J. (ed.) (2000) *Social Law and Policy in an Evolving European Union*. Oxford: Hart.

Shepherd-Robinson, L. and J. Lovenduski (2002) *Women and Candidate Selection in British Political Parties*. London: Fawcett Society.

Siim, B. (2007) 'The challenge of recognizing diversity from the perspective of gender equality: Dilemmas in Danish Citizenship' forthcoming in *Critical Review of Social and Political Philosophy*, 10 (4).

Sitton, J. (2003) *Habermas and Contemporary Society*. Basingstoke: Palgrave.

Skjeie, H. (2001) 'Quotas, parity and the discursive dangers of difference', in J. Klausen and C. Maier (eds) *Has Liberalism Failed Women?* New York: Palgrave, 165–76.

Skjeie, H. (2007) 'Religious exemptions to equality', in *CRISSP* (forthcoming).

Smith, G. (2003) *Deliberative Democracy and the Environment*. London: Routledge.

Smith, G. (2005) *Beyond the Ballot: Democratic Innovations from around the World*. A report for the Power Inquiry. London: The Power Inquiry.

Society for Human Resource Management (2004) 'Diversity management', available at: www.shrm.org

Spellman, E. (1988) *Problems of Exclusion in Feminist Thought*. Boston, MA: Beacon.

Squires, J. (1996) 'Quotas for women: fair representation?', in J. Lovenduski and P. Norris (eds) *Women in Politics*. Oxford: Oxford University Press, 73–90.

Squires, J. (1998) 'In different voices: deliberative democracy and aestheticist politics', in J. Good and I. Velody (eds) *The Politics of Postmodernity*. Cambridge University Press, 26–46.

Squires, J. (1999) *Gender in Political Theory*. Cambridge: Polity.

Squires, J. (2001) 'Representing groups, deconstructing identities', *Feminist Theory* 2(1):7–28.

Squires, J. (2002) 'Gender and international relations revisited', in H. Seckinelgin and L. Odysseos (eds) *Gendering the International*. Basingstoke: Palgrave, 208–31.

Squires, J. (2004) 'Gender quotas in Britain: a fast track to equality?', Stockholm University Working Paper 2004:1.

Squires, J. (2005) 'Is mainstreaming transformative? Theorising mainstreaming in the context of diversity and deliberation', *Social Politics* 12(3):366–88.

Squires, J. (2007) 'From gender to diversity: women's policy agencies in Britain', *Politics and Gender* 4(3).

Squires, J. and M. Wickham-Jones (2001) *Women in Parliament: A Comparative Analysis*. Manchester: Equal Opportunities Commission.

Squires, J. and M. Wickham-Jones (2002) 'Mainstreaming in Westminster and Whitehall: from Labour's Ministry of Equality to the Women and Equality Unit', *Parliamentary Affairs* 55:57–70.

Squires, J. and M. Wickham-Jones (2004) 'New Labour, gender mainstreaming and the Women and Equality Unit', *British Journal of Politics and International Relations* 6(1):81–98.

Staudt, K. (2003) 'Gender mainstreaming: conceptual links to institutional mechanisms', in S. Rai (ed.) *Mainstreaming Gender, Democratizing the State: Institutional Mechanisms for the Advancement of Women*. Manchester: Manchester University Press, 40–65.

Stephanopoulos, G. and C. Edley, C. (1995) 'Affirmative Action Review', Report to the President, Washington, DC.

Stetson, D. M. (ed.) (2001) *Abortion Politics, Women's Movements and the Democratic State: A Comparative Study of State Feminism*. Oxford University Press.

Stetson, D. M. and A. Mazur (2003) 'Reconceptualising the women's movement: discourses, actors and states', paper presented at the 2003 International Studies Association Annual Convention, Portland OR.

Stetson, D. M. and A. Mazur (eds) (1995) *Comparative State Feminism*. Thousand Oaks, CA: Sage.

Stienstra, D. (1994) *Women's Movements and International Organizations*. New York: St. Martin's Press.

Stienstra, D. (2000) 'Dancing resistance from Rio to Beijing', in M. Marchand and A. Sissan-Runyan (eds) *Gender and Global Restructuring*. New York: Routledge, 209–24.

Stoker, (1998) 'Governance as theory: five propositions', *International Social Science Journal* 50(1):17–29.

Stratigaki, M. (2004) 'The cooptation of gender concepts in EU Policies: the case of "reconciliation of work and family"', *Social Politics* 11(1):30–56.

Stratigaki, M. (2005) 'Gender mainstreaming vs. positive action: an ongoing conflict in EU gender equality policy', *European Journal of Women's Studies* 12(2) 165–86.

Studlar, D. and I. McAllister (1998) 'Candidate gender and voting in the 1997 British General Election: did Labour quotas matter?', *Journal of Legislative Studies* 4(3):72–91.

Studlar, D. and I. McAllister (2002) 'Does a critical mass exist? A comparative analysis of women's legislative representation since 1950', *European Journal of Political Research* 41:233–53.

Sunstein, C. (1991) 'Preferences and politics', *Philosophy and Public Affairs* 20(11) 3–34.

Swers, M. (2002) *The Difference Women Make: The Policy Impact of Women in Congress*. University of Chicago Press.

Swers, M. (2004) 'Legislative entrepreneurship and women's issues: an analysis of Members' Bill sponsorship and co-sponsorship', agendas paper presented at Annual Meeting of the Midwest Political Science Association, Chicago, 15–18 April.

Swift, A. (2001) *Political Philosophy*. Cambridge: Polity.

Swift, A. and G. Marshall (1997), 'Meritocratic equality of opportunity: economic efficiency, social justice or both?', *Policy Studies* 18: 35–48.

Tallion, R. (2001) *Where to From Here? A New Paradigm for the Women's Sector in Northern Ireland*. Belfast, Northern Ireland Voluntary Trust.

Teghtsoonian, K. (1999) *Centring Women's Diverse Interests in Health Policy and Practice*. Halifax, Canada: Centre of Excellence for Women's Health.

Teghtsoonian, K. (2003) 'W(h)ither women's equality? Neoliberalism, institutional change and public policy in British Columbia?', *Policy, Organisation and Society* 22(1):26–47.

Teghtsoonian, K. (2004) 'Neoliberalism and gender analysis mainstreaming in Aotearoa/ New Zealand', *Australian Journal of Political Science* 39(2):267–84.

Teghtsoonian, K. (2005) 'Disparate fates in challenging times: women's policy agencies and neoliberalism in Aotearoa/New Zealand and British Columbia'. *Canadian Journal of Political Science*, 38(3): 1–27.

Thompson, D. (1988) 'Representatives in the Welfare State', in A. Gutmann (ed.) *Democracy and the Welfare State*. Princeton, NJ: Princeton University Press, 131–55.

Threlfall, M. (ed.) (1996) *Mapping the Women's Movement: Feminist Politics and Social Transformation in the North*. London: Verso.

Tinker, I. (1999) 'NGOs: an alternative power base for women?', in M. Meyer and E. Prugl (eds) *Gender Politics and Global Governance*. New York: Rowman and Littlefield, 88–106.

Tinker, I. and J. Jaquette (1987), 'UN Decade for Women: its impact and legacy', *World Development*, 15(3): 419–27.

Towns, A. (2002) 'Paradoxes of (in)equality: something is rotten in the gender equal state of Sweden', *Cooperation and Conflict* 37(2):157–79.
Towns, A. (2003) 'Women governing for modernity: international hierarchy and legislature sex quotas', paper presented at APSA, Philadelphia, August 26–30.
Tripp, A., D. Konate and C. Lowe-Morna (2006) 'Sub-Saharan Africa: on the fast track to women's political representation', in D. Dahlerup (ed.) *Women, Quotas and Politics*. London and New York: Routledge, 112–37.
Tronto, J. (1993) *Moral Boundaries: The Political Argument for an Ethic of Care*. New York: Routledge.
True, J. (2003) 'Mainstreaming gender in global public policy', *International Feminist Journal of Politics* 5(3):368–96.
True, J. and M. Mintrom (2001) 'Transnational networks and policy diffusion: the case of gender mainstreaming', *International Studies Quarterly* 45(1):27–57.
Tully, J. (1995) *Strange Multiplicity: Constitutionalism in an Age of Diversity*. Cambridge University Press.
United Nations (1995) *Platform for Action and the Beijing Declaration*. New York.
United Nations (1997) 'Gender mainstreaming', Report of the Economic and Social Council for 1997 A/52/3, 18 September 1997.
United Nations (2002) 'Further actions and initiatives to implement the Beijing declaration and platform for action'. NewYork; available at: http://www.un.org/womenwatch/daw/followup/beijing+5.htmpara. 25
United Nations Division for the Advancement of Women (1998) 'National machineries for gender equality', available at : www.un.org/womenwatch/daw/news/natmach.htm
Van Roemberg, B. and S. Spee (2004) 'Gender mainstreaming', University of Antwerp, cited in A. Woodward, 'Too late for mainstreaming?', available at: http://www.rosadoc.be/site/rosa/english/pdf/athena/JESPoolateformainstreaming.pdf
Vargas, V. and S. Wieringa (1998) 'Triangles of empowerment: processes and actors in the making of public policy', in G. Lycklama, A. Nijeholt, V. Vargas and S. Wieringa (eds) *Women's Movement and Public Policy in Europe, Latin America and the Caribbean*. New York: Garland, 3–23.
Veitch, J. (2005) 'Looking at gender mainstreaming in the UK government', *International Feminist Journal of Politics* 7(4):631–38.
Verloo, M. (2000) 'Gender mainstreaming: practice and prospects', Report (EG (1999) 13).
Verloo, M. (2001) 'Another velvet revolution? Gender mainstreaming and the politics of implementation', IWM Working Paper, no.5. Available at: http://www.iwm.at/p-iwmwp.htm#Verloo
Verloo, M. (2002) 'The development of gender mainstreaming as a political concept for Europe', paper presented at the Conference for Gender Learning, Liepzig, 6–8 September 2002.
Verloo, M. (2005) 'Mainstreaming gender equality in Europe: a critical frame analysis', *Greek Review of Social Research* 117:11–32.
Verloo, M. (2006) 'Multiple inequalities, intersectionality and the European Union', *European Journal of Women's Studies* 13(3):211–28.
Verloo, M. and E. Lombardo (2006) 'Mainstreaming by political intersectionality: absence and bias in gender equality policies in Europe', paper delivered at the ECPR, Istanbul, 21–23 September.

Vincent, A. (2004) *The Nature of Political Theory*. Oxford University Press.

Vincent, L. (2004) 'Quotas: changing the way things look without changing the way things are', *Journal of Legislative Studies* 10(1):71–96.

Vos, S. (1999) 'Women in Parliament: a personal perspective', in *Redefining Politics: South African Women and Democracy*. Johannesburg: Commission on Gender Equality.

Walby, S. (1997) *Gender Transformations*. London: Routledge.

Walby, S. (2002) 'Feminism in a global era', *Economy and Society* 31(4) 533–57.

Walby, S. (2004) 'The European Union and gender equality: emergent varieties of gender regime', *Social Politics* 11(1):4–29.

Walby, S. (2004b) 'Gender mainstreaming: productive tensions in theory and practice', paper presented at the ESRC Gender Mainstreaming Seminars, 2003–4.

Walby, S. (2005) 'Introduction: comparative mainstreaming in a global era', *International Feminist Journal of Politics* 7(4):453–70.

Wängnerud, L. (2000) 'Testing the politics of presence: women's representation in the Swedish Riksdag', *Scandinavian Political Studies* 23(1) 67–91.

Wängnerud, L. (2005) 'Testing the politics of presence empirically', paper presented at the 3rd ECPR Conference, Budapest.

Wank, C. (2003) 'Different conceptualisations of gender mainstreaming in different institutional settings', paper presented at the ECPR General Conference, Marburg. Available at: http://www.essex.ac.uk/ecpr/events/generalconference/papers/

Watson, S. (ed.) (1990) *Playing the State: Australian Feminist Interventions*. London: Verso.

Waylen, G. (2000) 'Gender and democratic politics: a comparative analysis of consolidation in Argentina and Chile', *Journal of Latin American Studies* 32(3):765–93.

Waylen, G. (2006) 'Constitutional engineering: what opportunities for the enhancement of gender rights?', paper given at Political Studies Association Women and Politics Conference, Edinburgh, 11 February.

Weldon, L. (2002) *Protest, Policy and the Problem of Violence Against Women: A Cross-National Comparison*. University of Pittsburgh Press.

Weldon, L. (2002a) 'Beyond bodies: institutional sources of representation for women in democratic policymaking', *Journal of Politics* 64(4) 1153–74.

Weldon, L. (2004) 'The dimensions and policy impact of feminist civil society', *International Feminist Journal of Politics* 6(1):1–28.

Williams, M. (1998) *Voice, Trust and Memory: Marginalised Groups and the Failings of Liberal Representation*. Princeton University Press.

Williams, M. (2000) 'The uneasy alliance of group representation and deliberative democracy', in Will Kymlicka and Wayne Norman (eds) *Citizenship in Diverse Societies*. Oxford University Press, 124–54.

Wolff, J. (1998) 'Fairness, respect and the egalitarian ethos', *Philosophy and Public Affairs* 27(2):97–122.

Women and Equality Unit (2003) *The Business Case for Equality and Diversity*. Available at: http://www.womenandequalityunit.gov.uk/research/pubn_2003.htm#businesscase

Women and Equality Unit (2004) *The Cost of Domestic Violence*. September 2004 URN 04/600. Available at: http://www.womenandequalityunit.gov.uk/publications/update.htm

Woodward, A. (2001) 'Gender mainstreaming in European policy: innovation or deception?', discussion paper, available at: http://bibliothek.wz-berlin.de/pdf/2001/ i01–103.pdf
Woodward, A. (2003) 'European gender mainstreaming: promises and pitfalls of transformative policy', *Review of Policy Research* 20(1):65–88.
Woodward, A. (2005) 'Translating diversity: the diffusion of the concept of diversity to EU equality polity and the potential for an intersectional approach', paper presented at the conference on Theorizing Intersectionality, University of Keele, 21 May.
Woolley, S. (2003), cited in Nicholas Watt, 'Blocking of Asian candidate stirs row over Labour shortlists', *The Guardian* 29 January. Available at: http://www.guardian.co.uk/ guardianpolitics/story/0,,884344,00.html
Wrench, J. (2002) *Diversity Management, Discrimination and Ethnic Minorities in Europe: Clarifications, Critiques and Research Agendas*, ThemES no.19, Mangfaldens Praktik, Centre for Ethnic and Urban Studies, Norrköping.
Wrench, J. (2005) 'Diversity management can be bad for you', *Race and Class* 46(3):73–84.
Yeandle, S., C. Booth and C. Bennett (1998) 'Criteria of success for a mainstreaming approach to gender equality', CRESR Research Report funded under the Fourth Committee Action Programme for Equal Opportunities.
Yeatman, A. (1990) *Bureaucrats, Technocrats, Femocrats: Essays on the Contemporary Australian State*. Sydney: Allen & Unwin.
Young, I. (1990) *Justice and the Politics of Difference*. Princeton University Press.
Young, I. (1997) 'Unruly categories: a critique of Nancy Fraser's dual systems theory', *New Left Review* 222:147–60.
Young, I. (2000) *Inclusion and Democracy*. Oxford University Press.
Young, I. (2001) 'Equality of whom? Social groups and the judgement of injustice', *Journal of Political Philosophy* 9(1):1–18.
Yuval-Davis (1994) 'Women, ethnicity and empowerment', *Feminism and Psychology*, 4(1):179–198.
Yuval-Davis, N. (1997) *Gender and Nation*. London: Sage.
Yuval-Davis, N. (2004) 'Human/women's rights and feminist transversal politics', presented in the Bristol lecture series on the Politics of Belonging, June, 2004.
Yuval-Davis, N. (2005) 'Intersectionality and gender mainstreaming', *Swedish Journal of Gender Studies* (in Swedish) Kvinno-vetenskaplig tidskrift 2–3:19–30.
Yuval-Davis (2006) 'Intersectionality and Feminist Politics', *European Journal of Women's Studies*, 13(3): 193–209.
Yuval-Davis, N. and P. Werbner (1999) *Women, Citizenship and Difference*. London: Zed Books.

Index